MORE PRAISE FOR *POWER*

"How did Dave Power the man become J.D. Power the brand? It's all here: How his wife and kids mailed out early consumer surveys with quarters taped inside, always face up, to encourage responses. How he discovered the flaws of Mazda's rotary engine. How he maneuvered around Toyota's corporate gatekeepers, and persisted to crack Detroit's citadel with rock-hard data and his trademark congenial manner. The companies that heeded what Power's data revealed were winners. So are millions of consumers, in America and elsewhere, who enjoy quality cars thanks to Dave Power's pioneering work."

　　—**Paul Ingrassia,** automotive author and managing editor of Reuters

"GM was difficult to convince but Dave never gave up when it came to giving us the facts about what our customers expected. There is no question in my mind that GM is better off because of Dave, and this book charts his dogged efforts."

　　—**Jack Smith,** former chairman and CEO of General Motors

"This is a fascinating account of Dave Power's determination to bring the voice of the customer to the auto industry, but it's one that applies to all business segments."

　　—**Kenneth Beck,** CEO of CEO Connection and president of the Wharton
　　Club of New York

"Dave Power is the epitome of integrity. This book lays out how he provided advice—some of it unpopular—based on what his research told him."

　　—**Roger Penske,** founder and chairman of Penske Corporation

"Before Dave brought a precise, actionable measurement of customer satisfaction, there were only rudimentary systems for tracking the ownership experience. This book tells the story of the tremendous resistance Dave faced to bridge that gap with accuracy and compelling detail."

　　—**Jac Nasser,** former president and CEO of Ford Motor Company

"The market research that Dave Power pioneered remains an essential guide for savvy consumers—and an important benchmarking tool for companies focused on providing the highest levels of quality, value, and customer service."
> —**Carlos Ghosn,** president and CEO of Nissan Motor Company Ltd. and Renault S.A.

"This book is a reminder of the power consumer feedback has in creating global change when placed in the hands of a dedicated team and led by the principles of integrity, commitment, and a driving passion to ensure leaders at the top listen. J.D. Power and Associates has been instrumental in providing us with a thorough understanding of our guest expectations for both service and product quality."
> —**Jennifer Fox,** president of Fairmont Hotels & Resorts

"Dave has had a consistent vision for where retailing is headed. Based on what he's gotten right in the past, his thoughts are worth reading about."
> —**Mark O'Neil,** president and CEO of Dealertrack Technologies

POWER

HOW J.D. POWER III BECAME THE AUTO INDUSTRY'S ADVISER, CONFESSOR, AND EYEWITNESS TO HISTORY

SARAH MORGANS | BILL THORNESS

Fenwick Publishing Group, Inc.

Fenwick Publishing Group, Inc.
3147 Point White Drive, Suite 100
Bainbridge Island, Washington 98110

Fenwick Publishing produces, publishes, and markets custom publications for corporations, institutions, nonprofit organizations, individuals, and families.
www.fenwickpublishing.com

Timothy J. Connolly
    President and Publisher
Sarah Morgans
    Vice President
Kevin Berger and Angie Tomson
    Designers
Rachel Fisher
    Production Assistant
Dianna Stirpe
    Copy Editor
Marco Pavia
    Proofreader

John Kador contributed interviews, notes, and an initial manuscript draft that provided part of the foundation for this book. The opinions expressed in this publication are those of J.D. Power III and not J.D. Power and Associates, Inc., or McGraw Hill Financial.

First edition
Printed in the United States of America

22 21 20 19 18 17 16 15 14 13   1 2 3 4 5

Paperback ISBN: 978-0-9818336-7-5
Hardback ISBN: 978-0-9818336-8-2

Library of Congress Cataloging-in-Publication Data

Morgans, Sarah, 1974-
 Power : how J.D. Power III became the auto industry's adviser, confessor, and eyewitness to history / Sarah Morgans, Bill Thorness. -- First edition.
     pages cm
 Includes bibliographical references and index.
 ISBN 978-0-9818336-7-5
 1. Power, J. D., III. 2. J.D. Power and Associates. 3. Marketing research companies--United States. 4. Automobile industry and trade--Public relations--United States. 5. Selling--Automobiles--United States. 6. Consumer satisfaction--United States. I. Thorness, Bill, 1960- II. Title.
 HF5415.2.P6586 2013
 338.4'76292220092--dc23
 [B]

2013003414

CONTENTS

FOREWORD

I vividly remember the first time I met Dave Power. I was acting as master of ceremonies for a gathering of four or five hundred people in Southern California for my alma mater, California State University, Northridge (CSUN), in the spring of 2003. During the evening, someone slipped me a note that said J.D. Power was in the audience and would I please introduce him and ask him to stand and wave to the crowd.

My first thought was: What's a world-renowned business leader doing at an event for my beloved little state university? I had been living in the Northeast for a number of years and I didn't know that Dave had been an adjunct professor in our business school and served as chairman of the university's foundation board (a committee I am now a member of). I introduced him to the audience, and a tall, distinguished gentleman not unlike Jimmy Stewart stood and acknowledged the crowd's enthusiastic applause while I joked, "Yes, Virginia, there really is a J.D. Power."

Since then, Dave and I have become pals and we often run into each other at functions on both coasts. I was especially proud to serve as emcee during the evening in the fall of 2010 in New York City when one of his alma maters, the Wharton School of Business at the University of Pennsylvania, presented him with its Lifetime Achievement Award. Some of the biggest names in business were there that night, honoring him for building one of the world's most recognizable and respected brands, J.D. Power and Associates.

But here's the thing about Mr. J.D. Power III: for all of the power and prestige his name wields, he's just a regular guy. He and I had lunch one afternoon in the elegant dining room of a world-famous hotel in New York City. Our table was nothing special, and rather than throwing his weight around with the wait staff, Dave spent the meal making sure his guest was taken care of before he was. While we ate and chatted about family and our favorite getaway, Cape Cod, I kept thinking about Henry Ford's famous quote that customers could have any color car they wanted, as long as it was black. It was a take-it-or-leave-it attitude that the U.S. auto industry clung to well into the 1970s until people like Dave Power came along. I couldn't get over the fact that the man sitting across from me had had such a profound impact on the relationship between manufacturers and consumers—and, let's face it, on the world economy—and yet here he sat quietly sipping his soup, and nobody paid any attention to him. He has never stopped being the humble guy from Worcester, Massachusetts, who started his business at his kitchen table.

There are a couple of "firsts" in Dave's life that have been key to his success. One is family. He grew up in a house built by his grandfather, the first J.D. Power. And during the early days of his business, Dave's first wife, Julie, who passed away in 2002, was a partner in every way, joining him at the kitchen table as they pored over those first customer satisfaction surveys. And Dave and Julie both made sure that J.D. Power and Associates didn't come between them and their four children. As they grew, Jamey, Mary, Jonathan, and Susan were very much a part of the family business. When Dave decided in 2005 that it was time to sell, it was only fitting that the buyer he chose was another company with a strong family tradition: McGraw Hill Financial, whose CEO, Terry McGraw, is the great-grandson of the man who started the company in 1917.

The other first in Dave's life is the customer. J.D. Power and Associates was founded on a simple premise: the customer's opinion matters. He was way ahead of his time. When Dave started his business in 1968, few companies really listened to their customers, and that was especially true in the automotive industry. When Julie Power discovered that Mazda had a problem with the O-rings in its new rotary engines (because customers said so in satisfaction surveys), it put her husband's company on the map and a corporate revolution was born. Dave gets a lot of credit for the quiet persistence he used to grow his company, but for me the takeaway from this book is that J.D. Power and Associates was a success because it was armed with a very powerful tool: the truth.

Dave's ability to help the auto industry listen to the voice of the customer has had implications that have reached far beyond automotive, ultimately giving consumers around the world a greater say in a wide range of products and services. Striving to understand customer satisfaction—while providing the data and analysis to help businesses understand it as well—has been his life's work, and anyone who is interested in having satisfied customers would be wise to study Dave Power's career. He epitomizes entrepreneurial spirit, perseverance, and high ethical standards—values that he shared in his work with students at CSUN and are evident throughout the events recounted in the pages that follow. What shines through in his story is an individual who has succeeded in business by being a passionate and curious advocate of others in business, and it's a compelling journey for business leaders —and aspiring ones—in all industries to understand.

Power is an inspirational American success story that has all the ingredients of a Hollywood production about a humble guy who made a big difference. Too bad Jimmy Stewart isn't still around. He would have made a terrific Dave Power.

Bill Griffeth
The veteran CNBC anchor has covered Wall Street since 1981.

PREFACE

I have always had great respect for the American auto industry. The management and the workers of this powerhouse saved the world from utter ruin in the early 1940s by using their manufacturing expertise to create a powerful war machine, switching their attention from the production of millions of automobiles, trucks, and other vehicles to aircraft, tanks, and artillery. We could not have won World War II without the industrial might that was built up by these companies in the 1930s and 1940s.

After the war, they went back into commercial production and by the mid-1950s were in full swing to serve the pent-up demand of consumers. By 1955, automobile sales in the U.S., led by General Motors, Ford, and Chrysler—the "Big Three" of Detroit—reached a record eight million vehicles. GM was being challenged by some in government to split off Chevrolet because the company was approaching more than a 50 percent share of the market. Smaller auto companies, such as Packard, Rambler, Nash, and Studebaker, were going out of business. American Motors Corporation was formed to save some of those losers. The joining of Nash-Kelvinator and Hudson Motor Company into AMC was the largest merger the world had ever seen. At the time, Volkswagen, Fiat, Peugeot, and many other European manufacturers were exporting products to the United States, but these companies collectively had just 1 percent of the market, and the Japanese were not yet testing the waters in America.

At the end of the 1950s, the Big Three dominated. Many, including the leaders of the companies, perceived their success to be based on management and technical prowess rather than unprecedented consumer demand. Engineers and production people ruled the roost. "Engine Charlie" Wilson, CEO at General Motors, and Robert McNamara, president of Ford—who both held the job of secretary of defense after their Detroit offices— are excellent examples of the thinking and the mood at this time. Wilson was an engineer who valued efficiency and saw issues in black and white. From him came the famous statement, which is often misquoted, "what was good for our country was good for General Motors and vice versa." McNamara was also an analytical thinker and is credited with bringing Ford into profitability and an era of great expansion after the war.

But this expansion didn't hold. The market was dramatically changing after World War II, but manufacturers did not understand it. In the 1950s, the industry and its executives applied the same techniques they had used to perform so successfully during the war, but that was no longer the proper approach. Their plants were set up to build 200,000 units a year, but they did not make a profit until they had sold 175,000 units. So, they pushed the product on the dealerships, in a "command-and-control" method employed by all the companies. Automakers forced the dealers to take the vehicles, and then came up with schemes to get the dealers to try to sell more. Unfortunately, this system discouraged innovation. Rather than speaking out, people were pressured into just "playing the game," and there was much resistance to change.

It was in this type of environment that I entered the industry. I was indoctrinated into the top-down operations of the industry during my marketing studies in the MBA program at Wharton, but I've always felt there was a better way to do it, if you had better information. Since then, my entire fifty-year business career has been devoted to working with all factions of the automobile industry and helping them focus on their end-consumer needs and wants.

Over the years, many industry critics have laid the blame for the industry's problems on mismanagement by the executives in the top spots when the problems became insurmountable. I do not subscribe to that idea. Management at the Big Three was captive to the legacy culture of the industrial era. I don't know if, at the time, anyone was thinking about why they ran their companies this way—focusing on production and not understanding that consumer demand should drive their process. In the 1960s and 1970s, the Japanese car companies saw the change in demand and did a better job of meeting it. Their success was partly because they could adapt and American companies could not.

It has always been my intention to help the industry solve its problems. That is also the focus of this book. I have observed the trajectory of the auto industry through both its most productive and its most troubled times, and this book reflects my experiences and memories, as well as those of the dozens of others who worked with me at J.D. Power and Associates and the many who worked in the industry. This is what happened, as we remember it. It is my hope that providing this perspective will make the strong case that, in order to thrive, the industry must listen to the voice of the customer.

This book includes the perspectives of many colleagues, friends, and family, and I would like to offer thanks to everyone who drove with us down memory lane to recount the work we have done over the years.

Chief among my valuable collaborators and the people who influenced me are my dear departed first wife, Julie Power, and our children, Jamey, Mary, Jonathan, and Susan. Reaching even further back, my parents provided me with an upbringing that gave me the education and moral fortitude to do things in the way I felt was right. The strength provided by my family has led me into success beyond what I could have asked for or expected.

Clients, colleagues, industry executives, dealers, suppliers, and especially all the J.D. Power associates I have worked with over the years have also greatly influenced my thinking. Those ranks include many more people than the ones interviewed for this book or referenced in its pages, and I wish it were possible to mention everyone who has made such a great impression on me over the years. I have had so many friends and advisers in the ranks of automobile dealers and automaker executives, and I have been intellectually challenged by the writings of many great business thinkers, such as Alvin Toffler and Peter Drucker. I owe a deep level of gratitude to so many people—thank you.

Thanks, too, to the millions of car and truck owners for responding to the many mail surveys conducted by J.D. Power and Associates over the past fifty years. It is only through their participation that we gained an understanding of the problems and frustrations consumers were having with their newly purchased vehicles. Even though we were asking respondents to consider dozens of aspects of vehicle ownership in a substantial six- or eight-page questionnaire, we provided space for comments on anything else that would be helpful for us to consider in understanding their experience. Amazingly, 10 or 11 percent of the questionnaires came back with additional comments included. The comments we received were, as a general rule, mixed: some were negative and some were positive. When we started in the late

1960s, vehicles had serious quality problems and about 90 percent of the comments were negative complaints while only 10 percent were positive or even neutral. The negative comments often came with three or four pages of documents, including copies of dealer invoices, typewritten descriptions of difficulties in having repairs corrected, and even photographs of shoddy paint work or rusted trunk lids. (J.D. Power and Associates had a practice of sorting these comments by make and model, then sending them to the appropriate manufacturer for follow-up.)

Without the individuals who took the time to complete the surveys and send them back in, there would be no data for us to share with automakers to help improve overall customer satisfaction. By the late 1990s the ratio of the comments included with the surveys had shifted to only 25 percent negative and 75 percent positive or neutral. The credit for the spectacular turnaround in car quality that these comments reflected must not go only to our organization, which encouraged automakers to listen to the voice of the customer, or the executives who truly heard and made the tough changes that led to improvement; it was the customers themselves, who willingly, thoughtfully, and effectively made their voices heard, that contributed so significantly to this success.

J.D. Power III
March 2013

SECTION ONE
INDEPENDENCE

Many young Americans have learned early life lessons through stints in the military, and Dave Power was no exception. A young man fresh out of the College of the Holy Cross, the Roman Catholic Jesuit institution in Dave's hometown of Worcester, Massachusetts, Dave found opportunities for leadership, collaboration, and perseverance in the military. Fellow officers even offered valuable mentoring and career advice. But it was through adversity—in the form of an unreasonable senior officer—that Dave discovered an innate skill that would later propel him to success in business.

After graduation in June 1953, Dave knew that military service would be likely. The Korean War was being fought, and there was an active civilian draft of young men. Rather than allow his fate to be determined by chance, Dave chose to enlist in the Coast Guard because it was a smaller branch of the service where he felt he could have a greater impact. That fall, he was inducted into Officer Candidate School at the U.S. Coast Guard Academy in New London, Connecticut. Just over half of the sixty candidates graduated in February 1954, Dave among them.

He was posted to the icebreaker ship the USCG *Eastwind*, which was stationed in Boston and would sojourn to the Arctic and Antarctic to open channels, service weather stations, and explore the frozen seas. The lanky youth, who was nearly a head taller than many of the other recruits, had not spent much time on boats and certainly had no experience on a ship of *Eastwind*'s size. The candidates had been briefly trained in rowing and navigating the small lifeboats stowed aboard the ship, and just a slim portion of that training had taken place aboard a large sailing ship, the *Eagle*, berthed at the academy.

Dave's first drill on the *Eastwind* did not go well. He had been on a midnight watch, during which he contracted an intestinal problem from drinking tainted water. Although groggy, he was called to the deck at eight in the morning to participate in a man-overboard drill. He was to man the sweep oar at the rear of an eight-oarsmen boat, which meant maneuvering the boat through the drill and back to the Jacob's ladder attached to the ship. His docking did not go well, and he was summarily called to the bridge to meet the captain, a gruff man with a reputation for being difficult to serve under. "He said, 'I'm going to give you an opportunity to learn how to row a boat,'" Dave recalls. The captain had his own dingy lowered over the side, and sent Dave to it. Dave was ordered to row circles around the ship. "He had a megaphone and was shouting out to me, 'Row with your back!' and 'Feather your oars!'" As Dave, still weak, slogged along first the port and then the starboard side of the ship, the entire crew followed him to watch the spectacle. When he returned up the Jacob's ladder and reported to the bridge, the captain was not there, but a senior officer on duty commented to Dave that he'd never witnessed such behavior from a captain. Later, Dave heard rumors that the captain was trying to get him transferred off the ship.

But his service on the *Eastwind* continued, and soon the ship was outfitted for the Arctic. Dave was made exchange officer and put in charge of taking on a load of beer reserved for a later liberty leave in the far north, where the crew would blow off steam with a barbeque on the ice. Coast Guard rules prohibited sailors from drinking aboard ship. It was a lot of beer—two hundred cases—and was to be transferred from the *Eastwind*'s sister ship, the *Westwind*, which was berthed in New York and would rendezvous with them in the harbor off Nova Scotia.

It was pouring rain the day the ships met, but the crews began the transfer. The rain destroyed the beer's cardboard cartons, so hundreds of loose cans had to be gathered up in cargo nets and transferred. During the lengthy transfer, the captain called down to the crew bringing the beer across and told them they would each be allowed to have one beer while in transit. This was said in full view of the rest of the crew on board, Dave recalls. As the beer was being stowed, seeing there would be no way to accurately track the number of individual cans, some sailors slipped a can or two in their jacket pockets.

That night, at the weary end of his midnight watch, Dave was again called to the captain's bridge. He learned that two of the younger sailors, teenagers, had been found drinking beer in the engine room. The captain held a captain's mast, a shipboard disciplinary review, at which he found the young men guilty and punished them by revoking two nights of liberty at the ship's next port of call. Dave, as both a junior officer and the exchange officer in charge of the beer, stood as witness to the action. Afterward, the captain again called Dave to him, this time in his cabin, and told him how disappointed he was in Dave's handling of the beer stowage.

At this point, Dave Power took a chance. He saw—as he would many times in later years—a leader who needed a reality check, and he was determined to give it to him. With the captain reportedly already wanting him off the ship, Dave decided he had nothing to lose. He stood up to him and said, "Captain, I think you're the one who's at fault for having handled the crew the way you did from the bridge, allowing some of them to have cans of beer and others not." The young officer delivered his speech calmly and respectfully. The captain kicked him out of his cabin.

Dave felt his days on the *Eastwind* were numbered. Several days later, as they navigated through ice floes in Hudson's Bay, Dave was called to relieve the officer of the deck, who had been summoned to the captain's cabin. Dave performed the navigation. When the officer returned, he told Dave that the captain had been drinking in his cabin while addressing him. During the course of the conversation, the captain asked who was conning the ship in the officer's absence. The officer told him it was Mr. Power. Ten minutes later, they received a call on the bridge. The captain wanted Mr. Power to come down to his cabin. Dave warily complied. The captain, sitting in his bathrobe with a drink at his side, said unexpectedly, "I'm making you officer of the deck under way, icebreaking." Dave was stunned. This was an honor, and one not yet bestowed on officers senior to him. Through his straight talk he had won the trust of the captain, and so began his three-year stint on the *Eastwind*.

"I was often faced with this type of decision," Dave recalls. "Winning over the captain and having to overcome all his negative feelings was a challenging thing. But I did it, and it reinforced my thinking; and that's why I became successful in my dealings with the CEOs of the car companies. I stood up and, in a pleasant manner, laid the facts out to them." His congeniality in the face of bluster, presenting a calm argument that relied on facts and data, would be Dave's calling card.

CHAPTER ONE

THE OUTSIDER'S PERSPECTIVE

A seafaring career was not Dave's destiny, which he discovered toward the end of his three-year tour in the Coast Guard. He had held the title of "plank owner" for serving on the *Eastwind* longer than any other officer and had outlasted three captains. He had experienced many missions aboard the icebreaker, with its crew of two hundred and its storied history, which included capturing a German ship off the coast of Greenland in World War II. During Dave's time aboard her, the *Eastwind* had made three trips to the Arctic and one to the Antarctic, once getting frozen in the ice for two weeks. Dave had made the acquaintance of Admiral Richard E. Byrd when the famed explorer traveled on the ship on its way to McMurdo Sound. One mission was memorialized for Dave in a picture of him on the frozen deck with two-inch icicles hanging off the ship's rails. But with six months left in his tour, and the *Eastwind* about to depart on another long Antarctic expedition, he was transferred to a buoy tender in Boston Harbor. These ships maintain navigational buoys and perform other duties to aid navigation in America's waterways.

On board, Dave spoke to other officers about his next move. He could reenlist, which was the decision his superiors preferred. He was set on more education, though, and talked about pursuing an engineering degree. He had no specific goals, but he knew he did not want to end up teaching, a career for many with a liberal arts degree like his. The other officers steered him away from more undergraduate studies. "They said, 'You should be looking at an MBA degree,'" Dave says. "I had to ask them, 'What's an MBA?'"

He looked into it and decided to apply. True to his methodical nature, he researched the top schools and applied to six of them. The first to respond was the Wharton School of Business at the University of Pennsylvania. The dean wrote informally, encouraging Dave's application, because, he said, they needed liberal arts students as well as those with a business background. "So I immediately signed up with Wharton," Dave recalls. He later learned he had been accepted to three other schools.

He spent two years studying business and finance. It was a far cry from his studies at Holy Cross, where he had completed his liberal arts education by submitting a senior thesis on the philosophy of Don Quixote, the fictional character created by Miguel de Cervantes who "tilted at windmills," attempting to joust against imaginary giants. That iconic scene has come to symbolize fruitless effort, something a successful business leader can ill afford. But Dave's thesis took another approach to the famous jousting scene: he saw it as an idiom about Quixote's foolishness of sticking with the outmoded culture of a knight-errant while the world changed around him. This was a theme that would resurface regularly in Dave Power's later work with a seemingly immovable object: the U.S. auto industry. The industrial juggernaut clung to legacy product and manufacturing methods while informed consumers were beginning to demand something different.

Studying the Rambler

Toward the end of his MBA studies, Dave had his first professional involvement with the industry he was to serve. He was on a team of students responsible for analyzing American Motors Company (AMC) and what the automaker needed to do to make its Rambler a viable competitor in a U.S. car market dominated by the Big Three (General Motors, Ford, and Chrysler). AMC was formed in 1954 from the merger of Nash-Kelvinator and the Hudson Motor Car Company. Manufactured in Kenosha, Wisconsin, the Rambler—a legacy from Nash—was redesigned in 1956 in a bid to distinguish the model from those of the large automakers. AMC President George Romney was staking much on the redesign, which gave the car a lower look and bigger engine but still positioned it as a smaller, more fuel-efficient car.[1] This was the situation that Dave's team analyzed.

"It was my first rigorous exposure to the automobile industry, and I was fascinated," he recalls. He and his teammates would have long conversations about the Rambler and the auto industry in general. The team analyzed the Rambler business model, evaluated sales trends, and duly delivered a paper that was skeptical of the Rambler's prospects. For the first time, Dave was thinking about a profession, and the idea of a career in the auto industry proved an attractive one. "I learned that one out of seven jobs in the U.S. was somehow connected to the automobile industry," he says. "It seemed to me the automobile industry was the place to be." Intrigued, he carefully inspected the list of companies recruiting at the Wharton placement office and made it a point to interview with every car company. Of course, he also felt it important to consider the merits of other industries and he eventually interviewed with management consultant firm McKinsey & Company, an insurance company, and a number of government agencies.

Dave was particularly excited to meet the recruiter from General Motors, by far the biggest automaker and, at that time, one of the largest companies in the world. Furthermore, it was a company at which Dave had family—an uncle was high on the management team. But his excitement was soon replaced by disappointment at the New York–based recruiter's approach. "He displayed a superior attitude," Dave recalls. "He started the interview by asking me, 'What makes you think you can do anything for General Motors?'" It was as if GM knew it all and there was nothing Dave, or any student, could offer. Some weeks later Dave was in Manhattan and, from a pay phone, called the GM recruiter to follow up. Dave could tell that the recruiter was distracted, had no idea who was calling, and was too busy to take the time to talk with an interested applicant. Dave was so put off by the way he was treated that he crossed GM off his list of potential employers —another independent-minded decision, considering Dave's family background with the company.

His meeting with a Ford Motor Company recruiter left a better impression. The recruiter, a controller at Ford's assembly plant in Chester, Pennsylvania, had come to the University of Pennsylvania to meet with promising Wharton students to talk about the executive training program in Ford's finance department. The recruiter was curious about Dave's studies and treated the MBA student with respect. Dave said that his academic concentration was in marketing, not finance. The recruiter countered that Dave should seriously consider the finance training program because it would prepare him for anything, and then, after two years, he could transfer into marketing, if that's what he wanted to do. Dave thought this plan sounded workable. The recruiter put him in touch with a personnel manager at the Ford Tractor Division.

In June 1959, at the age of twenty-eight, Dave graduated with an MBA degree from Wharton, and within weeks he flew to Detroit. It was the first airplane ride for him, though soon he would be routinely flying more than a hundred thousand miles each year. In the Detroit area, he stayed with his uncle, Aloysius "Al" Power, general counsel for General Motors, and drove his aunt's Cadillac El Dorado to the Ford Tractor Division headquarters for a follow-up interview. Ford Tractor hired Dave on the spot.

His uncle was skeptical. "Why would you work for Ford," Al asked, "and not even Ford corporate, but the Ford Tractor Division?" Al added that he could help his nephew land a job that would put Dave on the fast track for success at GM. Uncle Al proposed to get him a job working in the New York finance office with the people who would one day likely run GM. In fact, two of GM's future CEOs—Roger Smith and Jack Smith (not related)—emerged from that office during that period. Al Power said he was heading to New York City the next day for a GM board of directors meeting and he was ready to arrange a job on his nephew's behalf.

Dave politely but firmly resisted. He struggled to make his uncle understand that while he appreciated the offer, it was important he succeed or fail on his own merits. Dave knew enough of GM corporate culture to know that any kind of authentic feedback about his performance was simply not possible for a nephew of one of the most powerful executives in the company. Dave didn't mention the cavalier treatment he had received at the hands of the GM recruiter. Nor did he tell his uncle that he was skeptical of the insular, old-boys-club spirit he knew existed at GM, a corporate culture that would frustrate him for much of his career. Al accepted Dave's decision.

That he was being hired to work for a division of Ford Motor Company and would not be based at Ford's headquarters in Dearborn, Michigan, didn't put Dave off in the least. "I always liked the smaller operations," he explains, "because I didn't want to be in a room with twenty MBAs pounding away on Friden calculators, which is what happens when you work at the headquarters." The Ford Tractor office was in Birmingham, Michigan, northwest of Detroit. While it was miles from Ford's corporate offices, Dave relished the autonomy he never would have experienced at Ford headquarters. "At Ford Tractor, they were short of people and they put me immediately into my own project."

Auditing at Ford Tractor

Dave started his career with the Ford Tractor Division in the auditing department, in a job that would later provide great insight into working with car dealers. Audits are vital to any accounting process, although, as Dave observed, no one would have known that by the level of respect the auditing department received within Ford Tractor. Nevertheless, he was determined to do a thorough job.

His first responsibility was to audit some of the tractor dealers in Michigan. The tractor business was just starting to pick up after slow sales during the recession of 1957–58, recalls Dave. During this economic downturn, Ford Tractor had offered a series of incentive programs to promote sales of tractors and tractor implements, such as plows and hay balers. By the terms of this promotion, dealers would receive $500 from the manufacturer for each sale made during designated months. Dave's first job was to audit the dealers to ensure they had earned each of the $500 payments they had received. In addition, Ford offered the dealers financing incentives to promote sales. Dave was tasked to audit this program as well. In both cases, the starting point was the same: physically visit each dealer and perform an inventory of the tractors on the lot. For tractors not on the lot and presumed sold, Dave required a sales receipt or a journal entry indicating a sale.

On a blistering summer morning, Dave and a colleague from the Ford Tractor distributor arrived at a small tractor dealer in

Pigeon, Michigan, to perform Dave's first inventory. "It was a crummy, run-down dealership," he recalls. On a clipboard, he had a list of tractors and implements the dealer claimed had been sold or financed. What he needed were the sales receipts or the journal entries indicating completed sales. The owner of the tractor dealer turned Dave over to the bookkeeper, a nervous woman who had much to be nervous about. Neither the sales receipts nor the journal entries could be produced. After some probing by Dave, the bookkeeper burst into tears. "Working for the bank didn't pay much, but at least it was honest," she cried. Dave was reminded of his mother, who had worked for a time in the early 1920s at a Ford dealer until she quit in dismay.

In due course, Dave delivered a report detailing the slew of irregularities he had discovered in the incentive program, but nothing much came of it. "I got the feeling that the practice was more or less okay with Ford Tractor," Dave says. "Sometimes dealers had to be assisted, they seemed to think. It was just the way business was done."

Nevertheless, Dave's managers decided to do a national audit. Dave was assigned to perform audits on Ford Tractor dealers in Illinois and Indiana, and later in Virginia, North Carolina, and West Virginia. He drove through the Midwest and the South, visiting dealers large and small. The views were beautiful as his comfortable Ford Thunderbird ate up thousands of miles of country roads. Everywhere he went for the Ford Tractor Division, he encountered varying degrees of corruption, from petty to more elaborate.

Sometimes the conduct of the tractor dealers moved from common corruption to outright fraud. One Michigan tractor dealer occupied an old farmhouse. When Dave arrived, the bookkeeper duly produced the documents Dave requested. As required, the sales receipts listed the registration numbers of the tractors. But then he took a closer look. The most recently dated sales receipts showed tractors with the lowest registration numbers—the opposite of what was to be expected. It was clear that the dealer had forged the sales receipts. Dave wrote a report and came away wondering if the Ford automotive division faced the same corruption.

Dave's education at a Jesuit school, which emphasized critical thinking and moral as well as intellectual formation, made him impervious to the rationalization of any impropriety being "business as usual."[2] "I saw it as a moral issue," he says. "Deceit for personal gain is wrong, even if the deception is petty and winked at. Ford Tractor, my employer, and thousands of honest and decent Ford employees and stockholders were its victims." Many months of this auditing work were exhausting. "But it was a useful education," he admits. "It made me more suspicious, especially of numbers."

It was also Dave's first opportunity to recognize how Detroit's orientation toward production—building as many tractors, or cars, as possible and then figuring out how to get them sold—was creating the inefficiencies that would eventually corrode the industry. In his groundbreaking 1960 paper published in the *Harvard Business Review,* "Marketing Myopia," Theodore Levitt identified the American auto industry as one of the industries subject to implosion if it did not alter its production-oriented perspective. Levitt wrote that in industries like auto manufacturing, "the enticements of full mass production have been so powerful that . . . top management in effect has told the sales departments, 'You get rid of it; we'll worry about profits.'"[3]

After completing the audit, Dave was assigned to evaluate Ford Tractor's two-step distribution system. In two-step distribution systems, the manufacturer works with a regional distributor rather than directly with dealers, and the distributors set up the dealer network.

This, Dave discovered, was a fast way to enter a marketplace but not an efficient system. "It took a lot of effort to set up the distribution," he explains, "so they gave the distributors the ability to run a territory and sign up the dealers." In the auto industry, Detroit's Big Three had a network of dealers in place since World War II, so they didn't need two-step distribution, but new entrants such as Volkswagen or other import brands needed it. "Otherwise, it would be an immense investment."

Dave credits this insight, gained through his study for the Ford Tractor Division, with giving him a valuable perspective on serving the auto industry. He saw Detroit's command-and-control way of running things, saw the market challenges faced by foreign manufacturers, and tailored his services to meet their unique needs. At the conclusion of that first study, he determined that Ford Tractor needed to eliminate the distributors, which eventually happened. As his training program continued, he took on more evaluative tasks, and he always tried to bring a broad, critical worldview to the work. He also never saw himself as the standard "company man." In an era when an employee typically stayed with a company for an entire career, Dave pictured himself apart from that track. He was curious to learn, driven to do well, and loyal to his employer, but he would not be tied to the organization. It was this attitude of detachment that gave him a trademark outsider's perspective possessed by few of his colleagues.

About twenty months into Dave's finance training program, he began to nose around for opportunities within Ford to do the kind of market research that had called to him when he was assessing the Rambler's chances in his student project at Wharton. His reputation for diligence and integrity opened doors to a number of opportunities. The vice president of sales and marketing at Ford Tractor suggested there was a spot on his team for a man of Dave's caliber—an opportunity, it seemed to Dave, for him to do market research—and he was interested. But for reasons Dave couldn't figure out, the job offer never quite materialized. He decided to go right to the belly of the beast and applied for a job working directly for Ford Auto Division's director of corporate research, a larger-than-life man named John Hay Brown. The interview was short and to the point, and Dave was too inexperienced to avoid a trap. "Dave, what would you like to be doing in ten to fifteen years?" Brown asked. Dave thought the corporate research head was testing his ambition. "In ten to fifteen years, I think I'd be qualified to be head of marketing for the Lincoln or Mercury division," he replied.

It was the wrong answer. Brown was looking for a career marketer researcher, someone who could be counted on to exhibit minimal ambition and remain in market research, doing at the end of his career pretty much what he had been doing when he started. It's inconceivable today, but in 1960 both employers and employees had a reasonable expectation that they were entering into long-term, very stable contracts. In no segment of the economy was this expectation more ingrained than the auto industry, a culture that rewarded stability, avoided conflict, and tolerated some very unproductive behavior from employees.

By the winter of 1961, Dave was a member of the Junior Chamber of Commerce in Birmingham, Michigan, and participating in one of its service projects, decorating offices for the holiday season. He held the ladder while another member of the chamber affixed decorations. The men introduced themselves, and Harold Adams, the man on the ladder, told Dave that he had once worked as a market researcher for the Ford division but was now happier doing the same thing at the Detroit office of Marplan, the research arm of the celebrated McCann-Erickson advertising agency and a subsidiary of Interpublic, at one time the largest advertising agency in the world.

Adams arranged for Dave to meet an executive at Marplan, C. Richard Johnston. The interview went very well and Johnston offered Dave a job. There was little to think about. Dave's salary would increase from $12,000 to $17,000 a year. Johnston had just one request: "If you accept this job, will you promise me that you won't go back on your word?" As he gave his word, Dave thought this was a curious thing to ask. But Johnston knew exactly what would happen. By noon of the day he turned in his two weeks' notice at Ford Tractor, Dave received two phone calls. One was from Ford's aerospace unit, offering him a job on very attractive terms. The second was from the Ford Tractor vice president of sales, dangling the position that had been elusive for so long. Dave told both men his mind was made up, honoring the assurance he had given Johnston.

Lessons from Marplan

Marplan was an excellent place for Dave to land, because the company regarded market research as an independent profit center. An afterthought at many organizations, market research at Marplan occupied the very center of the organization and was promoted as a resource, producing reliably independent research. Much of this flowed from the institutional mythology of Marplan. Marion Harper, Interpublic's legendary leader, who literally started in the mailroom, moved up through the ranks of ad agency McCann-Erickson by wowing clients with thorough and innovative market research methods.[4] Other ad agencies treated market research as an overhead function, and it often justified preordained results; whereas at Marplan, market research was billable to the client as an individual service and considered more independent.

Watching the executives at Marplan closely, Dave had two great insights about market research, a specialized field that had become formalized in the early twentieth century but was gaining more respect and interest as Dave was launching his career.[5] The first lesson was that market research was most effective if it got at the motivations of respondents. That required digging for information and not being satisfied with superficial results. The second lesson was fearlessness: never second-guess yourself; if you have the facts, use them. The moment a market researcher holds back because of implications concerning his or her own business, the business is on its way to being marginalized.

Dave took this message to heart. Many years later, John Humphrey, a colleague who helped Dave grow his own market research company, remembers an early pep talk from Dave: "We have no agenda," Dave told him. "We'll bring our clients the facts. You must never soften the message. Let the data do its work. It's not J.D. Power and Associates talking; it's the customer talking. They can choose to listen to the customer or not, but we're going to tell them what the customer says."

Dave was assigned to work on the Buick account, also a fortuitous development because Buick commissioned a lot of market research. He was hired just in time to participate in the very first product styling clinic for GM on behalf of the new Buick Riviera. The clinic compared the Buick Riviera, a full-sized coupe or personal luxury car, to its stablemate, the Oldsmobile Toronado. To the delight of the Buick marketing team, consumers demonstrated that they preferred the Riviera.

Dave learned a lot about market research at Marplan. He was exposed to a number of tools and techniques to help determine what people want, need, or believe as part of a coordinated marketing strategy. He learned more about market segmentation, customer analysis, statistical methods, survey and questionnaire implementation, and focus groups. All of these skills would prove very important when he started his own market research business.

But other lessons were evident too. He soon came to realize that not everything about the way Marplan conducted market research was as independent as the company professed. Too often the results of market research were skewed to support preconceived conclusions or to make the creative work of Marplan look good. Much of this, Dave felt, was more the result of laziness than dishonesty. "What I learned about market research at Marplan is that account executives had a problem with doing the hard work required to define the objectives of the market research," he says. "Unless you know ahead of time what you want to determine, you tend to interpret the data in opportunistic ways." It was very much in the tradition of how GM, and probably all captive market researchers, treated data. "You can't do a reliable market research study unless you define what you want—and that takes a lot of work. To get a client to do the heavy lifting of defining the precise questions to be answered is sometimes more than the client can manage. It's so much easier to say, 'Let's do some market research and take a look at what we have.'"

One study for General Motors, which was to evaluate advertising effectiveness, still stands out for Dave. "They had all the divisions—including Frigidaire—in the meetings," he recalls. "It was upwards of forty people in the meeting to design the questionnaire. And the process to generate the questionnaire was torturous. You'd get to one question in the questionnaire, and it would take all morning to finally get an agreement on what it was. And it was always a compromise. Then we'd go to lunch, come back in the afternoon, and go from question 2A to 2B, spend another few hours at it, and go home." With so many varying opinions, and compromise as a necessary result, the survey ended up "plain vanilla," Dave says, without the specifics necessary to really be able to analyze the returning data. In-house market research people preferred the data to be general, so they could interpret it in a way that would not be job threatening. Although the flaws in this process seemed obvious, it was standard practice at the time, and Dave felt he was the only one at Marplan who bristled at its ineffectiveness. It was another nudge toward the independence that Dave would demand in his own firm.

While Dave was learning so much at Marplan, his proclivity toward independence was also being tested. When his Marplan colleagues attended a party in the spring of 1962 to celebrate Dave's engagement to Julie Pierce, a vivacious young teacher who lived in an apartment in the same building as Dave, they were shocked to see senior GM executives Jim Roche and Dave's uncle, Al Power, walk in with their wives. Soon thereafter, Dave was asked to trade on his family connections to get Marplan an audience with more senior GM executives, a proposal that he quashed outright. He saw it as a turning point in his career at the agency. It created an atmosphere of tension and limited his opportunities for advancement because of his refusal. However, after he and Julie married, he continued to work there for two more years, learning about the auto industry and market research. But with the birth of their first child—whom they named James David Power IV and nicknamed Jamey—Dave knew he needed to look for his next opportunity. After a brief stint as chief of market research and corporate planning for J.I. Case, a farm implement company based in Wisconsin that was shifting into construction equipment, he was presented with another opportunity at Marplan, far from the Detroit office, and he took it. He moved his young family to southern California, where he would turn his attention away from the auto industry and work with companies in many fields, from banking to consumer products.

The Chainsaw Perspective

One of Dave's Marplan clients was the McCulloch Corporation, then the leading chainsaw manufacturer in the United States. Robert P. McCulloch, an engineer by training, had developed the first professional chainsaws, and his business prospered by serving professional lumberjacks, who considered McCulloch chainsaws to be the best tools available. But when McCulloch Corporation attempted to enter the residential consumer chainsaw market, its products met with resistance and failed to sell. The company asked Dave to figure out why. He found that the company had estimated sales based on the number of trees in each region. "But trees don't buy chainsaws," Dave pointed out to McCulloch, "people do."

He suggested that if McCulloch wanted to sell chainsaws to the residential market, it had to listen to what those customers wanted. Based on research findings, he suggested that home-use saws had to be much lighter in weight, easier to start, and quieter than their professional counterparts. Professional chainsaws were designed to survive two hundred hours of heavy use and were so finely tuned they required periodic servicing. Dave's research indicated that residential chainsaws were typically used only two to four hours per year, and six months would often go by between uses, at which point the consumer would expect the chainsaw to start. The chainsaws McCulloch injected into the residential market were wholly inappropriate for the targeted consumers. A homeowner did not need a chainsaw that would last one hundred years but he did need one that would start right up after a winter in the shed.

Dave's research-driven advice was not eagerly received by McCulloch engineers. As Dave discovered, engineers are notorious for concluding that consumers should accommodate themselves to well-engineered products. Nevertheless, McCulloch made its chainsaws lighter, quieter, and easier to use. Sales picked up.

His success with McCulloch earned him a new job: the chainsaw maker hired him away from Marplan to be their director of corporate planning. It turned out to be his last position before beginning his own company, and it also reaffirmed the basic tenets he would use to run J.D. Power and Associates: be objective, let the data speak for itself, and above all, take an independent approach, which allows you to see both the forest and the trees. Everything Dave had learned at Ford Tractor, Marplan, and McCulloch told him there was a better way to utilize market research. Dave transitioned into his own firm—with McCulloch as his first and by far his largest client—committed to following through on these ideas and creating a firm that would deliver market research in a new, better way—focused not on the needs of the corporation but on the needs of the customer. This focus on customer satisfaction would be one of the greatest distinguishing characteristics of Dave's company, which he christened J.D. Power and Associates.

Birth of a Company

Dave's entrepreneurial spirit kicked in one night in 1968, as he spent an evening with old friends from the Wharton School. They talked of embarking on a risky, exciting venture, and Dave let himself imagine what he could do with his own market research company. He considered giving up his stable position with McCulloch and discussed the idea with Julie, who by now was a full-time homemaker taking care of their three young children. Always his sounding board and most trusted adviser, Julie knew the decision rested with her, and she told him, "Let's go for it."

For most of its first four decades, J.D. Power and Associates was most closely associated with serving the automobile industry. It didn't start out that way. "To the extent I had a plan for the business," Dave recalls, "I anticipated we would conduct market research studies for the consumer goods and services segment." His young company, funded by a double mortgage on the family home, began to serve clients beyond McCulloch. The first clients of J.D. Power and Associates included U.S. Borax, Pacific Telephone Company, and firms working in the cosmetics, advertising, food, and glue industries. In the early years, Dave struggled to keep busy in any way he could. "If we had a strategic plan, it was to preserve cash flow."

That plan meant that everybody in the family pitched in. "Julie had more effect than anyone else on the company's start-up," Dave recalls. Julie and the children were an integral part of the company, and especially helpful in sending out and processing the many mailed survey forms. She served as the kids' "supervisor" and sat them down at tray tables in the living room, where they attached quarters to the questionnaires—an inducement for recipients to complete the survey—while she prepared dinner. When the kids were at school, and after they had gone to bed, Julie sat at the kitchen table, coding surveys and tabulating results, looking for patterns in the data. Dave was often stationed at that kitchen table, too, with pen and yellow legal pad, putting in the long hours necessary to get his nascent firm off the ground. The bedrock of Dave's company was infused with the sense of family.

Tom Gauer, who joined the young company in 1970 while still in high school, saw Dave and Julie as a consummate team. Gauer also saw Dave as a father figure and worked alongside the Power children processing surveys. Gauer then put himself through college by working at J.D. Power part-time, happily switching to full-time upon graduation. Gauer became known during the 1990s as employee number one because he was at that time the longest-serving employee who was not a member of the Power family.

"When you look at the two of them early on," Gauer recalls, "you'd almost look at Julie as being the one who wore the pants in the family, and Dave was sort of this soft-spoken, 'yes, dear' sort of guy." The dynamic was surprising "from the standpoint of the impact and knowledge he had regarding the industry." Dave was the knowledgeable, insightful visionary, Gauer says, "but in the day-to-day running of things I think Julie was more involved than a lot of us realized."

Linda Hirneise, who was recruited by Dave from her work as a business teacher at the high school Dave and Julie Power's kids attended, also became part of the extended Power family. While she had been a favorite teacher of the Power children, she and her husband also became friendly with Dave and Julie, who invited them to dinner when first encouraging Hirneise to join the firm. The social invitation was part of the vetting process for new associates, Hirneise recalls, as it was especially important to Julie that new associates fit into the family. "She would get to know the individual and get to know their values, and she was a very, very good judge of character." Julie was Dave's sounding board for vetting people: whom he could take a chance on, whom he could trust, says Steve Goodall, who succeeded Dave as company president. "I remember him saying a couple of times, 'This person is fairly good at this or that, but I was talking to Julie . . .'," Goodall recalls. "Or he would say, 'Julie was right about that person.' He said that more than once."

Over the years, Hirneise grew very close to Julie Power, also a former teacher. Julie gave her emotional support during her pregnancy and when she took maternity leave, but also guided her in the firm. "Julie taught me four principles very early on: passion, integrity, balance, and impact." She credits Julie as her "most revered mentor." As she grew to know her, Hirneise learned that Julie was gregarious and adventurous as well as driven to make the firm, and her husband, succeed. But shortly into their friendship, Julie was struck with a serious new concern, which traumatized the Powers and rippled into its extended work family: she was diagnosed with multiple sclerosis, and she would battle the disease for the next twenty years, even while she continued to be active in the firm and Dave's most ardent supporter.

Once the new associates came on board, Julie was also one to keep them on an even keel, Hirneise says. "Julie was tough. She was very strong, with high expectations. But none of us wanted to under-deliver." Of course, the rapidly growing firm attracted a lot of driven people, some of whom came on board with significant egos, and if an associate talked down about a colleague, "Julie would not stand for that," Hirneise says. "She would say either tell me more and back it up, or lay off." But along with Julie's strictness came a positive spirit. "That infectious smile encouraged us daily to do the best we could." And by Julie's side was soft-spoken Dave, the other half of an inspirational leadership duo. "The internal culture at J.D. Power was not driven by egos," Hirneise says. "It was driven by collaboration, by inspiration, by Julie having tremendous expectations, and by Dave creating this entrepreneurial environment, allowing us to take risks."

For a time, Julie Power had an office with her name on it, but that was not where her input to Dave or influence emanated from, says Steve Goodall. "I got a sense that most evenings, or at least a couple of times a week, he and she would talk business. It was not about meeting quotas, or the P&L. Almost always it was about people."

Julie's actions during those years stretched beyond being the matriarch to the extended Power family of associates. She regularly accompanied Dave when he gave speeches or presented plant awards or led company happenings, making fast friends with many industry executives and becoming essential to Dave as he grappled with the growing firm. "Every event, every roundtable, Dave had her at his side," recalls Pete Marlow, who became communications manager for J.D. Power and Associates in 1998. "He gave her all the credit for everything." Marlow remembers Dave often saying "I could not do it without my wife."

Julie would often be the one to say what they both were thinking, Dave recalls. "Where I was much more reserved in my comments, Julie would really say it like it is—to clients!" The couple would be having dinner with industry executives, perhaps Ford CEO Jac Nasser or Jack Smith, head of General Motors, and Julie would respond to one of their comments by asking "You really don't mean that, do you?" At times, Dave says with a laugh, "I'd want to kick her under the table and tell her to shut up!" Clients would notice Dave's discomfort in these moments. "They loved it. I guess they saw me squirming in my seat."

That straight talk endeared her to people across the industry as much as it did to company associates. "She was trusted by the clients," Hirneise says, adding, "I would travel across the world to client organizations, and there wasn't a time when a client representative wouldn't say 'How is Julie doing? Please give Julie our regards.'"

For many years after J.D. Power had created a worldwide network of offices, Dave held company-wide conferences at which Julie would appear with Dave to tell of the company's history, growth, and values, such as integrity and honesty. "Everyone talked about the J.D. Power family, the way we ran the company," Dave says. "Everyone felt they were part of the family."

Many felt they were part of a mission as well. Dave managed to instill in his associates a passionate belief in what they were collectively trying to accomplish. "Dave was clearly driven by the desire to represent the voice of the customer in an independent and impactful way," says Dave Sargent, vice president in J.D. Power and Associates' global automotive division. Sargent says that while the company had an enjoyable environment and the quality of work was satisfying, "there was this other dimension to it: the feeling that what you were doing was worthwhile and making people's lives better."

In those early years, Dave had a vision for how syndicated market research could be conducted for a profit. Back when he worked for Marplan and conducted a thorough market research study for McCulloch, he had an insight. Why not expand the study to include not only McCulloch products but also the chainsaws of all the major manufacturers in the chainsaw market? As he saw it, research that was narrowly focused on one client and purely proprietary could never help a company understand dynamic trends across an entire industry. "I wanted to do some studies on speculation, where we would own the data and sell the information to multiple clients," he says. "I made the case that if Marplan conducted solid market research at a cost lower than any one manufacturer could do on their own, then we could make a good economic case for selling our study." The company wasn't interested and Dave never got an opportunity to test that theory at Marplan. His opportunity would come just one year into doing business on his own, however, when he launched a syndicated study on the California banking industry.

Any number of factors contributed to the success of J.D. Power and Associates but none is was more significant than Dave's willingness to bet his company on the revolutionary market research business model of syndicated, industry-wide studies. By tradition (and this was true of Marplan and everywhere else Dave worked), market research was conducted on a strictly proprietary basis. Under the proprietary model, when an organization—a company or a group of companies working together—wanted market research, it commissioned a study, paid for it, and owned the results, which it considered part of its proprietary marketing information. This was especially true of automakers. "In the automobile industry," Dave explains, "the market research department had the term that you were a 'supplier.' They owned the supplier in the sense that they controlled them. They'd have four or five suppliers, and they would dole out studies to them. They would even design the studies and tell you how to run them."

Even in the rare cases in which two or more companies cooperated to share the costs of market research, the results were kept confidential. Under this business model, market research companies were held captive by the company sponsoring the research and were expected to work for that company exclusively. It was considered a conflict of interest for market research firms to serve competing clients in the same industry or market. "I did not want to be a supplier, and that moved us into the control of the data and doing studies industry-wide. The key element to it was that we covered the whole industry."

Dave established a new direction for automotive market research by being the first to conduct major syndicated studies for the auto industry. But the studies were possible only because Dave was willing to accept the risks of funding them himself, then trying to sell the results to as many subscribers as possible. The more subscribers he could get, the more profitable the study would be. There was a constant risk that any particular study would fail to pay for its sunk costs, a situation that could prove terminal for an independent company like Dave's. "Most of my key competitors asked, 'How can you afford to risk doing this? How can you afford to fund all of these studies? Isn't it a big risk?' But the big risk was doing it the conventional way."

Dave made plans to launch his first independently funded syndicated study by seeking an appropriate industry, an industry that served customers who would be both convenient and inexpensive to identify and survey. Looking around, he quickly zeroed in on the California banking market as an ideal segment to survey. "Almost everyone has a banking relationship," he says, "so I knew it would be relatively easy to identify and survey respondents. Since there were more than one hundred banks and S&Ls operating in the state, I thought the banking industry represented a good way to test the model of syndicated surveys."

Dave embarked on a prototype study of the banking industry to examine customer service issues in retail and commercial banking, including customer experiences with emerging technologies such as ATMs and credit cards. The idea was sound but banks did not prove to be receptive clients, and the project, which ran from 1969 to 1971, was not repeated.

That first attempt at a syndicated study, however, provided Dave with a number of valuable lessons. First, it foreshadowed a problem his company would repeatedly encounter: it wasn't safe to assume that client companies always welcomed facing the realities of their customers' experiences.

Dave had hoped that Bank of America, which had about 40 percent of the banking market in California, would subscribe to the study. In this hope he was wrong, but he learned another valuable lesson: his mistake was approaching the company through its in-house market research department. He quickly realized that in-house market research departments would be hostile to anything

J.D. Power proposed. At this point, Dave didn't have the contacts to go over the heads of the Bank of America market research managers, but he was determined to cultivate such high-level relationships so he could have other points of access into potential customers.

Despite Bank of America's intransigence, J.D. Power and Associates sold enough subscriptions to other banks in the study that they broke even on the project. From this outcome Dave took away a couple of other lessons that helped him hone his business model. "We needed at least three subscription sales to cover the costs of a survey. Four subscribers allowed us to break even, considering fixed costs. The fifth and subsequent subscriptions represented pure profit. So we needed to concentrate on industries in which there were at least five to six major players and a constellation of secondary players."

A Congenial, Data-Focused Approach

Dave had known that conducting market research was expensive, but he quickly found out that conducting independent market research was both expensive and risky. Whenever he authorized a syndicated study, he had no way of being certain the investment would repay its costs, much less make a profit for the company. The company's business model was persuading subscribers to buy the syndicated studies. That was its bread and butter. But while Dave had one eye on the bottom line, most of his energy was devoted to generating independent information that would assist manufacturers in making better products.

In a business that largely relied on cultivating personal relationships with the decision makers who would okay the research and select the company to perform it, Dave decided to take a different approach. "I didn't want to win by wining and dining," he explains. "I wanted to do it by providing information that an executive could

use, and that they respected. Of course, if you build up your reputation for being right and informative, it's easier to do."

John Humphrey, a longtime J.D. Power employee who worked
in the automotive research group and later opened the company's
offices in Shanghai, China, grasped Dave's priorities soon after
he joined the company in 1989. "I was immediately impressed by
Dave's passion for collecting information on behalf of clients,"
Humphrey says. "Yes, we were a business, but what truly made me
believe in the mission and the vision of the company was that, at
heart, Dave's vision was to get an unbiased view of what consumers
really experienced. Whether the results were accepted or attacked,
at the end of the day the results would help consumers get better
products and services."

Accurate Market Projections

After his first syndicated auto-industry project—a survey of trends
in the import car market—Dave boldly predicted that imports
would increase from less than 10 percent of the market to about a
third of the national market and half of the California market. He
was one of the first analysts to recognize market preferences for
smaller cars and front-wheel-drive cars. The results of the survey
were published in a 1972 issue of *Auto Age*, recalls Dave. In that
study, he also predicted the price of gasoline would increase to a
then-unimaginable two dollars per gallon. Few executives at the
domestic car companies believed him. That his predictions turned
out to be accurate didn't stop those executives from labeling Dave
Power as pro-import and anti-Detroit.

In 1971, he completed his second syndicated automotive project, a market research study of owners of front-wheel-drive passenger cars, such as the Honda 600 and entries from Subaru, to
gauge how well U.S. car buyers would accept them. Domestic car

companies took the position that front-wheel drive was inherently undesirable for reasons of safety and handling. "We showed that consumers were interested in front-wheel drive—if it performed well and was reliable," Dave recalled in a 1991 article in *California Business* magazine. "We did projections which pointed out the Japanese were moving fast in that direction."[6] It should have been obvious that front-wheel drive cars represented a significant market opportunity. Dave hoped that the domestic car companies would subscribe to the study, if only to get a better handle on a new technology that showed promise. He was disappointed that only Honda, Subaru, Mazda, and Peugeot subscribed. Still, it was enough for him to keep going. "With these studies, we found a niche and, best of all, the data belonged to J.D. Power and Associates," says Dave. "The clients subscribed to the report but the ownership of the data itself remained with us, and that became a strategic key to our independence."

He was vindicated. Within a few years, front-wheel drive became dominant in new car sales.

Charles Hughes, who would go on to lead Mazda and Range Rover in the U.S., first encountered Dave in 1976, when Hughes was working in market research for AMC. "I really admired Dave's take on market research and wished we could hire him," Hughes says. At the time, though, AMC—like all the Detroit car companies—didn't fully understand the value of the information Dave could provide. "American Motors spent a tremendous amount of money on very sophisticated consumer research, but it was mainly directed at getting consumers to buy the car rather than understanding whether they were happy when they got the car."

AMC also did not see the value of working with Dave because it was wrestling with a question that gripped all of the U.S. automakers at the time: was their customer the dealer or the driver? To the extent it was interested in drivers, AMC sent out a small customer satisfaction postcard survey to new owners with only a few questions. The most important question basically asked, "How do you like your car?" The postcard asked for responses on a three-point scale: excellent, fair, or poor. "In practice, we rated our performance on only how many people said AMC cars were excellent. We didn't do much with the other responses," Hughes says, "There was no intent to deliver a bad car. There were a lot of people throughout Detroit who were working as hard as they could to provide a good product. But they did not know what they did not know. There were gaps in their knowledge, and those gaps were filled in vividly by the first customer satisfaction study.

"The lion's share of the rising quality in the automobile industry can be laid at Dave Power's door. Dave transformed the automobile industry by making the syndicated research findings public. By providing consumers the ability to benchmark companies one against the other, the process drove companies into fixing their problems. When it was a secret—I hate to say it—companies didn't necessarily take care of things that should have been taken care of. Their sins were private. Once quality rankings became public, the incentives to raise quality became indisputable."

That customer-focused approach, along with Dave's independence, put J.D. Power and Associates in the position of uncovering problems automakers themselves had difficulty pinpointing. Often the executives' initial responses were a long way from gratitude, but Dave's focus on the independent data and his genial demeanor—the same tack he took in his exchange with the *Eastwind* captain about the errant beer cans—eventually persuaded many executives to view Dave as an adviser rather than a detractor.

Mazda O-Ring Breakthrough

A few years after Dave founded J.D. Power and Associates, he launched a small-scale, syndicated research study of how car buyers rated new car models. Determined to focus on products that appeared successful and innovative, he set his sights on the Mazda R100, powered by a type of internal-combustion power system new to American consumers: the Wankel rotary engine. Mazda was the first company to introduce a line of cars powered by an engine that replaced conventional reciprocating pistons with a rotary motion, providing increased power and better fuel economy. "The rotary engine was going to revolutionize the auto industry," Jamey Power, who spent most of his career at J.D. Power, explains. "It was akin to hybrid or electric motors today, and Mazda felt it had a shot at becoming the number-one import brand in the U.S. by employing that technology."

By the time Dave started studying the R100, Mazda of North America had sold more than ninety thousand rotary engine vehicles. Domestic manufacturers such as Ford began to take notice, and Detroit began making plans to adopt the technology.

Dave sent questionnaires to the first one thousand registered buyers of the Mazda R100. The company sold a number of subscriptions of the report to automakers. Mazda of North America, though, was not among them. The next year, Dave authorized a follow-up survey for the next one thousand buyers.

While tabulating the responses of Mazda drivers at her home's kitchen table, Julie Power noticed a pattern among purchasers who had owned the R100 for more than a year. A statistically significant number of buyers reported engine failure when their vehicles had between 30,000 and 50,000 miles on the odometer. Although J.D. Power had no way of knowing it at the time, the failure of the rotary engines would be traced to the failure of the O-ring gaskets designed to keep water from leaking out of the cooling system. When the gaskets failed, as they did on an astounding one out of every five cars, the rotary engines overheated and seized. Mazda, Dave realized, had a major problem on its hands, unless it quickly addressed the defect. The second report duly noted the problem.

Although each J.D. Power and Associates report included legal disclaimers stating that the data was confidential and for the exclusive use of the subscribers, the Mazda report was leaked to the *Wall Street Journal*, presumably by a competitor intent on embarrassing Mazda. The newspaper's Detroit bureau chief, Charles Camp, called Dave for a comment, which caught Dave by surprise. "He started asking me specific questions, and I could hear him flipping pages," Dave recalls. Clearly, Camp had an unauthorized copy of the report. To give himself some time, Dave said he had a press release that would answer most of the reporter's questions.

Dave had to scramble quickly. Not only did such a press release not exist, he had never written one before. He picked up a pencil and his trusty yellow legal pad and drafted his first press release, two pages, handwritten. His assistant found someone in the building with a telex machine (a precursor to the fax machine) to transmit it; they paid the telex operator five dollars to type it up and send it. The next day, the *Wall Street Journal*'s front-page headline said it all: "Wankel Engine's Durability Is Challenged By Research Firm; Mazda Attacks Data." The body of the article began, "A consumer survey by a California market research firm challenged the durability under U.S. driving conditions of the Wankel rotary engine used in the hot-selling Japanese-made Mazda car."[7]

The article positioned Dave as an expert. In that moment, J.D. Power and Associates was established as a national presence. Dave realized the value of this opportunity and subsequently sent the information to many other major domestic publications, from the *New York Times* to *Automotive News* magazine. "Within forty-eight hours, it had gone around the world," he recalls. It was at that point that his name became well known throughout the automobile industry, and when people spoke of the meteoric rise and decline of Mazda in the 1970s, Dave's role was often central to the narrative.

When the *Wall Street Journal* article quoting Dave was published, it caused a crisis at Mazda. Square in the crosshairs was the chief operating officer and general manager of Mazda's U.S. operations, C.R. "Dick" Brown. Dave had been trying to cultivate a working relationship with Brown for a year but had been continually rebuffed. Brown was, as Dave puts it, a command-and-control type who had been in the business many years with other companies. Only months before, an angry Brown had not only declined to subscribe to the original study but had dismissed the study as the product of a "two-bit research outfit." Now Brown had a choice to make: acknowledge that the rotary engine had a problem or muzzle the messenger. Brown chose to muzzle the messenger and embarked on a public feud with Dave Power. He asked Dave to come to Mazda's offices.

"Are you trying to kill us?" Dave recalls Brown asking as soon as he arrived. "No, I'm not," Dave responded. "This is a syndicated study, done independently. We did one earlier this year and you didn't purchase it. Nor did you purchase this one. But fourteen car manufacturers did." Dave stood behind the results and stated his credo: "These are the facts and there's no denying them." But that is exactly what Brown attempted to do. Mazda had copied the J.D. Power survey and conducted its own study. When Dave met with Brown, he saw the results: a stack of fifty thousand surveys piled in an office, all keypunched and run through a computer. Brown showed Dave the results and accused J.D. Power and Associates of inflating the Mazda failure rate, because the Mazda study showed that only two to three percent of owners had a problem with the O-ring. But Mazda's study had included all buyers, and Dave pointed out to Brown that the engines only started to fail at 30,000 miles. He asked Brown to run the data by mileage. When Mazda researchers reprocessed the surveys, filtered to just those owners, the results were similar to Dave's: 20 percent of the engines failed. "I knew that even a 5 percent failure rate was a major problem and would be an absolute disaster when it reached 10 percent," Dave says. When Brown saw the results, he was astounded, Dave recalls. "He didn't challenge me anymore."

Rodney E. "Rod" Hayden, at the time, was vice president and general manager of Mazda Central (and went on to serve as Mazda's chief operating officer in the U.S.). He recommended that the company be less defensive and work more quickly to correct the problem. He was tracking the costs of the warranty repairs for existing buyers, and the expense threatened to ruin the company. "We were replacing engines left and right, no questions asked," Hayden says. "It became more and more evident that we did have a problem. It seemed to me that J.D. Power and Associates was providing a service. Dave Power simply provided research for manufacturers that the manufacturers were neglecting to do on their own.

"Bringing the problem with the rotary engine to light was a blessing in disguise for Mazda," Hayden adds. "Sure, it was painful. But if it hadn't happened, if Dave Power hadn't been on the scene to bring the rotary engine's problem into focus, the problem would have gone on for a longer period of time, and it would have been much more expensive to overcome, if Mazda could have survived it at any cost. Through Dave Power's findings and the resulting consumer pressure, Mazda found the will to make the necessary changes and emerged as a stronger competitor."

Had Mazda accepted the criticism and quietly made changes (as it eventually was forced to do), the story could have quietly faded away. But because Mazda reflexively discredited the data and attacked the validity of the J.D. Power methodology, the story took off. The media thrived on the conflict. In the next few weeks, references to Dave and his fledgling company appeared in print, radio, and TV news outlets around the world. Overnight, Dave's research firm and its independent syndicated research model acquired global prestige. From then on, Dave Power's phone number started appearing in the Rolodexes and on the speed dials of business reporters around the world.

But as Dave's business was bolstered by the controversy, a valuable ally and friend was also being developed. Mazda executive Dick Brown, who had initially scorned Dave and rebuffed his independent report, saw the logic of the data and realized the value of the market researcher's approach. "Next time," Brown told Dave a month later, "I want you on my side."

CHAPTER TWO

END RUN TO THE DECISION MAKER

Shortly after Dave launched his new company in 1968, he got a lead on the automaker that was to become his breakthrough client. A friend from the McCann-Erickson advertising agency called and said, "You know, there is this car company from Japan that is trying to market their cars in the United States. They are located in Torrance, California, and they are looking for market research. It has a funny name." Thus Dave, within weeks of opening his doors, made a trip to the offices of Toyota Motor Sales U.S.A.

It was the first of many fruitless trips. The manager in charge of Toyota marketing and advertising, Jim Davey, would not even give Dave the courtesy of a meeting. Later, when Dave managed to get him on the phone, the manager curtly said that Toyota had interviewed a number of market research companies and had made its selection. "I think I have more experience in automotive marketing research than anyone west of the Mississippi," Dave replied, "and I only ask for a chance to show you." The offer fell on deaf ears. Nonetheless, Dave kept visiting Torrance in the hope that the manager would reconsider. One day, while cooling his heels in the Toyota lobby, Dave noticed one brochure among a number of brochures in a rack. It described some of the forklift trucks that Toyota manufactured. He suddenly had an idea.

In 1968, Toyota's entire U.S. presence was composed of about twenty people, including the advertising manager Dave knew was the most direct route to getting a market research contract. But now he thought he just might have another entrée into Toyota. He asked the receptionist if the executive in charge of forklift products was available. The receptionist directed him to a small outbuilding behind the main office. There, working out of a spartan office, were a couple of Japanese managers, led by a Mr. Okamoto and speaking halting English, who were pleased to welcome a visitor, with or without an appointment. Dave got right to the point. "I know more about the forklift truck market than anyone in California," he announced. He briefly described his experience with Ford Tractor and J.I. Case, explaining how Case's transition from agricultural equipment to construction and Dave's Ford Tractor study on two-step distribution gave him a unique perspective on the market trends and retailing of heavy equipment. "Would it be valuable for you to have an overview of the market for all of the U.S.?"

"We believe it would be useful to have such a report," Okamoto admitted.

"I can do one for you."

"How much will it cost?" Okamoto asked.

Dave thought strategically. This was his chance to demonstrate his value to Toyota beyond the forklift business and perhaps gain indirectly the business he had failed thus far to secure directly. "I can complete the report for six hundred dollars," he said. "And I can have it for you in two weeks." He got the green light to proceed.

A Green Light from Toyota

Dave was back with the finished report in three days. It was a three-ring binder full of summary charts and detailed information.

Okamoto was so delighted with his performance that Dave took the opportunity to ask for an introduction to Okamoto's Japanese counterpart in the automotive division. Okamoto picked up the phone and, after a flurry of Japanese, escorted him to meet Mr. Nagaya. Dave was beginning to understand that Japanese managers in the U.S. were more receptive, more open-minded, and certainly more courteous than their American colleagues. Dave quickly perfected one of the most important strategies of his career: if there is an obstacle, go around it. Over the subsequent decades, J.D. Power and Associates would have ample opportunity to benefit from this insight.

Nagaya very politely asked what Dave proposed to do for Toyota in the United States. As it was midday, Dave suggested that the conversation continue over lunch. Somewhat to Dave's surprise, the invitation was accepted and, in due course, he found himself at a small restaurant in Gardena. It was to be his first—but definitely not last—business lunch conducted over a Japanese meal. After the conversation, he drove back to the Toyota office thinking he would drop off Mr. Nagaya and be on his way, but another surprise awaited him. Nagaya invited him inside and escorted him to an empty conference room. After a few minutes, his host returned to introduce a slightly older Japanese executive whose business card, carefully tendered, identified Tatsuro Toyoda, vice president and general manager of Toyota Motor Sales U.S.A. Dave surmised, and would later confirm, that he was meeting with the son of Kiichiro Toyoda, the founder of the Toyota Motor Corporation. Tatsuro Toyoda would someday become president of the entire company, but at that moment, he leaned forward in a slight bow, awaiting receipt of Dave's business card.

Dave's business card identified him as the president of "J.D. Power and Associates, Marketing, Planning, and Consulting."

Dave watched Toyoda study his card. Looking back after years of working with Japanese executives, Dave suspects that Toyoda would have noted Dave's title and must have appreciated that he was dealing with a company president. At the same time, Toyoda must have surmised that Dave's operation was a small one. This realization, no doubt, gave Toyoda pause. Dave would come to learn that Japanese executives place a great deal of emphasis on organizational hierarchy, business stability, and structure.

Toyoda's next question surprised Dave. "I know you are just starting your business," he said. "What I would like to know is where are your files?" Dave hesitated in his response. "I actually did have some client files, but I decided it wouldn't be proper to show them." Instead, smiling, Dave tapped his temple. Toyoda smiled in return at this very American gesture and said, "I understand you have a good understanding of the U.S. automobile market and you worked in Detroit. Okay, what can you do for us?" Dave indicated he would come back the following day with a written proposal.

The next day, he presented the proposal and a number of copies to Nagaya, who then left the room to brief Toyoda. In addition to describing the study and its benefits to Toyota, the proposal included a typed contract, which already included Dave's signature and indicated a place for Toyoda's signature. In a few minutes, the signed contract was returned. It was clear to Dave that Toyoda had relied on the briefing and hadn't even read the proposal. "It was the easiest sale of my life," Dave recalls.

But perhaps the sweetest part of the victory was what happened next. "Mr. Power," Nagaya said, "before you leave there is someone I would like you to meet." Taking a copy of Dave's proposal, he led him down a narrow corridor of cubicles. At the end of the hallway, Nagaya stepped into a cubicle so small Dave was forced to wait in the corridor. It was then he noticed the nameplate on the smoked glass: Jim Davey, Advertising Manager. Nagaya had apparently put a copy of the proposal on Davey's desk. There was silence for about fifteen seconds and then Davey's angry protest emerged, complete with stomping feet: "You can't do that! We've already assigned a project to another market research firm." Nagaya ignored the outburst and led Dave away.

In that moment, Dave had his first glimpse of the complicated relationship between the Japanese and American managers of Japanese companies, a relationship often characterized by mistrust and mutual suspicion. He soon discovered that many Japanese businesspeople looked down on their American counterparts for focusing too much on the bottom line instead of on relationships and for being unprepared, litigious, and most of all—as Davey's outburst had demonstrated—rude. In the Japanese culture, where politeness is paramount, such lack of courtesy is inexcusable. In practice, this lack of trust between the American and Japanese staffs led to significant operational problems in firms such as Toyota, Honda, and Nissan.

Toyota's attitude was markedly different from the hubris that emanated from Detroit. In the late 1960s, Japanese engineers were well aware of the ongoing poor perception of their products in the United States. In the decades after World War II, "the label Made in Japan was not a compliment," explains Leslie Kendall, chief curator at the Petersen Automotive Museum in Los Angeles. Japanese goods were mocked for their shabbiness. The Toyopet, Toyota's first export to the U.S., was widely derided for its inability to withstand American highway driving. "It was a sturdy, small gas-sipper—very appropriate for rutted Japanese roads—but woefully underpowered," says Kendall. That first Toyota, like cars from other early Japanese entrants Datsun and Prince Motor Company (which would eventually be folded into Nissan), "couldn't keep up on American highways for any sustained period of time without the engines wearing out." In fact, Toyota was so affected by the failure of the Toyopet that it briefly abandoned the North American passenger car market altogether. "To Toyota's credit, they were able to say, 'This isn't working,' and pull out," says Kendall. "They then came back with a vengeance in the '60s with the Corona."

Dave understood that in giving him this market research assignment, Toyota was testing him as well as its own American staff. Toyota retained Dave as a countermeasure to the other market research firm, which they did not completely trust. He understood that Toyota would evaluate the market research he produced against what the other vendor produced for the American staff. "That made me work all the harder, determined to deliver the study before the other guys did." The clock was ticking.

Quarters, Face-Up

In a flurry of activity, J.D. Power and Associates established its first office in a windowless room on Wilshire Boulevard in Los Angeles. Meanwhile, Dave researched Toyota's main competitors in Southern California. Working on the living room floor, his children returned to taping quarters, face-up, on questionnaires. The Southern California Imported Car Buyers Study—J.D. Power and Associates' first study for Toyota—drew a 45 percent response rate, which is considered very credible. Every day, Dave brought a batch of responses home for his wife, Julie, to tabulate on a manual spreadsheet.

The study suggested some strategies for how Toyota could increase sales of its Corona model. At that time, the most successful import car was the Volkswagen Beetle. The study suggested that one reason VW was successful was due to its strong dealer network. While VW did not have many dealers, its dealers were well placed, disciplined, and had the necessary support for service and maintenance. In addition, the study suggested that the average buyer of the Corona was seven years older and more affluent than buyers of competitive imports models. These were significant insights Toyota would embrace on its road to market dominance. The study indicated a market position that would give Toyota leadership of the import market, and underscored a key factor in Volkswagen's success up to that point: an efficient, low-cost, and relatively small dealership body, which would come to characterize Toyota's success as well.

Dave was so eager to present the report that he was still collating the management summary in the back of the car as he was being driven to Toyota's office. He had beaten the other market research company by turning in his study first. In a big meeting room, he presented the study. There were about twenty American managers in the room, all managers Toyota had recruited from GM, Ford, and Chrysler, as well as importers such as Renault and Peugeot. Also in the room, sitting in the back, were five or six Japanese executives. The Americans, many dressed informally, were noisy and not very engaged with Dave's presentation. Questions were few. The Japanese, all wearing black suits with white shirts and black ties, sat quietly and wrote furiously in little black notebooks they all carried. When the presentation concluded, the American staff quickly filed out. The Japanese managers continued to ask questions and took more notes. Finally, one of the Japanese executives said, "Mr. Power, when can you go to Tokyo?" Dave blinked. He didn't even have a valid passport. Nevertheless, a passport and visa were arranged and, in due course, he made the first of more than fifty trips he would take to Japan during his career.

Jamey Power recalls the family's excitement about the first trip: "It was like a pilgrimage. It had the feeling of an adventure." There was much for Dave to share with Toyota's Japanese staff, but also much for him to learn. His first lesson came quickly: pack light. Dave's suitcase was too big to fit in the trunk of the car of the Japanese staff member, Mr. Taguchi, who had met him at Tokyo's Haneda Airport. As Dave got in the car, Taguchi was visibly excited. "Did you hear?" he asked. "Toyota just won the Deming Prize." The Deming Prize is given to organizations that exemplify quality. It was established in 1951 by the Union of Japanese Scientists and Engineers (JUSE) to commemorate W. Edwards Deming, the American statistician who had helped Japanese industry rebuild with a focus on quality after World War II. Deming's work continued to be highly valued by Japanese auto engineers, and winning the annual prize reinforced that focus. But all of this was unknown to Dave. Clearly, there was a lot to learn.

Making Inroads at Toyota

Dave repeated his presentation in Tokyo to about sixty Toyota executives, all young, all dressed identically in black suits, and all fluent in English. The presentation that took two hours in California required two days in Tokyo because of the relentless questions the executives asked. "The attitude of the questioners and the insight of the questions impressed me," Dave recalls. "They never once questioned my findings, but they had endless questions about every detail of the survey. With American audiences I always get more arguments disguised as questions." His presentation must have impressed the Toyota managers because he returned to the U.S. with three more projects.

These projects began years of consulting for Toyota, whose Japanese management wanted the type of research Dave was eager to provide: analysis and interpretation of data. Within three years, Toyota became Dave's largest client. The company wanted to know what it should do to become the leading import in the U.S.; Dave's advice was to put an emphasis on its parts and service departments. He knew from his research that customer satisfaction was a function of both manufacturing quality and dealer performance. Toyota quickly doubled its field staff and started instituting programs to strengthen its dealers' abilities to deliver service and parts. This was the first time Dave felt he had an influence on the top management of a global company.

Dave added value in other ways, too. For example, Toyota was interested in offering a pickup truck to American drivers. The light truck market was an area where the Japanese automakers saw potential not being tapped by Detroit, and Toyota believed it could find drivers for smaller, less expensive, and more fuel-efficient trucks. There was only one obstacle: a tariff that would erase the vehicle's profit margins. Toyota asked Dave for his counsel in avoiding the so-called "chicken tax," a 25 percent levy (ten times that of other tariffs) on light trucks and other imported goods that was a retaliatory response by U.S. regulators to a tax on American chickens by European countries. Instituted in 1963, the tariff had been removed on many products, but the tax on light trucks was maintained as a political favor to domestic car companies.[1]

Dave confirmed that Toyota could avoid the tariff by exporting an incomplete truck to the U.S., then finishing assembly with U.S. components when it got into the country. Toyota could ship the entire truck except for the cargo box or truck bed, adding the missing parts once it was in the U.S. Dave worked with Toyota to source truck beds and other components to complete the vehicles for sale as light trucks in the U.S. Other projects followed.

It was the beginning of five years of intense activity with Toyota. Dave's young company expanded, due to his innovative approach and his penchant for hard work. He began a career-long practice of working late hours at his office, which cut into his family time, but the creative entrepreneur had a solution for that, too. His young children, when they were not putting in hours to earn a paycheck (complete with payroll stubs) on survey processing, could often be found at the office, even accompanied by the family dog, playing near Dave's desk and generally having the run of the place after the rest of the staff had gone home.

During its early years, J.D. Power and Associates completed dozens of market studies that helped Toyota penetrate the American market and build a robust, well-disciplined dealer network. "By 1971 Toyota represented 75 percent of our volume, 100 percent of our profit, and 150 percent of my time," says Dave. He traveled to Tokyo three or four times a year, and even hosted Tatsuro Toyoda and his family at a birthday party for Dave's children, Jamey and Mary, in 1970. "My relationship with Toyoda was somewhat formal but very warm, in the traditional Japanese fashion." Many years later, after Jamey had become a J.D. Power executive and he and Dave visited Toyota in Japan, Tatsuro Toyoda's son, Tatsuya—now also a company executive—met with them and produced a photo from that long-ago birthday party where he and Jamey played together in the yard atop toy vehicles.

Despite the closeness of Dave's relationship with Toyota, it was not a sustainable one. Due to its rapid growth, Toyota started hiring new managers, many of them market research professionals from Detroit. One of Dave's biggest professional mistakes was to help Toyota recruit two ex-Ford managers to head up the Toyota in-house market research staff. Before too long, the ex-Ford managers started treating Dave as a vendor instead of a trusted partner, and they built in-house market research capabilities that gradually took business away from J.D. Power and Associates. Dave watched helplessly as his company's privileged position was dismantled. Now Toyota wanted multiple suppliers on a bid basis; it wanted J.D. Power to do data collection or tabulation only. This was exactly the business environment Dave had left Detroit to avoid. "We faced a nearly impossible situation," he recalls. "We faced a client base dominated by a single manufacturer who was now telling us they did not need the type of marketing research expertise that we were committed to provide."

The Customer Is the Company

The success of Dave's efforts in helping Toyota understand the American market was a key element in the company's growing sales and the expansion of its U.S. staff, and Dave soon realized that there were many other companies that could benefit from such insight, both foreign and domestic. So, he redoubled efforts to create syndicated studies and, over the next decade, completed dozens of them. "We would pick a hot subject, like the Mazda rotary engine, and mail out a thousand questionnaires on it," he recalls. Other early studies focused on the Nissan 240Z, Volkswagen's Rabbit, or the downsized luxury cars being offered by Lincoln and Cadillac. "Those studies went well because there were a lot of new introductions and a lot of manufacturers who didn't have information on their competitors." Dave's innate curiosity also helped. "I saw the changes going on in the industry and always wanted to understand how and why things were going on the way they were."

Central to Dave's approach with syndicated studies was the premise that he needed to serve both his direct customers— the car companies who bought his studies—and the ultimate consumers—the drivers who would benefit from cars that brought them satisfaction. But as the Mazda rotary engine study had done, future studies would irk some executives at the very companies Dave hoped it would help. That led the young market researcher to learn another lesson about independence.

"Independence is the ability to say it like it is," Dave says, "even when you suspect that saying it will be received with displeasure. I always wanted to make sure that my staff at J.D. Power and Associates understood that the client is the company, not the individual they are dealing with. This is very critical, because if you treat the individual as the client, you lose the very independence that you claim to offer."

Influencers and Influences

The quiet confidence that allowed Dave to share the unvarnished truth with the auto industry's top leaders came from his intellectual curiosity as well as his upbringing. There were brilliant leaders and management thinkers who were instrumental in shaping modern American business, and in influencing Dave. There were also key individuals in his youth who set the course for the leader he would become.

Before studying business and becoming an entrepreneur, James David Power III learned about life from family role models. His father, James David Power Jr., and his uncles, Aloysius Francis Power and Reverend John Power, were three men with distinct approaches to life and work who provided daily lessons in conduct, demeanor, and character. His mother added her own steadying force.

Dave was born on May 30, 1931, and grew up during the golden age of the American auto industry. In the 1940s and 1950s, when he was a teenager and then a young adult entering the workforce, General Motors dominated the landscape not just in his hometown of Worcester, Massachusetts, but across the country and much of the world. It's hard to overemphasize the impact of GM on the American economy. In 1955, for example, when Dave had just recently graduated from College of the Holy Cross and was thinking about his future, GM manufactured more than half the cars sold in America. The most popular brand in America was Chevrolet. In addition, GM built 43 percent of the nation's trucks, 60 percent of all the diesel engines, and, if that weren't enough, GM's Frigidaire subsidiary was the world's largest maker of refrigerators. GM was the biggest of Detroit's Big Three, with Ford trailing far behind and Chrysler the perennial third.[2]

GM loomed large in Dave's early life in unexpected ways. He delivered newspapers, with a canvas bag slung over his shoulder, and one of his most eager customers was his grandfather, James David Power Sr., who would immediately open the newspaper to the stock market listings to see the closing price of GM. His modest investment in equities was probably all invested in GM stock, which made sense in the late 1930s because no stock was more blue-chip and dependable than GM.

The primary influences on Dave's upbringing were his parents. His father, known as Jim, was born in 1899 in Worcester, where the Powers had been rooted since the 1860s. He graduated from the College of the Holy Cross in Worcester in 1920 and became a high school classics and English teacher. In 1930 he married Helen Chaisson, a young woman from nearby Fitchburg he had met on a blind date. They had four children; their first, James David Power III, was known as Dave. Jim and Helen put a lot of trust in their children and bestowed upon them the responsibility of living up to it.

Dave's mother was soft-spoken and frugal, yet she always dressed fashionably. She was an avid reader and challenged her children to stump her with a word she didn't know, a feat that was never accomplished. Helen had the distinction of being "the first in the family to work for the automobile industry," Dave says. Fresh out of high school, she worked as a secretary for the Ford dealership in Fitchburg. After her fourth child was born, she returned to work and held executive secretarial positions at an insurance company until retiring at age sixty-five. At work, she was known as meticulous and professional; at home, she provided the discipline to Dave and his younger siblings, Richard, Ann, and John.

Jim Power was a gentle, quiet man and "very, very good," says Dave's sister, Ann, of their father. He emphasized education over all else, and evenings would find him working with his children on their homework. His example of devotion to education was such that, as Dave recalls, "they almost had to carry him out" of his classroom at seventy, the school system's mandatory retirement age.

Jim provided Dave with a firm grounding of what it meant to be a productive, respectable man, even if he did not offer an exact blueprint for his son's career path. Although Dave was certain that he did not want to become an educator himself, he carried on the trait of encouraging ideas from anyone who shared a spark for insights and information.

Dave's father admired traits in Dave that he himself did not possess and expressed his respect for his son's early accomplishments in a way not all fathers were able to do, especially in the mid-twentieth century. "I remember my dad wasn't a very forceful advocate for his own situation. He was reticent to criticize people, and I know my mother was upset that he didn't stand up to a couple of things." When it became clear that Dave had the ability to speak truth to power, Jim openly commended him. "My dad would say to me that he was just amazed at what I was able to do."

Although life in Worcester was a far cry from Detroit, one member of the family had an intimate connection to the industry that would become Dave's life's work. Born a few years after Dave's father, Al Power—Uncle Al—also attended Holy Cross, and went on to law school at Fordham University in New York. In 1927, he took a job in the legal department at GM and, through loyalty, diligence, and patience, rose through the ranks, becoming chief counsel in the early 1960s. In this role, he supervised a global legal department of thousands of people. The GM board of directors relied on him for legal advice; few company officials had more influence and authority.

Al Power enjoyed the good life that an executive career at GM provided. His family lived in the most fashionable part of Detroit, near other GM executives, and he socialized casually with the most powerful men in the company. He often flew to New York on the company airplane to attend GM board of directors meetings.

He was also destined to play a critical role in the Chevrolet Corvair incident exposed by consumer activist Ralph Nader in his book *Unsafe at Any Speed*. The 1965 book skewered manufacturers for resisting safety measures, focusing most famously on the Corvair. A congressional hearing was later convened to review claims that GM had investigated Nader in an effort to discredit him. Al was forced to take responsibility for launching the investigation, and GM President Jim Roche offered a public apology. From Dave's point of view, Nader acheived impact by launching attacks on GM and other car manufacturers rather than what Dave considered more positive means. Seat belts were a good thing, but Dave believed there was a better way to engage with manufacturers to do what was good for customers. "Nader had a group of young college types known as Nader's Raiders," he says. "They did their own research to attack GM and others on their safety records, but their studies were flawed and unprofessional." Instead, Dave's work started by asking customers what they were experiencing, something that the self-appointed expert Nader never did.

Dave's other uncle, John, held great sway on his nephew's education. He was the oldest of the Power boys, four years older than Dave's father. Known to the family as Father John, he was a conservative parish priest, strict and demanding, but he cared deeply about the upbringing of all the Power children in the extended family. "He would tell me to stand up straight, shoulders back, things like that," Dave recalls. When Dave was a sophomore in high school, Father John suggested that the children be given a parochial education, so all were transferred to St. Peter's School, across town from the family home. As the oldest, Dave had the responsibility of driving them all to school in the family car and, as the only student with a car, the young driver was also pressed into service by the nuns to do errands or extracurricular duties. After high school, with the further support of Father John, Dave pursued college at Holy Cross, where the previous Power generation had studied and, like his father and two uncles, he pursued a liberal arts degree.

Thus, when Dave began in the working world, his character had been built on a three-legged stool of disparate influences: the strong guidance of one uncle helped usher him into a Jesuit college education, another uncle provided him with the example of hard work leading to success in the business world, and his parents instilled in him a strong sense of integrity and independence. He was well equipped to take on the Coast Guard, business school, and the apprenticeships in his chosen field, which led him to build his own unique and lasting professional firm.

Titans of Business Thinking

Since his youth, Dave had welcomed intellectual influences, and he continued to learn from others as he made his way in the business world. Four men in particular became significant influences on Dave's entrepreneurial approach: Peter Drucker, W. Edwards Deming, Alvin Toffler, and Walter Wriston.

Peter Drucker was a renowned corporate consultant, teacher, and author by the time Dave set his sights on the business world. His thinking was responsible for management theory becoming accepted as a discipline, and he was the first writer to examine the American corporation in scientific detail.

Born in Austria in 1909, and then earning a 1931 doctorate from Frankfurt University, Drucker escaped his country in 1933 as Hitler rose to power, and immigrated with his young wife to the United States before World War II. It was during his second teaching job, at Bennington College in Vermont, that he connected with the industry that would also become Dave Power's focus: Drucker was given the opportunity to study General Motors. He took a teaching hiatus and, after a two-year study of GM's management structure, wrote the best-selling *Concept of a Corporation*, published in 1946. Drucker's most lauded book, *The Practice of Management* (1954), put an even finer focus on the value and purpose of business.[3]

His entrepreneurial, practical approach, evident in that seminal study of the auto industry leader General Motors, had a great effect on Dave as a young MBA student getting his feet wet by studying the same industry. A number of ideas from Drucker's work resonated with Dave, and some of those tenets, including a commitment to putting customers first, became the very basis on which J.D. Power and Associates' services would be modeled. Drucker accepted Dave's invitation to speak at a dealer roundtable event in Palm Springs in 1991.

In W. Edwards Deming, a groundbreaking proponent of the focus on quality in business and industry worldwide, Dave Power found much inspiration. Deming (1900–1993) was a statistician who developed a career in academia and business by applying mathematical processes to industrial problems. Before and during World War II, he consulted with the U.S. government on programs at the USDA and the U.S. Census Bureau,[4] where he served as head mathematician.[5] After the war, the U.S. government tapped his expertise to help Japan recover its industrial capacity. His multiple trips to the war-damaged nation inspired a new generation of managers to focus on quality.

The Japanese people revered him for his work in helping to rebuild Japan and set the country on a course to prosperity. JUSE created the Deming Prize, an annual award for quality, in his name after his lectures to the organization, and it became a much-coveted affirmation of a company's focus on quality. Esteem for Deming was further cemented when Japanese Emperor Hirohito presented him with the Second Order Medal of the Sacred Treasure in 1960.[6]

Both Deming and Dave stood for improving quality and using data in innovative ways, but their approaches to that end were fundamentally different. Deming focused on analyzing engineering and production statistics to make incremental improvements to boost product quality. His process demanded measurements at every stage of the manufacturing chain to continually improve quality. He infused in the Japanese carmakers the conviction that they could attain a higher level of quality than anyone else in the world through the application of a statistical process.

By contrast, Dave's focus was on reflecting quality from the consumer's point of view. The data he generated concerned the experience consumers had with their cars. By providing specific feedback on what consumers expected and perceived in the automobile products they owned, carmakers had the opportunity to update their rigid design, engineering, and manufacturing processes. From Dave's point of view, satisfying the customer was the main goal of any quality-improvement process.

Dave had at least one thing in common with Deming, however. For many years, American car manufacturers ignored or resisted what Deming was doing in Japan, even as evidence mounted that the Japanese car companies were more successful in building quality products and every year were capturing more market share from Detroit. This was precisely the same view Detroit had of Dave's work. U.S. car company executives and engineers didn't think they needed lessons from a Dr. Deming in Japan or a Dave Power in California. The insularity of the Big Three car companies would not be breached until the gains of the Japanese car companies created financial pain that could no longer be ignored. (Ford's president, Donald E. Petersen, invited Deming to review Ford's operations in 1981.)[7]

Dave met Deming near the end of Deming's life at an Automotive World Congress, where the famed statistician presented a keynote speech from his wheelchair and kept the audience spellbound. "Even though American automakers largely ignored him," Dave says, "Deming was sure he was correct, and equally sure that American automakers who failed to stress quality would have a very difficult time. In this, as in most things, Dr. Deming was right."

Dave has always taken an inquisitive, forward-thinking approach to business, so it is no surprise that the work of the futurist Alvin Toffler, author of the best-selling books *Future Shock* and *The Third Wave,* resonated so passionately with him. Toffler, whose early career included work as an editor at *Fortune* magazine,[8] turned his attention to the coming technological revolution when consulting with IBM in the 1960s, at the dawn of the computer age. The project taken on by Toffler and his wife and writing partner, Heidi, examined how technology was producing a revolution for society and also for business, and Toffler became an influential voice for business leaders.[9]

Dave encountered Toffler's first book, *Future Shock,* in the 1970s when a Japanese executive at Toyota who was pursuing a master's degree asked Dave to help him write a report on the book. One of Dave's strengths is his willingness to be open to new information, and in this groundbreaking work, he found inspiration. Toffler asserted that vast structural change, on the magnitude of a revolution, was underway in society, an idea that resonated with Dave. Toffler argued that the evolution to a "super-industrial society" was overwhelming and alienating to people, creating what Toffler called "information overload."

Dave was later captivated by the implications of *The Third Wave* (1980) in which Toffler describes three types of societies. Using the metaphor of waves, Toffler suggests that each subsequent wave builds on and pushes aside the wave that passed before it. The first wave was the society that organized for the agrarian revolution, Toffler said, following the earliest cultures of hunter-gatherers; the Industrial Revolution signaled the second wave; and the third wave was the creation of a post-industrial society. Toffler's views on the role of information, adaptive organizations, and mass customization meshed closely with the emerging role of J.D. Power and Associates, and Dave was convinced his company would be integral in society's evolution to this third wave.

Toffler's third book, *Powershift*, released in 1990, focuses on who controls all these societal and business changes. Together, the books comprise a thirty-year trilogy, which define the evolution of the modern corporation.[10]

"His books," says Dave, who routinely cites Toffler as a mentor, "especially *Powershift*, encouraged me to organize my company away from the command-and-control structure he criticized, in favor of shifting decision making down to customer-facing employees. That required educating employees about my goals and strategies." Dave tried to make J.D. Power and Associates as decentralized as possible. If an employee came up with an idea, Dave was likely to encourage him or her to pursue it. It was not a very structured environment and those employees who needed a great deal of structure tended to move on.

Dave was so impressed by reading Walter Wriston's 1992 book, *The Twilight of Sovereignty*, he took more than forty pages of notes. Wriston (1919–2005) was the single most influential commercial banker of his time, the chairman and CEO of Citicorp,[11] and the author of three books. Wriston's thesis in *The Twilight of Sovereignty* echoed themes explored by Dave's other intellectual mentors. In the book, written in pre-Internet 1992, Wriston argued that humanity's most important resource is its intellectual capabilities. The information revolution, he said, would have massive geopolitical implications in countries around the globe.[12]

"The critical lesson I drew from Wriston is the value of freely flowing information as the world continues to become more globalized," says Dave. "I took heart in this because spreading information was a founding purpose and mission of J.D. Power and Associates."

As Dave sought to affect positive change in the auto industry, he relied on the influence of these thought leaders as much as his own ability to forge relationships with leaders within the car companies. Dave's reserve of congeniality and reliance on the data proved invaluable as he faced some of his more intractable challenges.

Taking It to the Top

Dave's focus on doing what was best for the client often spurred him to find creative ways to get his message across, especially if what he had to say was falling on deaf ears. When he came up against resistant staff at a client firm, he sometimes found a way to go around the obstacle, as he did when winning his first auto client, Toyota. In many instances, he proved quite successful at bucking bad news past the gatekeepers and taking it right to the top.

"What we had done was reach more people in the industry than anyone else," explains Dave. "We always looked to get to the decision makers. And we also had to fight, to struggle with the organization that was designed in the production-industrial era. Those people blocked us because we were laying the facts out. And at these companies, for an employee to make progress he had to play the game. If he was in engineering, he had to behave a certain way to work his way up the line. He had to defend the engineering department, for example, perhaps shifting blame to dealers when a car wasn't selling. This was true of every one of them."

Dave's boss at Marplan, Dick Johnston, provided an early role model in employing the tactic of sidestepping gatekeepers. Johnston had worked in market research at each of the Big Three, so "he knew all the ropes," Dave recalls. "When he was running Marplan, he went to the vice president and general manager at Buick, which was our account, and spent time with him. He did it in a different way than I did. He'd take them fishing in Alaska or Canada." This was not Dave's style, but the tactic was: connect with the decision makers.

"I couldn't do something like a fishing trip," Dave says. "I wouldn't have had the funds. But I also wouldn't want to win them that way. It's deception, in a way. I learned that you go straightforward with the facts, and that works just as well."

Often, Dave's studies would make the news, which gave him another way to get to company leadership. "The media and the press releases we produced helped reinforce our awareness among top management. When we were being blocked by the market research departments, and upper management would read in the *New York Times* an article about a study, it gave them a different perspective than what they were hearing from people down the line."

Executives Who Led

In the executive office, Dave sometimes found a leader with an open mind—someone who had already identified a problem within his organization and appreciated that Dave's data could help convince others of the need to act.

Often the internal issue the executives were working to fix from the inside was that of quality. In the late 1980s, Saab marketing executive Bob Sinclair initially rebuffed Dave's efforts as fruitless, saying that he had been unable to get the leaders at Saab's corporate office to understand the challenges of the U.S. market, where consumers were intolerant of poor quality and unacceptable designs. After empathizing with Sinclair, Dave encouraged him to let J.D. Power and Associates try to help. "We went to work on it, and I got an invitation to Sweden." After that presentation to engineers, the president of Saab Automobile AB at the time, Rolf Sandberg, stood up and started lecturing the engineers in Swedish. "He had his index finger out and was shaking it at them," Dave recalls. "'You'd better get on the ball,' was what I gathered the message was."

Dave had also worked with Mats Ola Palm, an engineer who headed up Volvo Cars of North America. Dave used results from a survey of owners of three-year-old cars to show Palm that Volvo was not faring as well on durability as the automaker's reputation would suggest. Palm acknowledged the slip in long-term quality and wanted to hire Dave to gather the data on how Volvo could regain its foothold. But sensitive to turning out poorly on "durability," one of the key hallmarks for the brand, Palm asked if Dave would name the study the Vehicle Dependability Study instead. Dave agreed and, as a result, found a stunning acceptance and demonstration of his company's influence. On the eve of Volvo's introduction of a new model, the 850, into the American market, the automaker decided to publish unalloyed facts from a J.D. Power and Associates Initial Quality Study (IQS), which charted customer satisfaction during the first year of ownership and had ranked the company's cars very low.

"We must become humble, swift, honest, brave," wrote a Volvo senior executive in the company's *Kvalitat Fakta* (*Quality Facts*) magazine, a technical publication that frankly discussed the results. "We have to dare to admit that a problem is a problem, and a customer complaint reflects our shortcomings in providing quality. Every problem brought to our attention must be taken seriously and solved."[13]

Other top executives recognized how J.D. Power and Associates could help aid their efforts in improving quality aspects of their business. American Honda President Yoshihide Munekuni was confident in the long-running reputation for quality the Japanese brand enjoyed, but he was concerned about the car-buying experience for Honda customers. In the early 1980s Hondas were in such high demand throughout the United States that dealers didn't have to put much effort into making customers aware of the vehicles' features and benefits. (In fact, Dave would learn, the strong sales of Honda models would pave the way for a kickback scandal that would later rock American Honda.)

"Munekuni asked us about the service aspects of the vehicles," Dave recalls, "and that's when we said we should find out how the dealers were handling the customers." He presented Munekuni with data that confirmed his suspicions: the sales representatives were resting on their laurels, and Honda customers were suffering for it. "He wanted to make sure his dealers were top notch and meeting the demands of their customers. He asked what we could do."

J.D. Power and Associates developed a dealer-by-dealer study for Honda that measured how dealers serviced their customers, and Munekuni committed to funding it and making the results available to all of its dealers. It would be Dave's largest proprietary project to date. The annual study was set up on a regional basis, so dealers could compare themselves to the average of other dealers in their area. Honda gave an award to those who were ranked at the top of each region. "It was very effective in improving the performance of the dealers. A key point in this was it created a competitive effort by most of the dealers who wanted to be in the top ranking. And that, I think, was a great contribution to Honda's success at that time."

Getting Close to GM

Getting J.D. Power research into the ensconced offices of the American car industry in Detroit, especially at General Motors, was a great obstacle, and hence a great challenge for Dave's go-straight-to-the-top approach. By 1988, after years of effort, the company had made minor inroads. Some GM divisions, such as Buick and Pontiac, had purchased J.D. Power syndicated studies, but it was tough going, especially at the corporate level. The GM market research people were determined to keep J.D. Power out of

GM. Dave knew that if he wanted to have a significant impact at the largest of the Big Three, he would have to get the attention of the GM chairman, who at the time was Roger B. Smith.

Dave suspected he would be blocked if he went through conventional channels; Smith was more isolated than most GM executives. But he knew Smith convened a weekly senior management meeting at ten in the morning. He also knew that GM President Lloyd Reuss met with his management team at eight that same morning to prepare for the meeting. And like most successful sales people, Dave understood that the best times to contact busy executives were before eight or after five, when their secretaries, who normally screen sales calls, were less likely to be at their desks. So, if a phone rings or a fax comes in during these times, executives tend to pick up the phone or fax themselves.

Dave was not about to phone Roger Smith or Lloyd Reuss. Instead, he launched a bold gambit, and the move paid off better than he could have imagined.

The night before the weekly management meeting, Dave faxed a two-page letter to Reuss. The letter was written to demonstrate the value to GM of buying the IQS. The April 28, 1988, letter started by highlighting GM's success, especially on the part of Buick, because Dave was aware that Reuss had been the general manager of the Buick Motor Division:

> Good news! From the preliminary finding of our initial quality survey (IQS), we find that General Motors' 1988 models have made a substantial gain in reducing the number of problems being reported by the owners during the first ninety days of ownership. Based upon our survey results, GM passenger cars on a sales weighted basis are now statistically even with Ford Motor Company's 1988 passenger cars.

The letter then listed a number of "interesting developments" from the study, including:

- GM was the only domestic automaker to post improvement in the number of reported problems per vehicle from 1987 to 1988,
- Buick and Oldsmobile saw significant improvements, and
- owners reported Cadillac had only 143 problems per 100 vehicles, which placed Cadillac ahead of the Japanese average.

Dave was banking on the notion that the one thing a company president meeting with a chairman could be counted on to do was to be the enthusiastic bearer of good news, particularly at a time when good news at GM was at a premium, and specifically when the good news happened to concern a GM division that would put Reuss in a positive light. The letter then went on to say:

> Lloyd, we are excited about the improvements we see happening and want to be able to help GM go on to bigger and better gains in customer satisfaction. As I said before, there is nothing more gratifying to us than to have our research findings make a positive impact. We want to make a difference.[14]

Dave ended the letter with a page of IQS summary statistics in tabular form comparing GM to Ford, Chrysler, and Asian and European imports. GM could be legitimately pleased with its performance for the first quarter of 1988 compared to the same period the previous year, and Dave suspected that if Reuss saw this the next morning, he wouldn't be able to resist making it part of his presentation to Smith. Nor would Reuss have time to massage the J.D. Power results into an internal market research product.

Dave was gratified to learn that Reuss not only picked up the fax when the president of GM arrived on the thirteenth floor of the GM building early the next morning, he also duplicated the letter and actually showed it to the GM chairman at the ten o'clock meeting. According to reports Dave later received from people who were at the meeting, Roger Smith was so pleased by the results that he said, "This looks very interesting. Do we have this study?" Reuss, momentarily startled, replied, "We're getting it."

Dave had hoped two things would happen in short order, and he was not disappointed. First, he received a telephone call from Lloyd Reuss's secretary, inquiring about ordering the IQS; a GM purchase order to buy the IQS would be issued. Next, he got a call from John Middlebrook, the head of GM's marketing and product-planning staff, the group that supervised the in-house market research function that had so long resisted Dave's overtures. With the apparent blessing of Roger Smith, J.D. Power had penetrated the inner sanctum of GM, and there was no way middle managers could ignore him any longer. He understood that injecting the J.D. Power research engine into GM the way he did would create major indigestion; that's why Middlebrook was on the phone. "Look, Dave, we have a problem here," he said. "The market research department reports to me, and this is causing me a lot of problems. I need you to come to Detroit right away."

As far as Dave was concerned, the situation was getting better and better, although the best was yet to come. A day or two later, Dave and Steve Goodall, manager of J.D. Power's Detroit office, were at GM headquarters. Dave found out that a team of GM managers had already met to discuss buying the J.D. Power surveys. The stated agenda of the meeting, Dave learned, was focused on whether GM should subscribe to the IQS and, if so, how the data should be used given that much of the information provided by the study was also available from an internal GM survey. The actual purpose of the meeting, Dave believed, was to let the GM market research management and GM divisions all save face. The market researchers were likely upset because Lloyd Reuss had made the decision, over their objections, to subscribe to the IQS. The general managers of the GM divisions were probably upset not only because Reuss had made the decision to subscribe to the J.D. Power studies but also because J.D. Power was charging each of their profit centers for the privilege.

By the time Dave and Steve Goodall arrived at GM headquarters for a second meeting, everyone was very tense. "What's being proposed is taxation without representation," Goodall recalls George Hanley, representing GM's Chevrolet division, yelling. And because the costs for the study were to be apportioned based on the revenue contributions of each division, Chevrolet—the largest by far of the divisions—would have to pay for almost half the subscription fee. As Dave and Goodall were ushered out of the meeting, Dave gathered that only two divisions—Chevrolet and Pontiac—were arguing against the purchase. With the political wind blowing from Chairman Smith's office, Dave calculated that resistance was futile. Goodall, a more pragmatic salesperson, wasn't so sure. "This wasn't a slam dunk," he says. "I knew the power that Chevrolet had historically played in such decisions."

Dave called it right. As the meeting came to a final vote, Dave and Goodall were asked to wait outside. Eventually, a group of mostly gray-faced men streamed past. Few made eye contact with the visitors. The one exception was Darwin Clark, head of strategy for the Buick division and a solid supporter of Dave's work. As he walked past, Clark surreptitiously gave Dave the thumbs-up sign. It was left to Vince Barabba, GM's chief of market research, to announce the committee's decision. "We have some interest across the divisions," Dave recalls him saying. "I want to go through this process only once. We want a three-year contract for the IQS, CSI [Customer Satisfaction Index], SSI [Sales Satisfaction Index], and Vehicle Dependability Study with discounts for the second and third years." Dave looked stricken at granting any discounts, but inwardly he and Goodall couldn't have been more delighted. "Here we were, working with all the other clients on a one-year contract," he recalls. The negotiation was a concession he was very willing to agree to. "It made our day."

GM already had large surveys in place, but the company ultimately found value in J.D. Power's studies. "We saw Dave's work as complementing what we did," Barabba says. The external analysis "was important for us to know," and was especially attractive due to the level of detail. "The real value to us is that we were able to get that information in a form that our engineers, who were working on new products and new programs, could see what was working and what wasn't. It was more the details of the information rather than the summary scores that drove our interest."

"The GM story is one that played out over years, not just one momentous event," Jamey explains. "It's a story about persistence, perseverance, about finding cracks, if you will, in the old foundation and working your way in, as a weed will." Dave worked into those cracks by identifying executives, often not initially at the highest echelons of the organization, where views of what needed to be done were compatible with the information the company could provide. "Dave had developed good relationships with people at GM, and you'd see the fruition when they became senior executives."

In the early 1980s, before all of the GM divisional zone offices were consolidated in a single regional office in Thousand Oaks, the Cadillac zone office was housed in the same building as J.D. Power and Associates, down the hall. "As will happen, you run into people in the hallways or parking lot, and it starts to foster relationships," recounts Jamey. GM's practice was to promote sales and marketing executives by moving them to one regional office, back to the Detroit headquarters, then out to another field office. "The idea of going to California to learn more about what was going on in this marketplace—from the dealers, from the customers, from the people who lived here—was seen as a reward. What also seemed to happen—I don't know if it was formal or not—was these executives were told, 'Be sure you get to know Dave Power.'" By the early 1990s GM had hired J.D. Power and Associates to consult on reigniting the California market, and several executives, such as Clark, Knox Ramsey, and Tom Shaver, who experienced a one- or two-year stint in California, returned to Detroit fans of the information that J.D. Power and Associates could provide.

Another individual who played a key role in helping GM see the value in listening to Dave and the data that J.D. Power and Associates provided was Roland Hill. Hill, who worked as the director of quality for GM North America, believed there were problems that needed solving and that Dave could offer some of the tools GM needed. Hill provided candid, cooperative dialogue to Steve Goodall, who was heading up J.D. Power's office in Detroit at the time. "Roland would describe how Dave's message was being received and would explain what GM meant by its responses," Jamey explains.

It was left for GM to figure out how to integrate the J.D. Power studies with its own market research. This was a problem because there was always some divergence between the satisfaction results as reported by J.D. Power and as measured by GM's own research. It would be extremely embarrassing for GM to try to explain such a discrepancy.

There also was the public nature of the J.D. Power and Associates data, which remained a sticking point for Barabba. "The manner that the information was presented publicly, I think, had a dampening effect on the amount of progress that was being made by the domestic manufacturers on their quality problems and battle for market share," Barabba says. But as the quality gap narrowed, GM soon concluded that there were real benefits in being able to present J.D. Power survey results to external audiences, while allowing it to maintain the privacy of its internal proprietary studies. Barabba saw a competitive benefit, too. "The real value in my mind of what Dave did was to come up with a process that allowed manufacturers to see how they were doing relative to all of the competition in a consistent and timely manner."

Dave was relentless in trying to get GM executives to understand how J.D. Power and Associates' services were different from their own in-house market research, and also in addressing GM's ongoing objections. One such objection was the old canard that GM's in-house market research people could provide all the data the company needed. Dave wrote the following to James Fitzpatrick, vice president of communications and marketing, to refute that objection:

> At J.D. Power and Associates we do not intend to nor do we encourage being at odds with the internal market research department. We would prefer to enhance their capabilities and efforts rather than clash with them. In the past, we have found that when our "data" appeared to be in conflict with the in-house research findings, we were often criticized for our methodology. In the past few years, as our methodology has been more readily accepted, the argument switched to the point that General Motors already collects the same data so why subscribe to another set of duplicate "data." It is interesting to note

that "data" (again, in quotes) is not what we bring to the table. It is information. It is data that has been transformed and enhanced through analytical skills and perspectives of multi-disciplined staff of professionals with many years of experience in the automobile industry. No other company or organization can easily duplicate our overall capabilities.[15]

Dave's efforts to convert GM into an enthusiastic client came full circle later that year, when Chairman Roger Smith quoted J.D. Power and Associates in a letter to stockholders reviewing GM's 1988 performance: "This extensive warranty coverage demonstrates our increasing confidence in the quality of new GM vehicles, a confidence that was confirmed when a 1988 survey by J.D. Power and Associates found that Cadillac, Buick, and Oldsmobile are among the ten most trouble-free cars sold in the U.S. They were the only American nameplates in the top ten."[16] In its annual report, the chairman of the largest company in the world was now referring to Dave's company as an authority. From that point on, GM began to treat J.D. Power and Associates with more respect, especially in the senior ranks of the organization.

Real-Time Influence in Europe

All around the world decision makers were coming to recognize the value of Dave's frank talk and honest facts. In the mid-1980s, he gave a speech at the Frankfurt, Germany, auto show, in an era when J.D. Power and Associates was working to build clientele in Europe that would utilize its customer satisfaction and quality surveys. Initially, though, "the general European mentality was not very open to what we had to say," Dave explains. "I can remember one German engineer saying to me, in a room full of people, that he thought that we were doing the research to promote the Japanese companies, primarily Toyota."

Some European companies were as hard to crack as Detroit. So, it was with some surprise that Dave received an invitation to meet with Ferdinand Piëch at Audi's German headquarters in late 1991. A grandson of Ferdinand Porsche,[17] Piëch was "perhaps the toughest engineer that I came across," says Dave. "However, he was open-minded. Every time we got to a chart showing the numbers comparing Audi to BMW and Mercedes, showing where Audi's trouble spots were, one of the guys sitting along the periphery of the boardroom kept getting up and giving a sheet of paper to Piëch. I think those papers were showing him that they had this information, too. Piëch just took the paper and didn't say anything to them. He also just took in our information from our presentation. He didn't criticize or challenge what we were presenting; he just took it in. That led us to working with them, and we had several more meetings with Audi."

At that meeting was Gunnar Larsson, a product development engineer who had worked for Saab and Volvo as well as with Piëch at Audi and Volkswagen. "Audi was at that time extremely engineering organized," Larsson explains. "Their slogan translated to 'Advancement Through Engineering Features.'" Dave also knew Audi's reputation for prizing engineering above the driver, which had been part of the reason he'd been so surprised that Piëch was interested in meeting with him. "I hadn't known who'd engineered my visit to make a presentation to Audi, until I walked into the room for the presentation," Dave says. "I saw Gunnar Larsson, and he just smiled. When I talked to him later, I learned that he'd set up the meeting because he felt that we could be very helpful to Audi in understanding how to build a car for the customer."

About a year later, Dave received a call from the homegrown head of BMW, Bernd Pischetsrieder. The Munich native, who had trained as an engineer and risen through the ranks at BMW, had just become its chairman.[18]

"He invited me back to give a talk to their engineers and product planning people," Dave recalls. BMW's Munich headquarters were near the site of the 1972 Olympics, and Dave dined with the executives on the top floor of their office tower, looking down on the sports park. The presentation took place in BMW's indoor amphitheater—complete with stage and big-screen projection—and the talk drew a crowd. "We must have had three hundred people there, sitting in stadium seating along the walls in a room like a gymnasium." Dave and Len Sherman, who headed J.D. Power and Associates' office in Connecticut, presented a slide show that offered a detailed analysis of BMW and also showed how Mercedes was doing. "We showed that both BMW and Mercedes were trying to outdo each other in terms of the latest technology," Dave says. "That was their market push." Unfortunately, it was backfiring. "The products were introduced without a lot of good testing, so they would have problems in their first year. They'd get it corrected after the second or third year, but we pointed out to them that they weren't paying attention to what the customers wanted." Dave once again was in the position of contributing a much-needed outsider's perspective, something that did not go over well in all companies, especially a European luxury carmaker. However, after the ninety-minute presentation, Pischetsrieder casually invited Dave to get more involved with the company, which began a long association between J.D. Power and BMW.

At the time, European auto executives routinely moved from one company to another, and in 1999, Pischetsrieder left BMW[19] and was soon head of Volkswagen. Volkswagen was another European carmaker not eager to embrace the desires of the American driver. "In the 1980s and 1990s they didn't necessarily look at the U.S. market as a primary market," recalls Jamey Power. "In a way, they didn't care as deeply what the quality was in the United States. There was a superior attitude toward the Americans, that Americans didn't appreciate some features, or that they were less sophisticated." J.D. Power and Associates had a staff member, Patti Hogan Sargent, assigned to work with VW full-time since the mid-1990s. But many in the auto industry observed that Volkswagen's new chief had been installed specifically to "shake up the organization," recalls Jamey. "Volkswagen was suffering from quality problems as well as products that were considered a bit stale and expensive to produce, and Pischetsrieder was brought in to help develop a new culture at VW that was more customer focused."[20]

Again, he invited Dave to come and speak to his engineers and product planners, this time at a Volkswagen plant in Emden, Germany, a port city that was the namesake of a famed World War I cruiser and would go on to become a stronghold of German manufacturing. The meeting was to discuss the Passat, a model that was not doing well. Pischetsrieder wanted a redesign from the ground up, and wanted Dave to review the new design and prototype. His chief engineer at the time was Martin Winterkorn (who would succeed Pischetsrieder as CEO in 2006).[21] "Winterkorn was in some respects very stern and opinionated about what the new model should be," Dave recalls. The team at J.D. Power and Associates, headed by David Letson, knew this would not be an easy assignment.

The chairman's plane was two hours late, and everyone at the meeting was uneasy. Pischetsrieder asked Dave to sit next to him. At Dave's other elbow was the company's head of engineering, Winterkorn. Pischetsrieder pulled out a cigar, and the work began in a more relaxed atmosphere. The team argued about small things, like the placement of a cup holder. "Winterkorn was arguing with Pischetsrieder over the design, and Pischetsrieder was sort of egging him on, was the way I took it," recalls Dave. The chairman was blowing cigar smoke around the room. "They finally started talking in German, and I couldn't understand a thing they were saying." Pischetsrieder graciously told Dave he could wait elsewhere until they got through the problems, but Dave remained until the meeting adjourned. Finally, they took him down to look at the car. "By this time, we had a program where we'd look at prototypes of the vehicles and point out any flaws we could tell from our research investigations that might be a problem once the car was produced. This was our first look at the Passat prototype."

Standing in front of the car, Dave realized how much his company's influence had grown. "That's when I felt we really had something going with product development," he says. "We were respected for having this capability." J.D. Power and Associates was seen as part of the carmaker's development team, a far cry from selling them market research reports, however valuable. Soon, Volkswagen's top executives "began to listen to our data because they realized the data they were using from Europe was limited and did not always reflect the voice of customers in the rest of the world." Dave attributes the success of Volkswagen globally today— especially in China and the U.S.—to the evolving perspective that the organization had to listen to the customer better, as well as to the leadership of Piëch (who is chairman of the Supervisory Board for the entire Volkswagen Group) and Winterkorn over the past decade.

Under Piëch and Winterkorn, VW not only came to value and utilize J.D. Power and Associates' input, but they contracted

with J.D. Power to continue to receive support through an ongoing consulting arrangement. The company educated Volkswagen
designers on the psychology of the American car buyer, including
driving habits and how Americans treated their cars, and on how
those traits can be affected by quality issues. "They understood
that J.D. Power and Associates knew what was happening in the
U.S. and China," explains Jamey, "and as a result they let middle
management know that it was okay to utilize J.D. Power to help
them." Their open-mindedness paid off. "From a sales standpoint,
they're going like gangbusters. They've taken the U.S. market very
seriously and have designed products that are tuned more deli-
cately to the American market's needs."

CHAPTER THREE

FORGING RELATIONSHIPS

Over the years, Dave Power captured the attention of more and more auto executives and won them over to his ideas of customer satisfaction based on solid market research. However, it often was an uphill battle, especially when it came to the world's largest automakers in Detroit.

Each of the Big Three American car companies developed corporate cultures with unique characteristics that defined the way they thought about their place in the world. "General Motors executives all had dark blue or gray suits, white shirts, ties—they all dressed like that," Dave recalls. "Ford had a more youthful and more current, rather than a conservative, style. If you walked into a meeting, you could tell if it was Ford, or Chrysler, or GM, just by looking at their clothes." By spending as much time in and around the auto industry as he did, Dave developed a connoisseur's sense of how the car companies— the Big Three in Detroit as well as the Japanese, Korean, German, Italian, French, and Swedish—differed in ways large and small. And Dave felt the conformity, evidenced by the Detroit automakers' de facto uniforms and reflected in their command-and-control management style, contributed to the economic downfall of 2009, when two of the three U.S. automakers declared bankruptcy.

"After you spend many years in Detroit," Dave says, "you pick up a lot of subtle clues about what makes automobile executives tick and how the cultures of the car companies evolved." The American automobile industry based in the Motor City is conflated as the Big Three, but of course they are individual companies with unique cultures and destinies. Perhaps the only thing they had in common in the early years was a desire to keep J.D. Power and Associates as far from their operations as possible.

"J.D. Power was the outsider telling it like it was," says Jamey. "For years we had been indicating the customer's dissatisfaction with the poor quality coming out of Detroit, but the American automakers acted as though J.D. Power and Associates was telling tales. There was a lot of disdain for us."

Steve Goodall, an early J.D. Power associate who would rise to become the president and CEO of the company, believes there was an informal agreement among the Big Three to freeze J.D. Power out. Dave stood for the right of customers to transparency and accountability, and the resistance he and his team met led them to believe that those were two attributes to which every one of the Big Three were ambivalent, if not outright hostile. "The fact that we owned the data, that we were therefore independent, irked the marketing departments of the Big Three," says Dave, "because they couldn't control us. They would say our data was flawed: we didn't have the right sample design; we didn't ask the right questions. They didn't like that we talked about the research in public. They didn't like all the work we did with the Japanese car companies."

"On the marketing side," says Bill Young, who conducted a marketing audit of J.D. Power, "the European and domestic manufacturers obviously didn't care for J.D. Power and Associates, because the Japanese in particular were using claims in licensed advertising. General Motors did not like J.D. Power and Associates or the way GM was reviewed. Chrysler had pretty much the same view, and Ford was extremely negative. They went even further and said the research was flawed. Many executives of those car companies thought that J.D. Power and Associates was nothing more than a mouthpiece for the Japanese manufacturers."

Dave was no stranger to being rebuffed by GM executives, so he was surprised when, in 1981, he was invited to deliver the keynote speech to an off-site meeting of Pontiac's top forty executives. GM didn't often reach out to J.D. Power and Associates, and Dave was delighted to attend. The event was held on a weekend in Northfield, a Detroit suburb. It was to begin with a dinner meeting on Friday evening to prep the executives for a full day of breakout sessions on Saturday. Dave was invited to present his market research about Pontiac at the dinner and then work with the group the next day. Attendees began to show up at about four in the afternoon, loosening their ties and easing into the cocktail hour, which Dave recalls stretched to about three cocktails before dinner was served.

The dinner progressed at an equally leisurely pace, and it was ten at night before Dave was asked to step to the lectern to present his slides. He pointed out some of the quality problems confronting GM in general and Pontiac in particular. Then he got to the last slide, showing GM market share projected ten years into the future. "By 1990, I had GM's market share below 30 percent, a ten-point drop," he recalls. This was too much for the Pontiac head of sales and marketing, sitting at a table just below the dais. He stood up and started arguing, in an emphatic, alcohol-fueled way, that Dave was not just mistaken but out of touch with reality. The executive sitting next to him—the head of Pontiac public relations—also stood up and joined the howling. Soon the room was filled with hoots and catcalls.

Dave remembers that this was too much for Bill Hoglund, an executive who held a high-level position at Pontiac, and who eventually would move up to corporate controller and chief financial officer at GM. He jumped out of his chair and made his way to the podium. He demanded silence. "Sit! Sit down and listen to this man," Hoglund roared. "We invited David Power here to tell us what he sees happening to Pontiac, and what he is telling you is that unless we change the way this division operates, that's where our market share will be. So listen and learn!"

Eight years later, Hoglund was group vice president of Buick, Oldsmobile, and Cadillac. Dave was invited to address a meeting of the three division general managers—Ed Mertz from Buick, Bill Lane from Oldsmobile, John Gretenberger from Cadillac— and, of course, Hoglund. Also present was William Ouchi, the author of the best-selling management book *Theory Z: How American Business Can Meet the Japanese Challenge*. Again, Dave played devil's advocate, suggesting that GM had to streamline the product lines for each of the divisions to prevent further deterioration of its image and market share. Once again, the general managers took issue with Dave's forecasts. At that point, Dave recalls, Hoglund stepped in and said, "Gentlemen, I appreciate the concerns you have about what Dave Power is telling you, but I've asked him to come and present his views. When he talks about market share, I want you to know that back in early 1980, he projected that GM would reach the 30 percent market share in ten years, and he was rebuffed for saying it. You know, Dave was wrong." The room grew quiet. "The market share was below 30 percent in *eight* years. So I, for one, never argue with Dave Power's numbers. I suggest you give him your full attention."

"The problem with Pontiac at the time was all the lack of communication between engineering, production, sales, and marketing. That's why Bill Hoglund decided to get all the various parties together and give me the chance to provide them with some external viewpoints that reflected the customer's point of view," says Dave. "I felt I could be helpful to them once they decided I could be helpful. It worked out well and changed the direction at Pontiac.

"Unfortunately, GM didn't pay attention early enough," Dave adds. "If they had paid more attention, they wouldn't have ultimately lost the midsized car market." GM eliminated the Oldsmobile brand in 2004[1] and killed the Pontiac brand in 2010.[2] "I certainly never felt I had an axe to grind, and I don't think Bill had the feeling that I wanted anything special from them. He allowed me to present the facts, and as it turned out, the facts ended up being pretty accurate. The numbers J.D. Power and Associates offered GM were not my numbers. They were the market's number and I think Bill knew that we had gleaned them with integrity and independence."

Dave always admired Hoglund's acumen as an auto executive. "He was an exceptionally gifted—and often ignored—executive at the top of the company for two decades," Dave says. Hoglund's eagerness to listen to external voices was rare in Detroit, according to Dave. Hoglund reached out to Dave and W. Edwards Deming, arguably the two most notable voices of the twentieth century advocating for quality in the auto industry. "I think that Bill felt that both Deming and I, looking at quality data from the outside in," Dave says, "brought GM good, actionable information."

Bucking "Command and Control"

From the early days of J.D. Power and Associates, skepticism about its survey data and Dave's interpretation of it was widespread, and

Dave was seen as a maverick. This was especially true in Detroit, partly because the Big Three had a more insular corporate culture than Asian automakers. In those days, external market research companies would do work for the domestic auto industry, but only as "suppliers"—glorified data entry firms who would handle the survey work but turn the information back to the client, which then owned and analyzed the data. In Dave's view, "the big risk was doing the survey in a conventional way, because you'd never get anywhere as an independent firm. But if you pushed it, you lost the business."

Dave came to know this particularly Detroit attitude as "command and control," where executives who were comfortable in their fiefdoms and did not want to rock the boat would support only the market research projects that fit into their existing format and could be kept under their authority. Their command over the work was absolute, and Dave observed much resistance to change, with employees required to "play the game the way it had always been played," he says. In an era when employees stayed with companies their entire careers, it was a deep-seated attitude. By the time Dave came along with his new ideas in the early 1970s, this entrenchment had been growing in the industry since the postwar boom of the 1950s. "The command-and-control people blocked us because we were laying the facts out," Dave says. He sensed that if the prewar industrial attitudes were to be dethroned for a customer-focused approach, they would not die without a fight.

Jamey Power recalls his father's company as going from "relatively anonymous" to "a thorn in the side" of the Detroit auto establishment over the course of the company's first two decades. By the 1980s, "there was strong animosity and negativity . . . almost a feeling that J.D. Power was this aloof counterculture company from California who was turning the world on its end." The image, fueled by the Detroit media, went even further to suggest that the company was going out of its way to help the Japanese automakers steal the business from American companies.

Dave and his company fought back the way they always had. "The way you win over hostile parties is through relationships," says Jamey. "Not glad-handing, 'let's go to a ballgame.' It was more through information and data, and finding people in Detroit who could see and understand the truth and weren't afraid to confront it."

To further counteract the aloof perception, Dave opened a Detroit office, to prove "the mission of J.D. Power was to help them do better, not condemn them," says Jamey. "Throughout the '90s, the more we were able to show that, we were really able to change those perceptions." Steve Goodall, who had been with the company for ten years at that point, was tapped by Dave to open the Motor City office. One month shy of being granted his MBA from the University of Southern California—intensive study that had been heartily supported by Dave and the organization—Goodall found the boss in his office, offhandedly saying, "Oh, I have an idea for you." Dave asked him, "Would you be interested in going and opening up the company's first branch office?" The offer presented twin challenges for the young MBA graduate: his friends thought he was crazy to take the assignment, that the company was banishing him; plus, his family had just endured two years of his all-consuming schooling, and now they were to be uprooted. But Dave sensed that Goodall wanted a challenge, and to Goodall, going to Detroit was quite the opposite of banishment. He tackled it with zeal. However, he soon discovered that the job presented a third, towering hurdle: nobody in Detroit wanted anything to do with J.D. Power and Associates.

"Dave was the air cover and I was the ground assault," Goodall explains. He went from company to company, "defending our methodology." To Flint, Buick's headquarters; to Lansing, for Oldsmobile; to Dearborn, where Ford's head of market research bluntly asked him, "But Steve, why are you here?" That first year, Goodall says, "People wished we would go away. I felt like a lobbyist." As time wore on, contacts stopped focusing on shooting the messenger, and the presence of local staff gave the company credibility. "It established a means of having a dialogue that was more in-depth, more around the data itself than just dismissing us."

"Steve did a phenomenal job of establishing the office, and building relationships out of almost nothing," recalls Jamey. One of the ways Goodall was able to navigate the culture of Detroit so successfully was with the aid of the first employee hired in the Detroit office, Pam Hill. The wife of a longtime GM executive, Hill provided perspective on a town so strongly rooted in the auto industry that a West Coast transplant could benefit from Hill's local knowledge and insight. "The person who, somewhat behind the scenes, held things together with calm focus and strong character was Pam. She was the backbone of the Detroit office at a critical time," says Jamey. "We wouldn't have been successful without her ability to both manage within the J.D. Power organization and provide Steve the perspective on the culture and people—as well as what the executives were thinking."

"Dave and the J.D. Power organization did something proactively that helped us develop a relationship with them," says Roland Hill, the husband of Pam Hill, who served as a quality director for GM North America before working for J.D. Power as a consultant and then retiring. "That was sending Steve Goodall to Detroit. After we got an opportunity to meet him and talk to him, J.D. Power was no longer just this unknown quantity. We developed a pretty good relationship with Steve: we could pick up the phone, chat about things, ask 'What is going on with this?' I think a big part of gaining the confidence in J.D. Power was the relationship we developed with Steve and, through Steve, directly with Dave Power."

Rebuffed by GM

But it would take decades of steady effort by Goodall, Jamey, and their teams to make those inroads at the nation's largest auto-maker, which had been flying high since World War II but was destined for a fall.

Decades of economic success had taught a generation of GM executives that the world was predictable. "This was an illusion, of course," Dave says, but an understandable one. The company's dominance lulled GM's executives into a false sense of compla-cency. When Dave Power came along with his independent sur-veys that revealed fissures in GM's success, he faced a risk-averse, highly controlled culture operating in an era when the company's fortunes were slipping. It's difficult to pin down the start of GM's decline as the greatest industrial engine in the United States. For more than thirty years after the end of World War II, GM had reigned supreme over an unprecedented boom in the world's larg-est car market, but by the 1970s the cracks in GM's façade had started to become obvious.

Given its culture of insularity, General Motors was a hard nut to crack for J.D. Power and Associates. It didn't help that, thanks to the relative open-mindedness of the Japanese automakers and the relatively high satisfaction ratings of cars from Honda and Toyota, J.D. Power was often perceived as being biased in favor of imported cars. Roland Hill believes the general feeling within the J.D. Power organization—that GM was actively opposed to working with Dave—was not entirely accurate. Rather, Hill says, the initial barrier to a relationship between J.D. Power and GM was GM's guarded view of outside measurements in general. "GM has historically been reluctant to fully embrace outside metrics of performance," Hill says, "preferring to utilize internal measures instead." Another barrier was the fact that Dave was an unknown entity, an obstacle that was eventually overcome as Hill and other GM executives came to know the organization. "Studies come floating in from all over the place," Hill says, "and here the J.D. Power studies were generated in California and they were published."

Over time, explains Hill, "that relationship grew and became a lot more comfortable. Once you know the people involved, accepting the studies becomes a lot easier. The early J.D. Power results were viewed with some skepticism, but in time, GM developed great confidence in the surveying process and results. Now, the J.D. Power studies are used as key metrics of quality and customer satisfaction performance across GM."

For much of J.D. Power's first two decades in business, GM tended to reject and rebuff the company. It generally declined to subscribe to J.D. Power's studies, choosing instead to question the methodology or challenge the outcomes.

"I came to GM in 1985 and there was no question that the vehicles had some quality problems at the time," recalls Vince Barabba, who was GM's executive director of market research and planning, "but they were working on them, and the information we got from Dave certainly helped identify what we needed to work on." But even as the company found it valuable, they bristled at the public charting of their problems, which was a comparison among brands expressed by J.D. Power and Associates as "X number of problems per hundred cars."

"Because it was problems per hundred, you could be listed as having twenty problems more than your competitors, but that's only two-tenths of a problem per car," Barabba explains, "and I don't think two-tenths of a problem is discernible. But . . . it looked like there were twenty problems, because it was per hundred cars. I think they should have published problems per car."

Whatever GM felt about the positioning issues, once they opened the door to J.D. Power studies, Steve Goodall recalls having detailed meetings with Barabba and his staff, painstakingly combing through the data to make sure it met their research standards and was reliable information. "And the good news is that J.D. Power's research stood up to that kind of scrutiny and test," Goodall says. "Vince would never have supported purchase of research that he didn't think was well executed and had validity."

The skepticism and battles continued, however. Barabba was concerned about the company using internal metrics and J.D. Power's data to view plant performance. One of the company's general managers who also disliked the idea of reviewing J.D. Power's data in addition to GM's own, memorably said, "When you go look at the time, you don't go look at three watches, just one." But, as Goodall recalls, that idea was turned on its head in the C-suite. "Jack Smith, who later became GM's CEO, ended up making the decision to only have one watch to measure vehicle quality, and that watch was going to be J.D. Power." General Motors had satisfied itself that J.D. Power's data was valid and reliable, and it had a further benefit: "Power had external visibility, credibility, and independence that their research would never have."

Smith, who became president of GM in 1992 and held that job until 2000, recalls his first encounter with Dave Power in 1976, when Smith was director of worldwide planning at GM. "I noticed that throughout General Motors, the J.D. Power rankings were not well received. Fundamentally, the basis for the resistance could be reduced to 'GM didn't do too well; there must be something wrong with the study.'"

From Dave's perspective, GM behaved just like every other client whose cars didn't show up well in the J.D. Power surveys. "The general attitude was that we didn't have anything of value to contribute. They thought they knew what their customers wanted and had the tools in place to measure product satisfaction. So, they criticized our methodology. But what really irked them was that we went public with the quality rankings. This was the part that drove them crazy."

It wasn't just idle handwringing at GM—this was a battle for market share with up-and-coming Asian automakers, and it seemed to Barabba that domestic cars were being painted as inferior by the data. Because buying that first foreign car might be a hard sell for some American shoppers, he says, "they would fall into a pattern that would seek out information that would support their decision and ignore anything that would question it—like twenty problems and not two-tenths."

Overall, Barabba believes that on balance Dave's data was useful for carmakers in comparing their quality efforts to their competition, but publicizing the data about problems per hundred cars "had a dampening effect on the amount of progress that was being made by the domestic manufacturers" in regaining quality. Nevertheless, Barabba credits Dave with "really getting the companies thinking about improving the quality and durability of their vehicles."

Oldsmobile's Botched Attempt at Diesel

While automakers had begun to address quality and customer desires, their actions in developing new cars were also driven heavily by economic events. In 1978, GM responded to the energy crisis by turning to diesel power. Diesel engines were attractive because diesel fuel at the time was less expensive and provided much better fuel economy than gasoline. GM directed its Oldsmobile division to develop a line of energy-saving diesel cars, from sporty to luxury models, to be alternatives to its large gas-guzzlers. But the new diesel engines were fraught with problems, resulting in a disaster from which Oldsmobile never recovered, and Dave got caught in the disarray that followed.

Oldsmobile created diesel versions of the Cutlass, an extremely popular car, as well as the larger Olds 88 and 98 models. However, the 1978 models of the 88 and 98 were a disaster. Oldsmobile had used the head bolts and attachment pattern from its gas-powered engine in the new 5.7 liter diesel V8 instead of additional and stronger ones that could withstand the higher cylinder pressure generated by diesel without breaking apart. The reason was production efficiency—Oldsmobile wanted to be able to use the same tooling as the gas engines—but the move was short-sighted. Proper testing would have revealed the engines' failure to stand up to normal use without causing catastrophic engine failures, but GM blamed tight deadlines and budgets for streamlined testing that didn't show the problems. The debacle spurred some state legislators to pen the first auto lemon laws and sparked a class-action lawsuit by owners seeking to recover engine repair costs.[3]

When word of Oldsmobile's diesel woes started to spread, Dave made two decisions. He decided to do a survey of the Oldsmobile diesels. Somewhat as an experiment, he also purchased one of the cars for his personal use. Had he completed the survey first, he might have spared himself the ordeal that followed. In any event, Dave bought an Oldsmobile model 98 diesel. At the time, Dave faced a total daily commute of eighty miles, and the long lines for gasoline following the oil embargos of the 1970s were still a fresh memory for him. He thought that owning a diesel car would hedge his dependence on gasoline; with the fuel efficiency of the diesel engine, he would have a range of four hundred miles between fill-ups. But from the beginning, the car gave him nothing but trouble. "The Oldsmobile diesel engines were notoriously unreliable," he says. "Within the first six months, I had it in the shop five times and ran up over $5,000 in warranty repairs."

His second decision made Dave's life even more complicated. In May 1979, J.D. Power and Associates published the Oldsmobile Owners' Experience with Diesel Engines study. The press coverage it generated was not lost on thousands of disgruntled owners of the Oldsmobile diesels and the attorneys they engaged. Dave received hundreds of calls and letters requesting that he be an expert witness in lawsuits against GM, which he definitely did not want to do. Dave even received subpoenas to give depositions in a handful of cases. All in all, it became a huge distraction.

Resistance to Risk

Humbling mistakes would eventually open GM's doors to outside ideas, but it would take time and much criticism of the company's culture for the automaker to change. "The resistance of the GM culture to risk-taking had a very dangerous flip side," Dave notes. Even the chairman of GM was frustrated by GM's truth-resistant culture. Dave first met Jack Smith (who was to go on to become GM's CEO), when they appeared on an industry panel together at an event in 1988. Smith was then in charge of running GM's European operations, and Dave suggested that he use J.D. Power's research to measure the quality of the company's cars in Europe. Smith agreed and ordered his staff to cooperate with J.D. Power in an industry-wide study of European carmakers. GM's active participation was needed to provide Dave's team with access to customers shielded by European privacy laws. The thoughtful, soft-spoken Smith was soon after promoted and he moved back to Detroit; six months later GM's European team declined to participate in the study.

Shortly after Jack Smith's ascension to CEO, Dave met with him again, and Smith asked him how the European quality program was going. When Dave told him that the European team had opted not to take part and the study had moved forward without GM, Smith was furious. "But that is the way it went," Dave says, explaining that there was no compunction about disobeying the boss's orders.

By the time Smith assumed the leadership position at GM in November 1992, the company's problems went far beyond cultural dysfunction. Market share had been dropping for years, and Smith announced aggressive policies to reverse the drop. But instead of the 35 percent market share Smith expected, by 1997 GM's portion of the U.S. sales market slipped to 31 percent. Although GM made a record $6.7 billion in earnings in 1997, it produced a net margin of just 3.9 percent. Ford, by contrast, earned $6.9 billion on sales that were $25 billion lower that year. Investors were quickly losing confidence in GM stock, and Smith stepped down in 2000.[4]

"It was too big a task for Jack to change the culture at GM," Dave recalls. Over time, he and Smith had become friends, and the CEO was especially close to Dave's wife, Julie. "I appreciated his friendship and his straightforward way of approaching things," Dave says. "I wouldn't criticize him for mistakes. GM was out of control, and it was a near-impossible job to bring it back."

Dave could see the problems; investors could see them, too. But the executives in Detroit seemed to be wearing blinders. "GM, more than the other car companies, developed a culture that favored loyalty over performance and bred a fierce insularity that made it impossible for GM to consider a full range of options when its prospects were screaming for a perspective only an outsider could offer."

Outspoken business leader Ross Perot concurred with Dave's assessment: "At GM the stress is not on getting results—on winning—but on bureaucracy, on conforming to the GM system," Perot stated in a 1988 *Fortune* Q&A. "You get to the top of General Motors not by doing something but by not making a mistake."[5] Nonetheless, Smith's successor—Harvard MBA graduate Rick Wagoner—was never really in doubt. In a February 2000 interview Wagoner said, "An outsider could never come in here and figure it all out." Wagoner started at GM in 1977, had served in upper management since 1992,[6] and would eventually put in seventeen years as a top GM leader.[7] However, Wagoner's insider status provided no insulation from the insurmountable challenges he would face, says Dave: "I think the ballgame was over by the time he took over and, as a matter of fact, by the time Jack Smith took over. The damage was going on and on, and the organization had built-in fiefdoms that were very difficult to overcome. I believe Rick Wagoner understood what his challenges were but he found it to be very difficult to come up with a program that would correct matters."

Low-Grade War with Ford

Dave founded J.D. Power and Associates with the intention of helping automakers better understand that customer satisfaction was a powerful tool that could help them build and market vehicles, and in this spirit he offered his services to Ford. If he thought his service at Ford Tractor would be a benefit, he was mistaken.

For the first two decades Dave had his company, Ford Motor Company fought a low-grade war to keep J.D. Power and Associates as far as possible from its Dearborn, Michigan, headquarters and any far-flung operations around the globe. Primarily driven by the Ford North American Automotive Operations market research department, this stonewalling gave rise to dozens of individual skirmishes. But all of the objections had one thing in common: reluctance by Ford officials to let outsiders measure the quality of Ford products and, by extension, their own performance. Over the years, the objections shifted in form but not in purpose. First, it was argued that the Ford market research department gave the company all the market research it needed. If that didn't work, the company challenged the statistical methodology and reliability of J.D. Power surveys. If that tactic failed, the position became that J.D. Power couldn't possibly understand an organization as unique and complex as Ford. Dave had to counter each of these objections before he could persuade the company that J.D. Power and Associates would actually be a partner in Ford's stated goal: "Quality is job one."

When Donald E. Petersen became president of Ford in 1980,[8] he had been out of the car business for ten years, heading up Truck Operations and Ford International. He knew that Ford trucks were generally well regarded by customers; the F-150 full-size pickup truck has been the best-selling truck in the U.S. for more than thirty-five years. Petersen wanted to see whether customer opinions of Ford trucks carried over to its passenger cars. He retained a Canadian researcher to conduct a number of product clinics and focus groups. Disguised as an average person, Petersen actually participated in a number of these activities. "I was struck by how uniformly negative customers regarded Ford cars," he says. More, he was astounded by the unmistakable conclusion that as far as customers were concerned, Ford built great trucks, but not great cars. "There's no way I would have been presented with that conclusion from an in-house market research study.

"It's the darnedest thing how people within an organization can get caught up in trying to block off factual information that is contrary to their assumptions," says Petersen, Ford's chairman and CEO from 1985 to 1989. Petersen is generally regarded as one of the most far-sighted executives ever to take the helm at Ford. He was named CEO of the Year by *Chief Executive* magazine in 1989, which hailed him for the company's "back-to-basics rebirth and emphasis on product quality."[9]

The profile noted Petersen's three guiding management principles: having concern and respect for workers, focusing on customer desires, and striving for continuous improvement. Tactics that combined all three would be needed to revive a company that had, in the late 1970s, seen its working capital and market share—and company morale—drop to perilous levels.

The company scrapped its new car development strategies for a team approach, customer research, and a focus on quality. Petersen even brought in one of Dave's influences, W. Edwards Deming, to coach executives in new methods of teamwork. The resulting twin models from different nameplates—Ford Taurus and Mercury Sable—spurred sales, made headlines, and energized the workforce. And the entire project came together because Ford focused on the customer.

Petersen had experienced many eras at Ford over his forty-year career, and he lamented that the company sometimes had an uneasy relationship with inconvenient facts. For instance, he found that he could not always rely on in-house market research, and this was a crucial lesson when it came to addressing quality and understanding the needs of the customer. "The in-house data tended to be very short term," Petersen says. "I couldn't get continuing estimations of quality across time. I had a lot of experience with the bias that crept into all kinds of research because [the market research department] was trying to score points with one executive or another. It got so that I personally couldn't rely on the conclusions being a true and accurate representation of reality." For that reason, Petersen was open to getting independent market research from firms such as Dave's. "The main thing that stays in my mind is that the end result was a reliable, unbiased source for information about how our products stood in quality relative to competitors."

In 1988, Petersen responded to an invitation from Dave to address a group of dealers. Petersen also knew that Dave had been trying for years, with scant success, to convince Ford to buy his syndicated studies. The letter that Petersen signed on February 15, 1988, was obviously written by Petersen's staff. Using boilerplate text, the letter declined the invitation and expressed the thought that Ford had sufficient resources to measure the quality of its products and the customer satisfaction of its customers.

But attached to the formal letter was a short note, dated that same day, which revealed the CEO's more personal attitude:

> I am aware that there are some differences of opinion on methodology between your people and our Marketing Research people concerning the calculation of your customer satisfaction indices.
>
> I also understand that they will be meeting before the month is out in an attempt to resolve the matter to our mutual satisfaction.
>
> I am most hopeful that this will be done. We are both highly respected sources of customer and market data and

I think it is in everyone's interest that we reach an accord on basic methodology, etc.

Kind regards, Don[10]

Intrigue and Backstabbing

In the early years of Dave's attempts to penetrate number-two automaker Ford Motor Company, the chairman was Henry Ford II, the grandson of company founder Henry Ford. "Henry had an imperial style enabled by the fact that the Ford family controlled 40 percent of the company," Dave notes. Ford's obituary and the opinion piece that accompanied it referred to his "autocratic management style"[11] and reported, "'My name is on the building,' Mr. Ford used to say to settle arguments."[12] Unlike GM, where most executives could hang on to their jobs until retirement, Ford managers served at the whim of the impulsive "Hank the Deuce." He famously fired President Lee Iacocca in 1978 with the line, "Sometimes you just don't like somebody."[13] (Iacocca went on to become chairman of Chrysler Corporation.)

In 1979, at the invitation of Ray Ablondi, director of market research for Ford North American Automotive Operations, Dave traveled to Detroit to attend a presentation on Ford's retail distribution. The meeting didn't go well. From the minute Dave walked into the room, he sensed a level of hostility unusual even at Ford. As the meeting proceeded, Dave was surprised to hear J.D. Power and Associates openly attacked as being disloyal and un-American. Dave was further perplexed when Ablondi said, "Dave, if you allow the Italian to use your data, you'll never do business with Ford again. You know the way out." With that, Ablondi, followed by the other participants, marched out of the conference room.

Dave was momentarily confused until he realized "the Italian" Ablondi was referring to was Iacocca. Then, as he was waiting for his flight at the Detroit airport, Dave fully grasped the source of Ablondi's resentment. The latest issue of *Businessweek* featured a two-page advertisement proclaiming that, according to J.D. Power and Associates, Chrysler was the highest-ranking domestic auto company. That episode set off a blizzard of correspondence between the two companies.

Dave and Ablondi would have many more difficult moments in the coming years. After that, Ford executives bristled every time J.D. Power surveys ranked Ford below average in customer satisfaction. Instead of recognizing that the market research reflected the perceptions of actual car owners and could be used to improve the quality of their product, Dave explains, Ford managers frequently sought the easier path of attempting to discredit the methodology underlying the market research. Dave chalked it up to the kill-the-messenger syndrome.

Inferiority Complex at Chrysler

If the effort to win over Ford was a battle, similar work to bring Chrysler on as a client could be considered at least a tussle. Chrysler, which was based in Auburn Hills, Michigan, outside Detroit, had been in business since 1925.[14] In 1987, it acquired American Motors Corporation (AMC).[15] The junior partner among the Big Three, Chrysler had an inferiority complex compounded by the fact that for most of the late-twentieth century it was, in fact, inferior. Dave felt that J.D. Power and Associates was there to help Chrysler improve.

Few Chrysler executives publicly supported Dave's work, but some privately relied on his data, and usually, Dave suggests, without paying for it. Although Lee Iacocca, for one, respected Dave, he delegated marketing responsibilities to executives such as Bob Lutz, whom a 2010 *Businessweek* profile called "the cocksure maverick who led a product renaissance at both General Motors and Chrysler."[16] From 1986 to 1998,[17] Lutz was responsible for Chrysler's product development and subsequently served as its president and vice chairman.[18] Lutz, who by all accounts did not care for J.D. Power and Associates at all, critiqued Dave's monthly newsletters with a red pen, making comments along the margins to the effect that J.D. Power was too hard on Chrysler, and then sent them back to Dave. Dave welcomed the exchange, figuring that being criticized was better than being ignored.

Dave thought there was a time and place for such criticisms, but Lutz had a different approach, one that got the attention of both Dave and legendary car designer Carroll Shelby at a function in the early 1990s. Dave was attending the annual Concours d'Elegance at Pebble Beach, California, which the *New York Times* likened to the Olympics of the automotive universe.[19] It features world-class collector cars displayed on the famous golf course's eighteenth hole, in a charity auction, and even in a race.

One event—a dinner for invited guests sponsored by Mercedes-Benz—was hosted by San Francisco superdealer Martin Swig, one of the first (along with Pennsylvanian Ron Ertley) to put multiple franchises under one roof. When Dave and Julie arrived for the dinner, there was only one seat reserved at the head table for Dave, which he declined so that he and Julie could sit together at another table. J.D. Power associate John Rettie took Dave's place. Another chair at the head table was reserved for Bob Lutz, who arrived at the last minute and went around the table getting introductions. When he heard that Rettie was with J.D. Power, he started haranguing him about the Power survey methodology. Keeping his head, Rettie said that perhaps Lutz should take his comments up with Dave Power, and he pointed to where Dave was sitting. "So, he comes over to the other table and starts in on me, pointing his finger and raising his voice," Dave recalls. "I had a group of people, some I knew socially, and I didn't think that was the time for someone from Chrysler chiming in about methodology when it was at a Mercedes dinner. So I got up from my seat and stepped off to the side." Lutz followed. "I said, 'Bob, I think it's foolish to discuss it here. I'll be happy to discuss it with you anytime, give me a call.' I sat down with Julie and we continued talking." Seconds later, Dave felt a tap on his shoulder. "There was a guy crouched down next to me, and it was Carroll Shelby," Dave says with a laugh, "and he said, 'Why the hell didn't you hit him?'" Dave downplayed the situation, but Shelby said, "Well, you put up with too much from him." The incident brought the two men closer. Dave notes, "We always used to talk about it when we'd run into each other."

But it wasn't just an angry Bob Lutz that got in the way of J.D. Power gaining traction in partnering with Chrysler. Constant turnover among Chrysler executives frustrated Dave's ability to create the long-term relationships he enjoyed at other car companies. As with every automaker, the market research professionals lobbied to keep Dave's company at arm's length. While Chrysler often purchased Dave's syndicated studies, the market research people usually succeeded in blocking the company from doing any proprietary work.

Support from Iacocca

Dave had a positive relationship with Chrysler chairman Iacocca. Iacocca, who became Chrysler Corporation president and CEO in 1978 and 1979, respectively, famously revived the company in the 1980s. Previously, as president of Ford Motor Company during a booming 1960s, he presided over the introduction of such iconic cars as the Mustang and the Lincoln Continental Mark III. At Chrysler, he solidified his reputation with the introduction of the minivan, which became a huge hit with consumers and the industry's best-selling vehicle for more than two decades. Iacocca became well known to Americans as the TV pitchman for Chrysler. A phrase from the ads later became his trademark: "If you can find a better car, buy it."[20]

Over the years, Iacocca participated in a number of events at the request of Dave. One particular event stands out in Dave's memory. It was September 5, 1975, and Iacocca was to speak to the Sales and Marketing Executives Club of Los Angeles at the Biltmore Hotel. It was the same day that an assassination attempt had been made on President Gerald R. Ford by Lynette "Squeaky" Fromme in Sacramento. Reportedly, the Charles Manson follower had a "hit list" that included Lee Iacocca. Out of an abundance of caution, Iacocca's security detail urged him to cancel the speaking engagement but Iacocca would have none of it. Nevertheless, Dave knew that the publicity would mean a much larger audience for the event and security for the meeting would have to be beefed up. While events for this organization usually had around two hundred attendees, six hundred signed up to hear Iacocca speak. On the day of the event, more than eight hundred people waited to be admitted. As arrangements were being made to move the event to a larger room, Dave and Iacocca spent close to an hour together in a small conference room. They spoke about the energy crisis, automobile retailing, and the future of the car industry.

While they were waiting, Iacocca told Dave that he was going to be speaking to a group of Lincoln-Mercury dealers in Southern California the next day, and he was at a loss for what to tell them about Ford's plan to address concerns about fuel economy.

While there was not time to help Iacocca determine a plan that night, Dave offered to assist Ford on its product development. "I sent a follow-up letter to him to let him know I was available. He sent the letter on to Ray Ablondi's boss, and the shit hit the fan. I got a call from Ford's market research department saying, 'How could you do such a thing? You're supposed to report to us.' But I felt that was the beginning of the breakthrough beyond the market research department." However, when a manager came out to meet with him, Dave was informed that there would be no work. "We had broken the rules," Dave says. It was not until a few years later that J.D. Power and Associates was brought on by the general manager of the Ford division to consult on the California market.

In the audience at the Los Angeles event that featured Iacocca was a man named Jerry Pyle. A graduate of Wharton a few years after Dave's time there, Pyle was serving as a Ford regional manager assigned to working with a young protégé named Edsel Ford II, Henry Ford II's son. Pyle was providing Edsel with background on the distribution side of Ford's West Coast business, which included accompanying him to Iacocca's speech. Pyle would go on to follow Iacocca to Chrysler before heading up Toyota's Gulf State distributorship. He and Dave developed a mutual respect for each other over the years, and Pyle would eventually serve as one of the few outside board members of J.D. Power and Associates.

Prickly Relationship

Chrysler was prickly in its relationships with J.D. Power and Associates. Chrysler executives could be counted on to take poor rankings personally and often reacted angrily to public comments made by J.D. Power staffers. For example, in a June 8, 1987, letter marked "Personal," Chrysler Chairman Bennett E. Bidwell wrote:

Dear Dave:

This kind of article adds insult to injury. It sure can give us a lot of problems with our dealer constituents all of whom read this periodical. I didn't need this one.[21]

Bidwell was referring to a full-page article in *Automotive News* reporting some comments made by J.D. Power executive John Hammond when he spoke at a conference in Detroit. The comment that Dave believes Bidwell took most exception to was "'Chrysler is in more trouble than GM' in terms of sales, market share, and excess plant capacity." The article provided figures Hammond shared to support this conclusion: "For Chrysler, Hammond predicted sales will fall from 1.3 million units (including captive imports) in 1986 to 800,000 units in 1991. He looks for market share to drop from 11.5 percent in 1986 to 7.3 percent in 1991."[22]

As Chrysler's reputation for reliability and influence grew under Iacocca, the relationship between Chrysler and J.D. Power and Associates became friendlier. Nevertheless, it was often frustrating to have Chrysler as a customer. In May 1989, Dave suggested to Bidwell that Chrysler would benefit by subscribing to the 1989 IQS. Bidwell wrote back:

> The points you make on the importance of quality in this industry are valid and I agree with you. Nevertheless, we have decided not to purchase the 1989 IQS.

He reminded Dave that Chrysler had its own quality studies "tailored to our needs" and that previous comparisons showed the internal survey produced similar results to the IQS. Therefore, he said:

Our decision not to purchase the IQS survey should not be construed as an abandonment of our pursuit of quality, but simply as a solid business decision.

The letter was signed "Ben" and he had added the following in a handwritten postscript:

Dave, don't take this too hard, please. As told, we will be doing more business with you in the New Year.[23]

Just as Ford Chairman Donald Petersen had done earlier, Bidwell had appended an encouraging personal message to the company's formal letter of rejection.

By 1996, the relationship between J.D. Power and Chrysler had improved to such an extent that Chrysler Chairman and CEO Bob Eaton actually agreed to endorse Dave's company. Eaton, who served as Chrysler's chief executive from 1993 to 1998, wrote:

In 1996, the domestic auto industry reached its 100th birthday, giving us a once-in-a-lifetime opportunity to recognize and celebrate the most influential vehicles, people, milestones, and companies of the past century.

J.D. Power and Associates has a special place on that list. While relatively new to the automotive stage, Power's impact on the industry has been significant. The company's unique research and analysis redefine the standards for vehicle quality and customer satisfaction. In so doing, Power and Associates has come to be recognized—both by the industry and the car- and truck-buying public—as a leader in its field.

If it is true that the automobile is "the machine that changed the world," then it is equally true that J.D. Power and Associates is one company that helped change the machine for the better.

Things became easier for J.D. Power in 1998 when Chrysler was taken over by Daimler-Benz AG. Dave enjoyed very good relations with Daimler CEO Dieter Zetsche, and for some years Chrysler was a loyal subscriber to J.D. Power studies. "Dieter Zetsche was a young, successful executive moving up quickly through the ranks at Mercedes-Benz," Jamey recalls, "and he was assigned to handle the Chrysler integration." A colorful character with a walrus mustache and a German accent who for a time took on spokesman duties for Daimler Chrysler as "Dr. Z," "he was a really strong supporter of J.D. Power and Associates," Jamey says. Although Zetsche assigned direct communications with J.D. Power and Associates to his staff, Zetsche consistently backed up Dave's efforts.

European Resistance

Despite Dave and his team's difficulty in winning over the Big Three, Detroit was not the hardest market to crack. In the 1980s, J.D. Power and Associates attempted to expand its customer satisfaction surveys to Europe. In trying to do so, the company encountered open, severe, and orchestrated resistance by the European automobile manufacturers, which could generally be expected to agree on few things. But in keeping J.D. Power and Associates out of the European market, the manufacturers seemed unanimous. Jamey recalls that a senior executive at BMW provided a friendly but candid assessment of what the firm was up against. "There are only two things the German manufacturers agree upon when they get together," a BMW executive acknowledged to Jamey at the time. "The first is keeping new car warranties to no longer than one year; the second is keeping J.D. Power and Associates out of the car industry in Europe."

Jac Nasser, who, before being named chairman of Ford Motor Company in 1996, headed up Ford operations in Europe, saw that same resistance. "The European carmakers simply did not want J.D. Power because, to some degree, it was American, but more fundamentally, because they felt that the J.D. Power market research was not an accurate measure of true quality. There was a suspicion that the surveys were largely influenced by such American idiosyncrasies as the size of the cup holder."

To the European car manufacturers, Dave felt his firm's commitment to empowering consumers with open information represented a grave threat. J.D. Power was, after all, considered responsible for prompting big European companies, such as Renault, Peugeot, and Fiat, to leave the U.S. market. The manufacturers did everything in their power to deny J.D. Power and Associates access to new car owner registration information. In the U.S., registration data is readily available through a company called R.L. Polk, which contracts with the departments of motor vehicles to collect and sell data for research or analysis. European nations, many on the forefront of consumer privacy protection, restricted such information. The European car manufacturers were happy with the situation and weren't inclined to help J.D. Power by providing access to any internal data collected on owners.

As for their own internal market research needs, the European car manufacturers established secret agreements to share new-car-buyer information among themselves. They cooperated on the design and the rollout of their own syndicated market research and quality surveys. They called themselves "the Club," Dave recalls, and it was a very restricted club at that. "The Club would meet periodically to decide which surveys to conduct. Everything they discussed and decided upon was kept strictly confidential." Unlike the J.D. Power surveys, the summaries of which were designed for wide dissemination, the surveys sponsored by the European car companies were held in extraordinary secrecy. "Reports were strictly numbered and controlled. Each marketing manager would get only one or two numbered copies of the final report. They would keep control of who in their respective company could see the results. Everyone was under special instructions to not reveal the findings to the news media or public. The whole enterprise was kept very private."

Dave was frustrated in his attempts to penetrate the European market until 1988. Then he moved swiftly and secretly to grab two small windows of opportunity that had briefly opened. Very early that year, he learned that he could obtain new car owner registration data in Belgium. Belgium was a special case because it was one of the few nations in Europe that had a more diverse array of car brands sold—European as well as Japanese—and it had a less restricted market structure due to fewer protective duties and tariffs on vehicles sold there. Working quietly so as not to alert the car manufacturers, J.D. Power and Associates was able to purchase the data and mail a questionnaire to thousands of new car buyers to ask about their experiences. The questionnaire was similar to the one it used in the U.S., but it was translated into French and Flemish, two of the predominant languages spoken in Belgium. The company was lucky to have acted quickly; by the following year, Volvo and Renault opened assembly plants in Belgium and further access to registration data was denied.

A report rating the customer service experience in Belgium was released in the spring of 1988. J.D. Power and Associates convened a meeting in Brussels to announce the findings, inviting representatives of the twenty European and Japanese car companies covered in the survey to participate. The study, even though it was destined to be a one-off, turned out to be a financial success. All the Japanese companies purchased the study and participated in the presentation. Of the European car companies, only a representative from Mercedes-Benz registered. Dave assumed that this representative would take delivery of the study and immediately depart, and that is exactly what happened. Dave was certain that this registrant represented the Club as much as Mercedes-Benz, and in violation of the license for J.D. Power reports, he would immediately make copies of the report for all the members of the Club.

At about the same time, Dave tried to obtain new-car-buyer registration in the United Kingdom. Government officials—citing consumer privacy concerns—would not make the data available for purchase. No matter. Dave found an alternate path at *Top Gear*, a top-rated British Broadcasting Company (BBC) television show at the time. "The TV show was a pretty creative way of doing an end run around the restriction," Dave says.

Top Gear was a television series broadcast on the BBC from 1977 to 2001 before being revamped in 2002. The show focused on topics such as new models and road safety for the British market. A print magazine of the same name had been spun off from the show in 1993.[24] [25] The widely watched show became so influential that manufacturers saw *Top Gear* reviews impact sales. Dave saw in a partnership with *Top Gear* the opportunity to get around the Club. Instead of "pushing" its questionnaires by buying registration information about new cars and mailing questionnaires, J.D. Power and Associates employed a "pull" model, whereby viewers of *Top Gear* who recently purchased a car would be invited to contact J.D. Power.

Win-Win Partnership

For seven years, J.D. Power and Associates enjoyed a successful partnership with *Top Gear,* explains Dave Sargent, vice president of J.D. Power's global automotive division. Beginning in 1994, the annual *Top Gear* J.D. Power Top 100 survey captured the experiences of tens of thousands of U.K. residents and their car-ownership satisfaction. The team created a survey called the "*Top Gear* J.D. Power Top 100" and *Top Gear* on-air hosts presented J.D. Power satisfaction data. It was a win-win partnership, at least for the first few years: J.D. Power and Associates for the first time managed to get access to a significant number of new car owners throughout the U.K., and the TV show benefited from the prestige and expertise of J.D. Power. On the show, the presenters gave viewers the opportunity to participate in a customer satisfaction survey. The TV screen flashed a toll-free telephone number. Operators, as they say, were standing by to get the following information: name, mailing address, license plate number, and make and model of the vehicle. It was important to get the license plate number because, in the U.K., the license plate itself told J.D. Power the registration period of the car. In that first go-around, the company wanted to hear from owners with "J" plates. "We had no idea of how many people would call," Sargent says. In fact, about 75,000 people called in the first few hours, overwhelming the telephone system. "It was a painful process to collect all the data, but once we did we were well positioned to validate respondents and send out surveys by mail."

When the results came out, there were very few surprises. The Japanese car manufacturers (particularly Toyota and Honda) outperformed the European-made models, Ford, and GM. The study validated the general impressions of quality and dealer service. Still, some of the car companies howled in protest.

From the first, J.D. Power was criticized for cooperating with an increasingly aggressive entertainment-based car show that didn't hesitate to throw punches. (That aggression would terminate the company's association with *Top Gear*, but that came later.) The car manufacturers were very uncomfortable with *Top Gear's* approach. The market research community was outraged because the *Top Gear*–J.D. Power survey methodology involved "volunteers" instead of a strictly random sampling. "All in all," says Sargent, "there were many parties with a vested interest in us not succeeding."

The partnership between J.D. Power and *Top Gear* unraveled after the show's producers went too far. For some time *Top Gear* had been growing increasingly bold in taking potshots at the companies at the bottom of the J.D. Power ratings. They ignored Dave's discomfort with this practice. Dave always insisted that his ratings be used to promote quality, not to beat up manufacturers who occupied the lower half of any particular ranking. The last straw came when *Top Gear's* spin-off magazine illustrated the ten lowest ranking car manufacturers by showing key fobs adorned with the logos of the ten companies disappearing down a flushing toilet. It was a graphic entirely in violation of J.D. Power's value that its reports be used to improve automobile quality and customer satisfaction, not shame the companies struggling to catch up.

Many car companies, not just the ones humiliated, were furious with J.D. Power for being associated with such a stunt. Honda was one company whose logo was not pictured, but a key executive there called Dave to say that J.D. Power needed to distance itself from *Top Gear*. Dave agreed that this was no way to treat respected companies, such as Ford, GM, Fiat, Renault, and Volkswagen, even if they were not quite as highly rated as others. He expressed his displeasure, but the producers of *Top Gear* defended their stunt. So, after seven years, J.D. Power pulled the plug on *Top Gear*.

When one door closes, another one opens. After years of fruitless appeals to the British Driver and Vehicle Licensing Authority for access to new car registration data, the agency reversed course. Within a few weeks, the parties struck an agreement that allowed J.D. Power to utilize official new car registration data. There were many restrictions. For example, the company never received physical possession of the data. Rather, it provided the questionnaire and set the sampling parameters, and the Driver and Vehicle Licensing Authority sent out the questionnaire. This was actually ideal for J.D. Power because no one could argue that the methodology was tainted by self-interest since it was an agency of the British government that sent out the surveys. Dave Sargent was a bit worried that these "official" results wouldn't align with the results of previous years, but the results in fact stacked up almost perfectly.

An Evolving Relationship with Toyota

Although Dave's relationship with Toyota, once the primary focus of his business, changed significantly once Toyota brought their studies in-house and Dave realized he needed to diversify, Dave continued to maintain ties with Toyota and its leaders and occasionally still conducted studies for Toyota's Japanese staff.

In the early 1970s, Tatsuro Toyoda returned to Japan. "It changed the relationship, not having Tatsuro Toyoda any longer in that job," says Dave. "They appointed Norm Lean as general manager in charge of parts and service. And he got the organization better prepared for growth and expansion. But his staff, the American staff, still disliked the fact that I was going to Japan and we were doing a lot of projects for them." Toyoda was replaced by an interim executive until Yukiyasu Togo was brought in from Toyota's Canada operations. "He was more aloof to working with J.D. Power," says Dave. When Bob McCurry retired from Chrysler and joined Toyota, Dave says, "we had a lot of trouble connecting with Toyota's American staff." For the next three decades, J.D. Power and Associates had less day-to-day and proprietary interaction with Toyota.

During those three decades, Toyota faithfully subscribed to the whole portfolio of syndicated studies offered by J.D. Power in the United States and most other markets in the world—except Japan. In particular, the studies that focused on quality and customer satisfaction were used extensively, and where Toyota managers could, they promoted Toyota's good scores in advertising and other marketing arenas to burnish the automaker's brand image of quality and dependability. Toyota enjoyed wild success with its cars, trucks, and new luxury division, Lexus.

The relationship with Toyota was complex and it became apparent that Toyota welcomed J.D. Power's help with listening to the voice of the customer so long as it wasn't that of the Japanese customer. As a matter of fact, the voice of the Japanese customer wasn't being heard by anybody. In Japan, the challenge to conduct an independent, syndicated study like the ones J.D. Power and Associates ran in the U.S. was formidable because outside companies were not allowed to use government registration files to contact customers. Perhaps, Dave thought, those rules could be modified, but it would require the support of the country's leading company, Toyota. Dave knew that if he could convince Toyota of the value of opening up access to its new vehicle buyer lists, the other manufacturers in Japan would follow suit. In the mid-1990s, he requested a meeting with a senior market research executive at Toyota in Japan. The meeting included Aki Funayama, a long-time associate of Dave who was the general manager of the J.D. Power office in Japan. Funayama served as translator at the meeting.

"It was a non-meeting," Dave recalls. "Nothing was advanced out of it." Then the party went to lunch, and Dave, in his earnestly convincing way, continued to probe the executive's thinking and coax him into seeing the value of the partnership. The executive spoke some English and talked with Dave directly, but at one point turned to Funayama and said something in Japanese. It was clear to Dave that neither of them wanted him to know what was said.

After the lunch, Dave asked Funayama what the executive had said. "He said you're like the black ship in the harbor," said Funayama. Dave immediately understood the reference, which was to Commodore Matthew C. Perry, a U.S. Navy commander in 1853 who, sailing into Edo (now Tokyo) Bay in a black-hulled frigate, became infamous in Japan for threatening a naval assault if the Japanese did not accede to American demands to open its ports to trade.[26] Dave, far removed from his seafaring days, was seen by the executive as a modern-day Perry, aggressively trying to get them to share their information against their will. The idea was dead in the water, says Dave. "I knew we weren't going to get anywhere, so I stopped pressing it."

Around that same time, leadership changes at the very top of Toyota shifted the focus of the corporation. Dave could see that the modest organization he first encountered in 1968 was becoming bolder in its goals—particularly those surrounding growth, sales, and Toyota's role in the world. Toyota was successful but Dave was concerned. Dave has always analyzed the marketplace. With reams of data on all aspects of the industry coursing through the halls of J.D. Power's office, it was often possible to chart the path of a trend for a company or even the entire industry—and prognosticate when asked, which, Dave admits, "is always where I get into trouble."

Such a situation arose in November 2000, when Dave was asked to give a talk to the automotive writers of Northern California. He attended their dinner meeting at a restaurant near the San Francisco airport and told the sixty or so journalists assembled his view of the industry at the time, mainly speaking about the distribution system. Later, during the question-and-answer period, an audience member asked him for his take on Toyota—whether the company would continue to grow and what its effect would be on the domestic companies. Dave thought for a moment about his old mentor, Peter Drucker, who had spoken in 1991 at a J.D. Power and Associates event. Dave had asked Drucker about General Motors, and how such an industry-leading company could make such missteps. He had also asked about Toyota, a company that had been on the rise but was struggling with growth.

"Drucker said, 'Dave I'm not going to mention either of those companies by name, but I'll tell you one thing: when the gods want to get even with a company, they'll give them forty years of good fortune.'" Dave understood that Drucker's message was, "The people who had built those companies to this great level have left, and now there are new people in charge. They feel they're the ones who made it that way, and that's why they won't change."

Dave related a version of that idea to the automotive writers. "I said that I feel that there are signs at Toyota that they're putting too much emphasis on sales and not enough on adapting to the business conditions and the consumers of today." He related his idea that "there was a bit of smugness at Toyota, that they were in control." Thinking back to Drucker's comments, he felt that the company had to be careful of that overconfidence, especially because "the people who really built Toyota are long gone from the scene."

Shortly after the talk, Dave went to the Christmas party at the Toyota Motor Sales U.S.A. headquarters. The top U.S. executive, Jim Press, came to up to Dave. "He said he'd heard I was taking potshots at Toyota's management. One of his public relations people was at that meeting." Dave had to admit that it was true. But also, he felt his comments were correct.

Eventually, Toyota started to have a few quality issues. Then came the accusations of cars exhibiting unintended acceleration. Dave watched to see what would happen next but felt that Toyota's managers had taken their eyes off the ball and emphasized sales over the core values that had gotten them into the top tier of automakers worldwide. Those missteps were catching up with them.

Another Toyota executive became the recipient of the truth that J.D. Power spoke to power, a trait that Dave instilled throughout the company and that continued to be a hallmark of longtime employees even after Dave sold the company in 2005. Loretta Seymour, a senior director at J.D. Power and Associates, felt she needed to voice the hard truths when Toyota's quality was brought into question.

Seymour was preparing one of a series of J.D. Power presentations to Iwao Nihashi, Toyota's Japan-based chief quality officer, who was visiting J.D. Power's headquarters for the first time in 2007. She was alarmed by her data analysis on quality workmanship, and although Power's Japanese staff members counseled against it, she felt the analysis must be shared. "I basically said this needs to be put forward. I don't care if he's not going to like it; we need to speak from the data."

In the presentation, she shared with Nihashi that "the perception of quality workmanship from Toyota had been dropping over the past few years. I wanted to put this forward and say, you know, it's not just about watching our IQS, because what's happening is you've got a drop in the buyers' general perception of Toyota quality."

Nihashi listened with his arms crossed, recalls Seymour. "His immediate reaction was not real positive. But he thought more about it, and then, when we went back later in 2008, he wanted to know more about it." Through assistants, he asked, "What is this quality of workmanship, what's going into it, why is it declining?" But, despite Nihashi's inquires, the data showed the decline continuing. "And then, of course, the recall happened in 2009." Toyota lost respect and market share, and needed to embark upon a massive effort to rebuild its place among premier automakers.

The data provided an early warning, and although the client could not turn the problem around to avoid a disaster, Seymour felt she had raised the issue and "put a line in the sand to say, look, this is really something important for you to recognize and be aware of."

In the long run, the Power effect was again on display. "When Mr. Nihashi retired," Seymour recalls, "he sent me a letter saying I really brought a new perspective to him and had him focus on some things he'd never looked at. That's an example of what Dave would do."

It was a rough period for Toyota, and Dave now expresses hope that the company is on another upswing: "They've discovered a lot of the problems and have gone back to look at things, formed committees, and are reorganizing. One of the grandsons is taking charge again. So, it is much more family controlled. And the relationships in the United States have changed dramatically for the better."

Perhaps it is not surprising that even Dave's first automotive client, Toyota, had to swallow hard at times when the J.D. Power reports came through the door, because when an automaker was not doing well, and the data showed it, the J.D. Power staff had no choice but to deliver the truth to the client. It was what Dave required. It was the basis of his business and always guided the company's development. The unblinking directness that Dave first exhibited when he calmly gave his Coast Guard captain the hard truth would continue to drive his actions as he led his company. And that famous independence was the first leg upon which the J.D. Power and Associates reputation was built.

SECTION TWO
IMPACT

Dave Power not only wanted to remain independent in his efforts to help automobile manufacturers improve by listening to the voice of the customer, he also wanted to have as big an impact as possible on consumers and clients. Dave's drive, as the company grew, became infectious. "There was a sense among many people that the work we were doing was both important and valuable to greater society," says Dave Sargent, vice president of global automotive at J.D. Power and Associates. "We were one of the catalysts that made consumers' lives better. They had more reliable vehicles and better service at car dealers because we created a situation where the players in the industry competed to achieve a higher level of satisfaction and therefore raised the bar for everyone.

"You did feel like you were contributing almost to a public service. That was exciting, and you felt good about going to work every day. I felt like I was having a direct, positive influence on the quality of vehicles in the marketplace."

In addition to Dave and his team's efforts elevating overall car quality, Dave quickly understood that listening to the voice of the customer could also help manufacturers understand what drivers want and need in their cars. Ignoring the voice—or even listening to it ineffectively by conducting research in-house or crafting ill-conceived studies—would be at manufacturers' peril.

Two situations that occurred in 1975 showcase the fact that an automaker's ability to fully listen to its customers can steer the introduction of successful new vehicles, while its failure to listen in a way that accurately captures the voice of the customer can have disastrous effects on its product line.

Ford Motor Company showed signs of innovation when it decided to test the market for a minivan in 1975. The United States was just coming out of a recession that had been touched off by the 1973 oil crisis. Cost increases at the pump and rationing sent Americans streaming for smaller imports, and the Big Three were left wondering what their next move should be. "There was a tension in the industry," explains Jamey Power. "Were these short-term issues, even fads, or were these real trends? Detroit was still trying to figure this out while imports were going gangbusters." The type of vehicle christened the minivan—sized between a station wagon and a passenger van—had never been tried, but the industry was buzzing with the idea. Ford's market research department decided to run its own study in three cities and hired two external firms it had worked with in the past to perform the Midwest and East Coast studies. Without another firm left in their stable, Ford contacted J.D. Power and Associates about holding the Los Angeles focus group to test the idea. Ford marketing executives were uncomfortable with Dave's firm because their cars sometimes came out lower in J.D. Power's survey results, which they feared was the result of a bias for Japanese imports. "We had worked with Ford on a couple of proprietary studies, but had never done field research for them before," Dave recalls. "But this was an emergency, and they asked us to help out." Although wary of Dave's company, Ford issued a contract.

Upon hearing how Ford wanted to structure the field study, Dave became wary of the arrangement as well. He and his team were to get responses to a full-size model of the proposed vehicle used for display, with fake wheels and no engine. Ford wanted to recruit drivers from three segments considered likely targets for the new model: people who owned large vans, large pickup trucks, or large station wagons. "I tried to object to interviewing these people," Dave recalls, "because we said they aren't the ones who would be in the market for it, and never will be." He suggested that Ford allow him to recruit from the general *car*-buying public because, in his estimation, the large-vehicle owners were very unlikely to want to downsize. "Our projections came through." The vehicle bombed with the limited demographic that Ford requested.

Engineering had a big role in how the situation played out, he recalls. Ford—and General Motors, too—had separate teams of engineers for their passenger cars and their trucks, "and those groups did not interrelate well," Dave explains. Ford had tasked the truck engineers with creating the minivan, but they knew little of the car-buying public, so the design did not appeal to that group of customers. Ford's president, though, was not deterred. He was Lee Iacocca, destined to become head of Chrysler after being fired by Henry Ford II. A few years after he went to Chrysler, that company came out with a small, front-wheel-drive minivan, which became its best-selling line ever and led to a massive change in the U.S. market.

In the wake of Chrysler's success, Ford rushed out a minivan, but it was rear-wheel drive and not successful. Front-wheel drive was, in the 1970s, still a feature of imported cars despite creating a roomier passenger compartment. Chrysler had two small front-wheel-drive cars, the Omni and the Horizon, but it was making a leap to use its K-car platform for the van.

Also in 1975, four-wheel-drive was nonexistent on passenger vehicles, until one import company took Dave Power's customer-driven advice and saw its fortunes forever improved by it.

Subaru had been trying for years, unsuccessfully, to make a bigger break into the American market. Its small cars commanded a fraction of the market compared to their Japanese brethren from Toyota and Honda. But Harvey Lamm, Subaru's U.S. chief, came to J.D. Power and Associates for a number of studies, including one regarding a new vehicle with four-wheel drive built off a front-wheel-drive chassis, making it less expensive to produce. The Japanese parent company, Fuji Heavy Industries, had created a four-wheel-drive station wagon for use by Japanese forestry workers. "They thought it wouldn't sell in the United States," Dave recalls, "but Harvey thought it would. He said he had to come up with a good evaluation that he could take back to Japan and sell them." Dave's forecast of potential customers and dealers showed that such a car would sell, in fact, 30,000 to 40,000 units a year, a whopping number for Subaru at that time. Dave recalls that when Lamm took the report to Japan, the company reluctantly agreed to follow Dave's results, and the car was brought in. "In the first year, they met our forecast." It was an innovation that became Subaru's hallmark and triggered decades of U.S. success.

Providing research that more closely connected the company to its customers "helped transform Subaru from being a relatively unsuccessful, also-ran Japanese company into a distinctive brand," says Jamey. The automaker used four-wheel drive as a point of differentiation from other car companies, even to the point of becoming the official car of the U.S. Olympic Ski Team, a unique corporate sponsorship in the sporting world.

Both those cases, as in all of Dave's market research, relied on properly listening to customers and evaluating what they were saying. Ford missed the opportunity to be the trailblazer in a lucrative new market segment because it did not heed Dave's call for listening to the voice of the customer (VOC) in the most effective way. Subaru's success, on the other hand, was utterly defined by its acting on Dave's insights into VOC. Not only has J.D. Power and Associates' research into customers' perceptions of a potential product proven effective in boosting an automaker's success in the marketplace, but the company's impact has also been solidified by its handling of survey results: J.D. Power and Associates' awards for quality and customer satisfaction have emerged as the automobile industry's best proxy for VOC.

CHAPTER FOUR

THE GOLD STANDARD OF QUALITY

The 1980s saw J.D. Power and Associates' influence grow almost as fast as the company itself, which was in continual hiring and expansion mode. Company surveys guided the actions of automakers as they sought to grapple with a fast-changing industry or introduce new brands and models. With the end of the Voluntary Restraint Agreement that had limited Japanese imports, the U.S. market became entirely open, and a worldwide battle ensued for market share. The Big Three might have been reluctantly studying J.D. Power's surveys, and European car companies were just showing signs of swallowing their pride as they tried to better address the American market, but Japanese automakers continued to rely on the company and view its market insight as an essential asset.

Dave increasingly interacted with automakers in ways that utterly transformed the manufacturers' trajectory. In many cases, he served as direct adviser to executives at the highest levels, but in all cases his influence was transformative, especially in the area of quality. "Cars . . . don't have the kinds of glaring faults they had in the 1970s and early 1980s," Andrea Adelson wrote in an October 1997 *New York Times* article. "That is a change for which many inside and outside the industry give Mr. Power much credit."[1]

"I firmly believe that J.D. Power and Associates has done more to encourage improved vehicle quality and customer satisfaction than any other organization in the world," says Dave Sargent, who managed the company's London office before moving to a senior role in Detroit. "We created a competition that everyone wanted to win. And, like the Olympics, people work harder and compete better, and that improves standards for everybody. And that, in turn, makes the world a better place for consumers."

Quality as a Measure of Customer Satisfaction

By virtue of countless quality surveys conducted by J.D. Power and Associates, customer satisfaction is now part of the common vocabulary of the auto industry. In many ways, Dave was responsible for making the auto industry consider customer satisfaction a fundamental metric, equal in importance to units produced, return on investment, time-to-market, and other measures of performance. "One of Dave Power's biggest achievements," says Carlos Ghosn, Nissan's chief executive, "is the insight that no matter what an automaker's internal indicators of quality are, at the end of the day the only indicators that matter are what customers regard as important."

Other industry visionaries have recognized Dave's contributions. "Power discovered a niche in the industry many years ago, when [customer satisfaction] wasn't the top-line issue that it is today, and quantified it," commented George Borst, then vice president of strategic and product planning for Toyota's U.S. sales operation, in a 1992 *Fortune* magazine article. "I think Power has changed the auto business forever," agreed William Pochiluk, who from 1985 to 1997 led the Autofacts consulting firm in West Chester, Pennsylvania. "There was a time when he was the only guy in the business making these kinds of pronouncements, and he grabbed the attention of consumers."[2]

One reason the auto industry started paying attention to Dave was the realization that there were real benefits to scoring high in the J.D. Power rankings. Carmakers watched sales take off after festooning the windows of dealerships with decals reading "J.D. Power and Associates Number One Customer Satisfaction Index." Another reason was that Dave's research was ultimately affordable. "Most car companies, " Dave says, "understood that it was more economical to buy our study than to go out and do such a study themselves."

While Dave and his company were having much influence over the auto industry and individual companies, they were also developing a series of customer satisfaction measures that would guide and back up the company's suggestions. Over the years, J.D. Power and Associates developed more than two dozen syndicated market research studies and reports for the automotive industry to utilize in understanding the voice of the customer. The two most influential studies are the Customer Satisfaction Index (CSI) and the Initial Quality Study (IQS).

Satisfied Customers

As Dave was building the young company, the most common question he had to wrestle with was, "What is customer satisfaction?" In his many presentations around the world—the notes for which were penned by Dave on his ever-present yellow legal pads and then typed by daughter Mary (because she could read his handwriting)—Dave worked hard to define what customer satisfaction measured and what it did not. An October 17, 1990, presentation Dave made to Mazda is typical of his precision:

> It is important to understand that in measuring customer satisfaction we are measuring the difference between the individual customer's *expectations* and what that individual customer *perceived* he received in terms of the product and/ or service. It would be impossible to get a true measurement

of "absolute" satisfaction levels since expectations vary widely from one individual to another and even with an individual his or her expectations change over time. By measuring relative differences between expectations and perceived results, we can make valid comparisons between different makes and models of cars. For example, Mercedes owners have higher expectations than do [Subaru owners], but each manufacturer in this case has to meet the respective expectations of their own customers.[3]

In other words, customer satisfaction is determined by perception and expectations, two constantly shifting values. One goal of market research is to point out the gap between the promise a company makes and its ability to deliver on that promise. Fundamentally, satisfaction with a product or service is a function of two factors: the expectations a customer has going into a business encounter and the experience itself. "The fact that expectations play an important role in determining customer satisfaction carries numerous important ramifications for business," says Jamey Power. In a book he co-authored, *Satisfaction: How Every Great Company Listens to the Voice of the Customer*, he outlines three issues that emerge from rising expectations:

- Consumers have learned to continually expect more, which means that customer satisfaction is a moving target. Standing still is not an option. A company must improve or be passed.
- Consumers have heightened expectations for each touchpoint. It is not enough to improve product quality; companies must also offer exciting new features and better service.

- Today's "wow" factor is tomorrow's standard equipment. A company can gain a short-term bump in customer satisfaction and sales by introducing a new service or product feature, but soon enough the competition will introduce the same or better. Thus, the new breakthrough product or service quickly becomes a baseline expectation.[4]

"Customer satisfaction is always a relative measure," Dave notes. "We simply assessed what the individual customers expected when they purchased a car and how the reality of owning the vehicle compared with those expectations."

The original measure of customer satisfaction, the CSI was an annual survey of new car and light-duty truck owners, identifying the most important issues to customer satisfaction during the first year of ownership. (Today, the study covers the first three years of ownership experience.) The focus of the CSI is on product reliability as well as the levels of customer service provided by auto dealers. The company calculates an index score for both makes (for example, Chevrolet) and models (Impala) as a way to compare performance. The CSI emerged in 1981 following successful one-time syndicated studies on new innovations, such as the minicar and minivan, and a decade of performing market research for Toyota and Honda. Both Japanese companies were interested in studying how their franchised dealers were treating customers and helping low-performing dealers do better. J.D. Power and Associates acquired considerable experience in surveying registered buyers of cars to determine how they rated the reliability of their vehicles and their experience with the dealers in getting those cars serviced.

Both Toyota and Honda were satisfied with the market research Dave's company conducted on a proprietary basis. Both companies benefited from being able to distinguish low-performing dealers from those that consistently satisfied customers. The studies allowed the companies to identify best practices as well as isolate those behaviors that customers rated negatively, allowing them to propagate the former and minimize the latter. But Dave understood that the market research was limited. For example, it could not provide an answer to the question of how the average Honda dealer compares to the average Toyota or Mercedes-Benz dealer. "That's an important question to be able to answer," Dave says. He decided to syndicate a study comparing makes, models, and dealers across manufacturers to generate industry norms and averages. In 1981, the industry-wide CSI was born.

For the first CSI, J.D. Power and Associates mailed out approximately two thousand questionnaires. Within a few years, the company was sending out more than one hundred thousand questionnaires, allowing it to generate statistically significant results for more than a hundred and thirty different models of cars and trucks. The mailings went out about twelve to thirteen months after a person bought a new car. Detailed questions focused on the quality of the vehicle and the service after the initial purchase. With all this data, it was inevitable that J.D. Power would create an indexing system to rank the makes and to release the top ten finishers to the media. Dave realized that publicly ranking the performance of the carmakers would force them to be more responsive to the quality issues identified by the car buyers, but the indexing method would give them a means to learn exactly where they needed to improve. From a problem with the tires to a salesperson not properly educating customers on new technology, this detailed index of customer satisfaction became a powerful tool.

"With the CSI, we were able to move the needle on the consumer's decision to buy again," explains Linda Hirneise, who joined J.D. Power and Associates in 1982 and went on to become its first female partner. "We showed a tight relationship between first-year quality and how that appealed to the pocketbook of the consumer."

Initial Quality

Introduced in 1987, the IQS is an annual study of the new car and light-duty truck market as measured by the incidence and repairability of problems during the first three months of ownership. Originally, approximately ninety problem areas were covered in the study. Information is available on several levels: manufacturer, country of origin, model, and final assembly plant. The basis for comparison is "problems per one hundred vehicles."

Within ten years of the study's launch, the impact on car quality throughout the industry was striking. In 1987, the average number of defects per one hundred vehicles in the IQS was 166; by 1997 that average had dropped by more than half, to 81.

In 1990, J.D. Power and Associates had formalized a program to present IQS awards to assembly plants in North America, then expanded it to Asia and Europe. The awards recognized that cars flowing from these plants exhibited the fewest defects. Taking a cue from the Olympics, Dave awarded the best-scoring assembly plants with gold, silver, and bronze awards. "It got the various plants to appreciate the teamwork required for quality," Dave says, "and to stimulate other plants to get the award." A platinum award was given to the best overall plant in the world.

The first time Dave was invited to present the plant quality award in person was in 1991 in Canada. He and Julie traveled to Cambridge, Ontario, to take part in the ceremony. He was overwhelmed by the celebration, which was conducted during a change in shifts to allow all employees, each of whom was given a wristwatch by Toyota, to attend the ceremony. As Dave was joined onstage by line workers—not executives—selected to receive the award, "that's when we began to see that this was a tremendous opportunity for us to help educate the employees on the fact that quality matters to the consumer."

Earning an IQS award became a major point of pride for the assembly plants responsible for quality. Honda was the first Japanese company to establish an assembly plant in the U.S.; the first Honda Accords rolled off the line at a plant in Marysville, Ohio, in November 1982. Honda had announced its plans to begin manufacturing in the U.S. in 1980 to stave off criticism about the gains made by Japanese imports—criticism Honda feared would lead to congressional restrictions.[5]

On July 13, 1995, Dave went to the Marysville plant to award the workers there the Silver Plant Quality Award earned by superior results in the IQS. With sixty-six problems per hundred cars, the Marysville auto plant ranked number one in the U.S. and finished second in North America, topped only by Toyota's Cambridge factory. The assembly line was shut down for Dave's address. "This study is based on a survey of Honda's owners versus all the other models out there on the market," he told the assembled workers. "It's important to understand that your customers are giving you this award, not J.D. Power and Associates. Time and again, when people ask me what the biggest determinant of quality is, they expect me to talk about technology improvements. I have to tell them that it's the people who make the difference. Every associate at Honda American Motor is responsible for getting this award. Congratulations!" Only two years later, in 1997, the plant received the platinum award.

Evolving the IQS

In the early days of J.D. Power's first big surveys and clinics, the firm made various adjustments to its processes in order to improve the accuracy of its results. When Dave began his syndicated studies, carmakers were skittish because the surveys and the results were not under their control; nor were they proprietary or kept secret. Critics were many, and the press often listened to them, Dave recalls. "At first they'd tell us that the survey methodology was incorrect. We overcame that. Then they'd say, 'Your questionnaire wasn't designed properly.' They'd find different reasons why it wouldn't work. We fought that for forty years."

One of the biggest criticisms originally was that mailed surveys were not reliable. "We devised ways to make it more effective," Dave says, "and this effectiveness and efficiency were what we had to continually prove."

Once market researchers began relying on J.D. Power surveys, they wanted the surveys to remain the same, or nearly so, from year to year so the carmakers could get longitudinal data from model year to model year. They complained that J.D. Power changed the items on its surveys too frequently, making such long-term studies impossible. Dave says the company tried to keep the questions unchanged for a five-year period, but the surveys had to change to measure the changing nature of owner expectations, technological advances, and new features and equipment. "In the beginning of the IQS, for example, many of the questions concerned the quality of engines and transmissions, because that's where most of the quality problems centered. But over the years, those problems by and large receded, and owner complaints centered on such items as wind noise and windshield wipers. We had to change the questions to keep up with overall improvements in quality and reflect new concerns. More recently, we added questions to measure satisfaction with new features, such as audio and entertainment systems, GPS systems, and remote locking systems."

Often, clues to the evolving concerns of car buyers could be found in a catchall survey category called "all other," which allowed the survey respondent to write in their own notes. That's how Dave learned about a unique problem with key fobs. "Originally we had a lot of problems with those," he recalls. On a Mercedes-Benz model, for instance, "if you dropped the keychain and the key fob hit the ground in a certain way, it threw off the programming." Dave duly reported these comments in IQS reports and began tracking the issue. The key fobs improved. "They changed the design to make it more reliable if you dropped it."

Sometimes the IQS studies could result in changes the automaker would make during the existing model year. "We finished the study and published it in May—eight months after the new model year started. They were making cars throughout the year, and they would change some quality issues right away." Of course the survey results were also useful for future model years, but J.D. Power's quick work on the IQS provided insight never before received by automakers; previously they would have to rely on warranty work and other slower methods to decide what changes should be made. This ability to get direct feedback from customers soon after they purchased their cars was a key feature that interested Dave's clients in the studies.

Becoming a Client's Coach

One of Dave's prime precepts has been to use market research to help companies improve their products, manufacture as close as possible what the customer wants, and deliver what the customer perceives as quality. In Dave's mind, it was a natural step to use his and his company's expertise to interpret the surveys for the clients who bought them; thus, the company started delivering the survey results with presentations that brought the data to life. That step added relevance and made the expensive, sometimes lengthy, complex surveys more immediately useful to management. The next step was to use those survey results to advise clients about where they might improve customer satisfaction. In that, the company opened itself up to criticism.

"We began to take heat from some people, who would say, 'How can you be fair about judging the horse race and then coaching one of the horses?'" recalls Jamey Power. "My father didn't think it was a legitimate criticism." Jamey explains that the survey department was scrupulously separate from the new training arm. "We set up the organization like church and state, and didn't let the people who were managing the measurement really interact with the people who were doing the coaching and training." And, he says, to counteract the critics, "our research methods were really an open book."

Dave Sargent recalls that the conflict perceived by critics was never a gray area internally because of the guidance Dave Power provided to the associates. "We basically had two audiences," explains Sargent. "One was the client, who provided revenue and ultimately paid our salaries. The other was the consumer, who depended on us to provide them with independent information, as the *New York Times* would say, 'without fear or favor.' The best way we could serve our clients was to represent the customer voice as independently as we possibly could. Dave was very good at aligning the two missions we had and identifying that these two things were not in conflict, but by serving one we served them both."

Another fear held by J.D. Power's automaker clients, as Jamey recalls, was "that we were taking ideas from one client and running to the next." It is a concern for any company that hires outside consultants specializing in an industry and with many clients in that field. But, he says, "I think we did better than what you had at the traditional consulting companies."

Providing consulting services helped the J.D. Power staff feel it was contributing more value to the industry and to its clients' customers. "We derived more personal satisfaction and confidence by playing this role," Jamey says, "and it made us a better company, because we were always experimenting and improving."

Helping Volvo Face Facts

Halfway around the world, another respected automaker was concerned about its standings in the J.D. Power and Associates studies, and the company took a direct approach to the situation.

Swedish automaker Volvo got its official start in the automobile business when its first car rolled off the line in 1927. Durability was paramount for Volvo from the beginning, when a Volvo could be likened to "a tractor: unexciting but solidly built, a serf on wheels."[6] Dave first engaged more deeply with Volvo in the early 1990s, during a critical period in its history when the carmaker sought to upgrade its image and compete with Mercedes and BMW. It was poised to introduce a new model, the 850, to the U.S. market.

But Volvo knew it was in trouble in 1991, following the release of the annual IQS rankings to the media. In that study, Volvo cars ranked twenty-sixth in quality—just below archrival Saab. The CEO of Volvo was blindsided by these results and demanded answers. Volvo management scrambled, and within a month, Dave was on his way to Sweden to present the facts. "There was a small faction, a revolutionary force, who spoke up at Volvo," Dave recalls. This was the group, led by middle managers, who had facilitated the invitation to present to the company's board of directors. It was the first of many trips Dave took to the

Scandinavian country as he began a front-line consulting role that was to have a lasting effect on the automaker.

"Volvo had not subscribed to all of our studies at that time," Dave recalls, "so this was a wonderful opportunity to show top management our capabilities. We were very confident in our data and could show Volvo management precisely why Volvo cars ranked as they did." For two hours, going through a series of charts, he laid out how Volvo cars—model by model—compared to the competition. "Through the survey results, I was trying to show Volvo executives how Americans felt about their cars and each of the important attributes."

Over the years, Dave has given variations of this presentation hundreds of times. Usually his audiences resist accepting difficult facts, as well as his prescriptions—no one welcomes bad news—and it was difficult for Volvo management to consider the results. However, at Volvo "a light bulb came on," Dave says. They finally agreed there was a problem and coalesced around a common set of facts. "Few words were necessary," Dave recalls. "The charts showing the trend information spoke for themselves. Volvo managers assumed that the image of Volvo as a very durable and dependable car would sustain sales. My presentation noted that in the previous five years, Japanese cars had set new standards for durability and dependability. Volvo was being left behind." His presentation demonstrated that Volvo sales and profitability tracked below the industry average. It also emphasized specific quality issues, especially Volvo's problems with its engines, air conditioners, and heating systems. The quality data were segmented not only by model, but also by assembly plant.

"The presentation to Volvo was one of the easiest and most impactful presentations I have ever given," Dave says. In addition to purchasing two other reports (the Vehicle Dependability Index and the Vehicle Performance Index), Volvo engaged J.D. Power and Associates in a consulting capacity. The engagement with Volvo represented the beginning of J.D. Power's consulting practice; the firm's consulting relationship with Volvo lasted until 1996.

Based on the IQS, Volvo executives learned that its cars were ranked as low as twenty-sixth out of thirty-four makes. At the time, Lexus and Infiniti had approximately 75 percent fewer problems than Volvo. Volvo clearly had a major problem on its hands. But unlike many of their counterparts, the senior leaders of Volvo did not flinch from the facts. Instead, Volvo used the disappointing results of the IQS in a broad-based internal campaign to inspire the need for fundamental change. In an in-house technical periodical called *Kvalitet Fakta* (*Quality Facts*) dated August 1991, the Swedish automaker published a cartoon depicting a Volvo 850 sedan sinking into the ocean. Above, thunderclouds labeled IQS, JDP, and CSI emitted a lightning bolt. It didn't require translation for Dave to understand the message.

Never before had Dave seen so starkly the emphasis carmakers placed on ranking well on the J.D. Power customer satisfaction and quality indexes. His eyes widened as he read the unfiltered internal comments of a Volvo senior executive to his subordinates:

> We (directors and colleagues) have not reached our goal to earn the top spots in J.D. Power's rankings for the 1991 model year! This is by far the most serious problem for our company, since it is customer evaluations which decide our future and makes possible our survival in the auto market. . . . My challenge to you as a manager and colleague is for you to familiarize yourself with the J.D. Power results and use them as the basis for your plan to improve your areas of responsibility.[7]

At Volvo, the J.D. Power results became internal metrics. Dave was both stunned by this demonstration of his company's influence and impressed by Volvo's willingness to publish unalloyed facts only a week after J.D. Power and Associates released the results in Los Angeles.

The *Kvalitet Fakta* magazine represented a new understanding that Volvo's best solution to its problem was to change its secretive corporate culture. The magazine stood for the start of open and honest reporting on the quality situation at Volvo. Before, such information had been tightly controlled. Now the automaker's in-house magazine would publish previously confidential information. By the time Dave got his hands on a copy, the magazine had a distribution of 2,600 people and served as an important tool in Volvo's quality initiatives, providing results, analysis, and comment.

Dave took a small risk and shared his own perspective that a customer satisfaction initiative cannot be sustained without involvement from top management. "Without top management visibility involved on a day-to-day basis, it is difficult to change the organization's behavior," he wrote to Volvo President Lennart Jeansson on September 17, 1991. This letter was more prescriptive than Dave usually allowed himself to be. The letter continued:

> I respectfully request that you demonstrate your personal commitment and involvement in improving the quality of the products and services. This can be done not only through simple means like letters and written directives but most of all through physical appearances at any meetings on the subject of quality and/or customer satisfaction. I know that the people in your organization are dedicated to an "improvement process" but they need the *stimulation* and

leadership to help them make the organization move faster toward continual customer satisfaction improvement.[8]

At Volvo's request, J.D. Power and Associates brought to the surface problems that consumers had with the automaker. The results showed that Volvo did not live up to the image of quality and dependability the company thought it enjoyed. "Volvo was most outstanding in its ability to face the truth," Dave says, amazed that his team received absolutely no push-back from Volvo executives in Sweden. Nor was there an attempt to "spin" the results. "It was eye opening for a European car manufacturer to accept the seriousness of the problem so openly," Dave says. Jeansson disseminated the results widely. He later wrote to Dave about his understanding that customer satisfaction is not just a production issue, but also a management one.

Dave agreed completely. In his experience, good intentions alone were not sufficient to change the culture of an organization. True change must start at the top with concrete, visible action. "My experience with several manufacturers who have demonstrated a leadership role in automotive quality and customer satisfaction shows that it is essential for the senior executive to become the visible champion of customer satisfaction throughout an entire organization." Only when the "tone at the top" is visible and consistent can change initiatives gain traction.

Dave saw the pay-off of this strategy at Volvo where, he says, there was a "transformation" at a scale unseen at other carmakers. Volvo's actions were widespread and quickly implemented. Under J.D. Power guidance, the company addressed many of its processes and refocused them on quality and customer satisfaction.

Volvo took immediate steps to implement Dave's suggestions. The 1992 issue of *Kvalitet Fakta* showed the new car model headed up a set of steps toward the number-one spot at the top, with a listing of total quality management and other initiatives the company was using to get there. Within five years, Volvo had improved scores in quality and customer satisfaction. In 1996, for the first time, Volvo was ranked among the top three in the IQS and the SSI (Sales Satisfaction Index). This dramatic improvement was not the result of any single change. "Volvo was an organization ready to change," Dave says. "All we did was encourage the change, give them some objective data to justify the change, and point them in the right direction."

For example, as part of his recommendation to make quality more visible throughout the organization, Dave suggested that Volvo encourage internal competition. Dave knew that vehicle quality was both a top-down and a bottom-up effort. That's why he wanted to help Volvo recognize outstanding achievement. "Our goal was to make quality more visible throughout the organization and give Volvo more opportunity to motivate the team."

Volvo workers at two assembly plants were delighted to receive prestigious awards from J.D. Power and Associates. There was much celebrating among the workers of the Volvo assembly factory in Ghent, Belgium, when in 1996 it learned that J.D. Power had ranked it first in Europe. Workers at the Torslanda, Sweden, plant took satisfaction in being ranked third for two consecutive years among stiff competition. (The Mercedes plant in Sindelfingen, Germany, was ranked second.)

In the May 1996 issue of *Kvalitet Fakta*, Volvo Vice President of Quality Stellan Flondin congratulated the workers on this accomplishment. "This year's results, with [Ghent] taking first place as the top European plant and Torslanda taking third place, show that we made the right decision in making quality a priority. It has now been definitely confirmed by the only really important judges, our customers, that last year's results were not a fluke but the reward for a coordinated, systematic, and very consciously targeted effort."[9]

In rankings of the SSI, which tracks salesperson performance, delivery activities, and initial product condition, Volvo climbed from twenty-third in 1991 to third in 1996, making it the top European brand in the U.S. market. In the IQS, Volvo ranked immediately behind two luxury models in North America, Toyota's Lexus and Nissan's Infiniti. However, in the final ranking of all manufacturers with sales in the U.S., Volvo ranked first with only seventy-one problems per one hundred cars, followed by Toyota (seventy-seven), Honda (seventy-nine), and Nissan (eighty-one). This time, the graphic accompanying the article on Volvo's results showed the company's rank spiking over the dropping "problems" index, with a line showing the "best practice" level. Five years earlier, the story had included storm clouds and a sinking car; this time, a simple line graph evoked a runner jumping over a hurdle.

Transforming Quality at General Motors

Not all automakers were as introspective and responsive when presented with J.D. Power and Associates studies. GM had for many years been a reluctant user of the studies. During the 1970s and 1980s they purchased them only piecemeal, so the surveys and indexes had trouble reaching all corners of the huge organization. The company culture at the time did not encourage external review. "GM was insulated," recalls Jamey, "they lived in a bubble." He likens the attitude to a simple, black-and-white early television show, such as *Leave It to Beaver*, whereas reality was a colorful, more complex world where times had changed. For instance, Jamey says, "they couldn't fathom that people had other choices, that they would buy a Japanese car." Although particularly strong at GM, the attitude was endemic to the Big Three culture in Detroit.

But as the rankings in J.D. Power surveys were treated with more prestige by many other companies, the public, and the media, GM took notice. The automaker had seen the impact made by Dave's research, and it realized how far it had strayed from being the icon of the automobile world. It also learned from experience how much it had to lose. By the mid-1990s, the J.D. Power rankings were so critical that automobile companies introduced new processes based on actual J.D. Power surveys to help them detect defects before cars were released to customers. GM, for example, established the Customer Acceptance Review and Evaluation (CARE), a quality verification process aimed at preempting the types of customer concerns that would cause the automaker to rank poorly in the J.D. Power Initial Quality Study. As part of CARE, every car that rolled off the assembly line was systematically reviewed by a team of GM plant personnel for nearly all the points addressed in the IQS questionnaire. "We couldn't test for everything; for example, we couldn't check for wind noise inside of the assembly plant, but checking whether everything worked right, fit right—we could get at all of that," explains former head of GM's quality department, Roland Hill. "We even put bump tracks in the lot so that when the car drove out of the back of the assembly plant it went over some chatter bumps so that we could check for squeaks and rattles.

"The premise with CARE was that if a customer could find a defect, we should be able to find it first and contain it to the vehicle assembly plant. . . . We wanted to improve our quality so we used J.D. Power's IQS as a checklist of the things we wanted to make sure we got right. We used IQS as a guide for improving our quality of out-the-door products. So with the CARE process, there was not only a quality element to that but a customer satisfaction and economic element as well.

"Dave and I talked about CARE, and he thought it was a step forward in improving quality. And as we did this, our quality did in fact improve."

The advent of quality awards being given to top-performing manufacturing plants created a breakthrough at GM. When J.D. Power announced that a GM plant landed in the top three and would be given one of the awards, the company invited Dave to come and present it in person. "The fact that GM brass was saying 'we're proud we won this award' meant they were giving their approval that the J.D. Power methods were acceptable," observes Jamey. Another GM plant handed out commemorative watches to employees who had helped the plant earn that year's award. Over the years, Dave, Jamey, Steve Goodall, and other J.D. Power executives took time out to travel to award ceremonies all over the country, where they would then spend time with more of the company's executives, further strengthening bonds. Dave's direct involvement with celebrating awards helped cement the relationship with GM's truck operations, according to Jamey, who was by then heading up the J.D. Power office in Detroit. "The light truck group was actually leading the passenger car divisions in using J.D. Power and Associates as an independent measure of quality," he says. At one point, Jamey and the staff were invited to present the latest IQS data to the mid-level managers of the GM truck division. Heretofore such presentations were centralized at the GM division level. "Suddenly we were visible to work groups on a local level," Jamey says, crediting support dating back to the 1980s from key executives such as Lloyd Reuss and continuing through the late 1990s with Jack Smith and Rick Wagoner for paving the way for this development. "Along the way my father built some great relationships with guys like Don

Hackworth, Ron Haas, and Gary Cowger, who championed the ideas of using more customer-based data and were demanding that the GM organization adapt to the changing marketplace faster.

"It was a great experience for me and the company to get into places such as assembly plants in Flint, Michigan, or Janesville, Wisconsin," says Jamey. He and his team used IQS data to drill down to the local level, showing managers how products being assembled at their particular plants were contributing to customer satisfaction. Sometimes the audience for these presentations was just the plant manager and his senior reports, but at other times, salaried workers were invited. In the GM plant in Fort Wayne, Indiana, where Chevrolet and GMC pickup trucks were assembled, Jamey actually presented to two different shifts of workers. "Up until that point, there was a lot of suspicion about J.D. Power and our findings, but I was thrilled by the warmth and appreciation that these workers expressed. It was clear they welcomed the information and felt that we were validating issues that they had already identified."

By 1996, the transformation of GM's relationship with J.D. Power and Associates was complete. In a newspaper article in the business section of the *Ventura County Sunday Star*, a GM spokesperson was quoted as saying of J.D. Power and Associates: "We know their surveys are going to be accurate, not biased, and that the name J.D. Power is synonymous with credibility. Over the years, its studies have become one of the key points that we look at overall in terms of building and selling our products. We manufacture our products in a very competitive world and have to be able to satisfy our customers. Anything we can find to help us understand what customers want is a very big plus."

By the late 1990s, GM was taking the customer-focused results of J.D. Power and Associates surveys so seriously that it became a stated corporate objective to seek improved J.D. Power ratings. When GM adopted the IQS data as an official company metric, quality as defined by the customer became an official General Motors goal.

Challenging Hyundai to Improve

Dave's efforts probably had more effect on Hyundai than any other manufacturer, but just as with some of the Big Three customers, a relationship with Hyundai did not immediately take hold. The company's long relationship with J.D. Power and Associates began in 1974, when Hyundai executives were first thinking of bringing their cars to the United States. They invited Dave to make the first of what would be many trips to South Korea. Based in Seoul, Hyundai Motor Company had become the most profitable of the top six automakers in the world by 2012.[10] But early on, when they began to market cars in the U.S., explains Jamey, "Hyundai wasn't that attuned to customer issues and had an extremely production-oriented view of the world."

The Excel, a compact passenger car first imported into the U.S. in 1986, initially met with remarkable success, selling nearly 169,000 units that first year,[11] an industry record for an import car distributor in its first year.[12] "Hyundai marketed the Excel on price alone," recalls longtime J.D. Power employee John Humphrey, now senior vice president of J.D. Power and Associates global automotive division. For a time the Excel was the lowest-priced product in its category. But had Hyundai executives been paying closer attention, they would have heard grumblings about the quality.

On the Customer Satisfaction Index, which measured product quality and dealer service, Hyundai fared below average. When J.D. Power conducted its first long-term reliability survey of Hyundai, it finished thirtieth out of thirty-four brands. The only brands to finish lower were AMC, Merkur (an imported line of Ford of Europe), Peugeot, and Yugo—all of which were soon withdrawn from the U.S. market. Many industry watchers predicted that Hyundai might face the same end.

"The tragedy of the early Hyundai story is that its quality nightmares were not primarily due to problems in design or manufacturing," says Jamey. "Hyundai was in a position to deliver quality vehicles. What it was struggling with was an ability to understand what the American consumer needed." Some of the decision makers at that time were obstinate and arrogant, not unlike what Dave first encountered in Detroit, Jamey says, and had an insincere interest in what Americans wanted and liked in their cars.

Worse, shortsighted and fearful managers hoarded customer satisfaction data, the mechanism by which any organization understands the needs of its consumers. The U.S.-based Hyundai staff was determined to control the message to serve their own narrow agendas. Dave suspected that his warnings were being filtered or intercepted before they reached the decision makers in Seoul with the power to make real changes.

Middle managers in Korea were equally determined to keep bad news from their superiors. For example, Jamey Power went to Korea to deliver the results of the latest study but was "immediately shuffled off to lower-level managers who simply did not want to listen to bad news. These managers refused to even acknowledge they had a quality problem, and most certainly did not want us giving such a message to their superiors," recounted Jamey in his 2006 book *Satisfaction*. "Time and again they would tell us that they priced their car so low that quality shouldn't be an issue. They blamed their troubles instead on mistakes made by their U.S.-based (and staffed) sales and marketing division. More than once they even blamed the fact that there were too many women drivers in the United States."[13]

While Dave had very good, trusting relationships with several of the leading American COOs, such as Rod Hayden and Doug Mazza, once again he decided to bypass channels and appeal directly to Jerry Shin, an executive at Hyundai Motors of America. Dave was blunt: there was compelling evidence that Hyundai had a big problem, they needed to fix it soon or their position in the U.S. marketplace would no longer be viable, and the message was not getting through. Dave's forthright approach worked. In 1996, Dave and John Humphrey were summoned to South Korea, and something was different this time. Instead of being shunted off to junior executives, Chairman Chung Ju-Yung himself agreed to a meeting. Dave didn't pull any punches. He presented a report that directly correlated Hyundai's sales decline with poor vehicle quality. It was clearly an embarrassing moment for Hyundai management not used to such straight talk. But Dave let the facts speak for themselves, and the chairman was so impressed, he asked Dave to repeat the presentation to the top designers at the R&D center. It was not on the agenda, but of course Dave agreed. For Dave, there was no better audience for his presentations than the designers directly in charge of quality.

To its credit, Hyundai management immediately began making changes. "I believe this was the turning point," Humphrey says. "Hyundai was a price-play company that began to transform into a company that now injected VOC into the design of the product. Subsequently the brand showed consistent improvements in quality, and Hyundai is now seen as a quality car. It took a while for Hyundai to turn quality around—you can't fix things overnight— but they made real improvements, thanks to Dave's persistence and Chairman Chung's willingness to champion change."

Hyundai also improved its relationship with customers by offering a ten-year warranty, a move that Dave strongly supported. "Hyundai was the first to offer such a warranty," he says. "It put everyone in the organization, from manufacturing to sales, on notice that if Hyundai was to survive, they would have to change the way they conceptualized and delivered quality. It was as much an internal challenge to improve quality as it was an attempt to show car buyers how much it stood behind its cars."

The auto industry even noticed the change. In a 2004 *Automotive News* article, which revealed that Hyundai had topped the latest IQS results, the paper reported, "Once a byword for badly built cars, Hyundai finally broke through. It was as if Yugo had shot past Mercedes on the Power charts. Everyone knew Hyundai's fit and finish had improved, but here was a sensational stamp of approval." The article pointed out the impact of the Power data. "Hyundai has focused specifically on doing well in the J.D. Power arena. Task forces were set up . . . with the explicit purpose of improving the initial quality score."[14]

Going forward, the role of J.D. Power and Associates at Hyundai was very specific. "Our goal was nothing less than to change the corporate culture," Jamey says, "so that, above all, it integrated the voice of the customer as a filter through which all decisions were made." Hyundai had a lot going for it. It had some of the best auto engineers in the world. "All they needed was to break the information barrier that prevented VOC information from reaching those executives who were in a position to turn the company around."

Another article described the evolution of Dave's guidance of the company, and how Hyundai had been poised for change. Dave had seen the writing on the wall when he first started consulting with Hyundai in the mid-1990s. "I saw what they were investing in," he told *American Way* magazine, "and I knew that was eventually going to have a big effect on the quality level of the vehicles."

The magazine described Dave's visit with Chairman Chung and how Hyundai needed a new approach: "To make sure they didn't forget, Hyundai managers have kept a copy of Power's advice on a conference-room wall—vowing to keep it there until they are given credit for surpassing Toyota's reputation for quality."[15]

"More than almost any other car manufacturer, Hyundai took Dave's advice to apply the voice of the customer to product planning, engineering, production, and vendors," agrees Jerry Shin, now vice chairman of Hyundai Motor. "In the early 1990s, no one paid attention to Hyundai and no one thought Hyundai would succeed, except perhaps for Dave Power. His trips to Korea and his presentations to Hyundai executives had a real influence on the success of Hyundai. His constant focus on the VOC made an impact." In 2000, Hyundai developed a quality management focus with dedicated executives and top management support. As a result of continuous improvement efforts and the strong focus on quality, Hyundai achieved the number-one ranking among non-premium brands and came in third overall in the 2006 IQS. "Dave provided the path to improved quality and the data that supported it," Shin says. "The message was clear: listen to the voice of the customer."

Maybe Korean culture can be chiefly credited with the swift pivot, Dave told *American Way*. The attitude from the top down has been to learn from mistakes and make whatever improvements are necessary. "To change the management thinking is the most important thing—to have them understand that the consumer is the one calling the shots today. That's why some of the manufacturers have fallen behind the others."

In the decade following its embracing VOC across operations in 1998, Hyundai's initial quality improved 59 percent, far more than any other brand sold in America. Most important, sales rebounded accordingly. In 2004, Hyundai sold more than 400,000 vehicles— more than Volkswagen and Mitsubishi combined. "[P]eople now buy a Hyundai because they *want* one, not just because it's the *only car they can afford*," wrote Jamey in *Satisfaction*. "The lesson from this story is simple: break down any political silos that exist between the collectors and the users of VOC data. Do not allow something as critical as VOC to be spoiled by the personal agendas of a few or, in Hyundai's case, middle managers who were so afraid to bring bad news to their superiors that they nearly allowed the company to fail."[16]

Creating a New Normal at Mitsubishi

The data from customer satisfaction studies often provided stark examples of customers' woes, and such was the case when Mitsubishi Motors Corporation began to build its cars in the United States. Mitsubishi in 2012 ranked as the sixth largest automaker in Japan by global vehicle production.[17] The company has long had a strategy of growth through alliances with other automakers. Thus in 1971 it partnered with Chrysler in a deal that allowed Chrysler to have a piece of the fuel-efficient compact car market by selling Dodge Colts manufactured by Mitsubishi.[18] However, quality ratings for the Colt were low, as were the other models sold in the U.S. under the Mitsubishi brand when the company launched American distribution in the mid-1980s. Despite not being able to offer vehicles that met the same high level of quality that its Japanese automaker brethren were producing, Mitsubishi determined that it would make economic sense to build an assembly plant in the U.S., just as Toyota and Honda had, explains Jamey. "Some might speculate that one of the reasons for setting up an assembly plant in the U.S. was not just for an economic reason but also an attempt to start with a clean sheet of paper, hoping that they could provide a higher quality vehicle. But they struggled." Mitsubishi looked to J.D. Power and Associates for help. "Mitsubishi cars—both those sold by Chrysler and under the Mitsubishi mark—were perennial laggards in the quality race," Jamey says. J.D. Power made presentations to Mitsubishi to help it understand why it was failing, but other than subscribing to the IQS, Mitsubishi didn't engage Dave and his team intimately at that time.

"The assembly plant in Normal, Illinois, had many problems," says Dave. "It was not the first transplant [assembly plant in the U.S. manufacturing foreign cars], but there were growing pains. Mitsubishi was handed poor cards and it didn't play them well." J.D. Power studies reflected the mounting quality issues facing Mitsubishi. Dave was frustrated that increasingly critical recommendations were being ignored or slanted in ways that diluted their value.

Dave had been in this position many times and knew what to do: he had to directly get the attention of Mitsubishi's chairman, Dr. Hirokazu Nakamura, and ensure he understood the seriousness of this situation so that he could take the steps needed for improvement. "This was one thing Dave was very good at," says Phil Pincus, the J.D. Power associate who was responsible for working with Mitsubishi on quality and was on site in Normal from 1994 to 1995. "It's easy for senior executives to say, 'Thank you very much, we'll think about it.' Executives find it easy to trust themselves first and everyone else second. But Dave had a way to crack that. When Dave was able to speak directly and without a big audience, the results were quite remarkable."

It couldn't have been easy for Dr. Nakamura to read Dave's letter. Nakamura was a power train engineer by training and it must have stung to read Dave's report that the Mitsubishi power train had quality problems. In Normal, the engineering team ran the factory; it was not acceptable to say that there were fundamental problems with the engineering. Nevertheless, Nakamura asked Dave to come to Japan for a personal briefing.

At that meeting, Dave laid out his concerns—the assembly issues, the quality issues, the buck-passing, the deliberate concealment of problems. (Years later it was revealed to the public media that Mitsubishi's Japanese staff routinely covered up complaints from customers.)[19] After about forty-five minutes, a visibly shaken Nakamura asked Dave to accompany him to a larger conference room around the corner where eight members of his internal board of management were quietly waiting. After Nakamura instructed Dave to repeat his presentation on the problems, Mitsubishi began facing and correcting quality issues with new resolve.

Jaguar Reaches Out

The parent company of Jaguar was another carmaker that saw the value of engaging with J.D. Power and Associates. British Leyland Motor Corporation Ltd. (BLMC) included such esteemed brands as Land Rover, Rover, and Jaguar, as well as the best-selling Mini. In the early 1980s the company called on J.D. Power and Associates to help it sort out a number of long-standing quality issues, starting with the Jaguar. Since its introduction in 1922, the Jaguar brand has evoked prestige and comfort. But by the time John Egan, the new chief executive of BLMC, called J.D. Power, both the BLMC and Jaguar were in deep trouble.[20]

Jaguar owners were a paradox. They were at once the car's most vocal defenders and its ever-kvetching critics. Dave had heard the jokes that Jaguars were so unreliable that one needed two of them: "one to drive while the other was in the service shop."[21] Yet Jaguar owners were astonishingly loyal, appreciating the design, appointments, and driving experience while holding out hope for better reliability.

Dave could empathize with the problems of Jaguar owners for the simple reason that he owned a Jaguar, too. Dave had accepted the suggestion from Michael H. Dale, senior vice president for sales and marketing at Jaguar Cars Inc., that the best way to know about a car was to drive it, so he had purchased a car at full list price. The styling was excellent, but in his second month of ownership, the car broke down on the freeway as Dave was heading to the airport to attend the Automobile Import Dealers Association meeting in Washington, D.C. The Jaguar XJ6 had just 1,400 miles on the odometer. As a result, Dave missed his flight and arrived just in time for the first day's dinner meeting. Dale was there with his colleagues from Mercedes-Benz, BMW, Honda, and Toyota. When Dale saw Dave walk into the room, he recognized an opportunity to score points for Jaguar. "Dave Power! How do you like your new Jaguar?" he asked, making sure everyone knew what kind of car the chairman of J.D. Power and Associates chose to drive. Dave didn't want to embarrass Dale, he recalls, but the truth was the truth. "Mike, it isn't good," he said, and he detailed his experience to the deeply mortified sales executive. It turned out the car's problem was a piece of sandpaper that had been left in the crankshaft. The sandpaper had jammed in the bearings and stopped the flow of oil, seizing the engine. "I had an excellent example of what Jaguar customers were going through," Dave says.

According to Dale, who documented Jaguar's recovery in a 1986 article for *Fortune* magazine, Egan realized that if Jaguar was to be restored to profitability, he would have to focus on the American market, the only one big enough to provide the volume needed for a turnaround. Jaguar retained J.D. Power and Associates to conduct in-depth research to reveal all the ways Jaguar, especially the new XJ6 model, was frustrating owners. Dave set up an interviewing center in Westlake Village, California, to exclusively interview Jaguar XJ6 owners. "I was flabbergasted at how many problems the owners identified," Dave recalls. "Interviews that for other car models took ten to fifteen minutes required up to an hour each as Jaguar owners listed in painstaking detail the numerous issues they had with their vehicles. It was clear that Jaguar owners loved the styling of the cars but were frustrated with deep-seated quality problems with the cars and especially the dealer experience." For almost two years J.D. Power and Associates conducted and recorded telephone interviews to expose customer complaints. These audiotapes became part of an action plan for Jaguar.

"The chorus of complaints we heard gave us all an all-too-clear picture of what it meant to own a Jaguar: dirty service department waiting rooms, incompetent mechanics, indifferent dealers," Dale wrote in *Fortune*. "I got so angry listening to some of those tapes on my way home in the car that my wife made me promise to play them only in the morning so as not to wreck our evenings." Dale wanted everyone at Jaguar to hear those tapes and channel the collective anger into improving customer satisfaction. His insider's account of how Jaguar pulled itself out of the ditch in the U.S. market continued:

> I distributed the tapes to middle management. Hearing the customers' own words energized everybody. We then began

to feed it all back to the district service managers, who in turn went to the customers to find out if their complaints had been dealt with. All too often, we learned, nobody had fixed the problems. We began to take customers down to the dealers by the hand, confront the dealers, and say, "We are going to address these on the spot. Give the customer a car, let him drive away." The message started to reach down right away from the top of Jaguar: "You'd better satisfy the customer, because we are not going to be content with anything else." Since we had begun to cut back on our dealerships, the message had to be taken seriously.[22]

John Egan's commitment to hearing the absolute truth is a rare trait among auto company executives but was absolutely imperative to reversing Jaguar's fortunes. After also listening to the tapes and studying the J.D. Power market research, which identified about 250 distinct defects, from peeling paint to faulty steering mechanisms, Egan set about changing the culture of Jaguar. Reserving the top five trouble spots for himself, Egan assigned every board member a set of faults to address and correct. Suppliers were put on notice: they would be required to pay replacement costs and labor charges for any parts with excessive failure rates. Egan revamped the Jaguar dealer network to raise the quality of service and the assembly plant to improve productivity. "Egan's program worked," says Dave, who visited the assembly plant on a number of occasions and could see the changes for himself. Sales and productivity rates tripled. Partly for the turnaround of Jaguar, Queen Elizabeth II knighted Sir John Egan in 1986.

For Dale, Jaguar's success story was most evident in J.D. Power and Associates studies. "The results in terms of customer satisfaction and sales have been, to say the least, gratifying," he wrote in the summary of his *Fortune* piece. "Power reported in 1984 that we had made the biggest one-year leap in customer satisfaction in the study's history, and we had moved into sixth place. In 1985, we moved into fifth place, behind Honda and ahead of Mazda."

Despite the improvements, Jaguar was still in trouble when Ford acquired the automaker in 1990. Ford paid more than $2 billion for the company, whose physical assets were estimated at half a billion dollars, because Ford was looking to pump up its share of the luxury market. Ford initially tapped Bill Hayden to run the division, but in 1992, Nick Scheele was brought in as chairman and CEO of Jaguar. An "affable, portly, silver-haired bear of a man," as one profile described him, Scheele had been working for Ford in the United States when he was tapped to return to the U.K. and lead Jaguar.[23] It was there that he first met Dave, and their friendly relationship continued after Scheele became president and COO of Ford Motor Company. Ford would go on to sell both its Jaguar and Land Rover lines to Indian automaker Tata Motors in 2008 for $2.3 billion.[24]

Reuniting Quality with Luxury at Mercedes-Benz

While some manufacturers accepted Dave's voice-of-the-customer satisfaction surveys and changed course to address issues brought up on the surveys, other European carmakers were less receptive. Although J.D. Power and Associates frequently worked with such European-based luxury car heavyweights as BMW and Jaguar, Mercedes-Benz was the luxury carmaker most difficult to win over. It was also the European automaker with which Dave had the most personal involvement.

It was commonly accepted that German engineering, led by Mercedes-Benz, ruled the European market. "It was good engineering," Dave says, "but I don't think Mercedes executives necessarily understood what the consumer wanted today in terms of customer satisfaction. It is one thing to assume to understand what discerning consumers should want. It's quite another to actually ask them."

Dave's central lesson is that the customer is the only legitimate source of measuring quality, and it was an insight that Mercedes-Benz engineers did not swallow easily, especially coming as it did from an American. Bill Taylor, CEO of Mercedes-Benz U.S. International and a Canadian who had first worked on the line for Ford Motor Company, was sympathetic to Dave's philosophy, but he had a difficult time persuading his colleagues in Stuttgart, Germany, to heed the voice of the customer. Having joined Mercedes to open its first North American assembly plant in Alabama, Taylor had previously been recruited by Toyota to manage its first North American assembly plant in Cambridge, Ontario, Canada. From his stint as vice president of manufacturing at Toyota Motor Manufacturing Canada, Taylor understood what Toyota had accomplished by listening to Dave. So, Taylor asked Dave for help in the initial planning of Mercedes's Alabama plant, engaging him in numerous conversations about the drivers of customer satisfaction and how they could be planned for from the ground up.

Taylor also tried to pave the way for acceptance of Dave's message in Germany. It was a lesson that Mercedes-Benz initially resisted. "Mercedes-Benz is a proud culture," Taylor notes, "and at first there was a lot of denial and somewhat of a filtering process about what news went to management. The way bad news was handled was with such finesse that it almost became indistinguishable from good news. You weren't a popular person if you brought bad news to the table." Meanwhile, according to Taylor, Mercedes-Benz quality was no longer matching customer

expectations of the premier brand. "The bar was rising fast on quality, and we needed to move quickly."

"They got distracted from a quality standpoint," recalls Jamey,
"and we started to see that happen." The grand old blue-chip company wanted to keep its chin up and feel it was above such work-
aday issues as consumer concerns, but it stumbled. "The world
kind of caught up to them in terms of styling, quality, prestige,
and technical sophistication."

In 1994, Taylor asked Dave to travel to Mercedes's headquarters in Stuttgart to meet with the product development group for
the M-Class. Dave stood before the team of engineers charged with
developing a luxury midsize SUV that would be a hit with the
American consumer, the target for this increasingly popular category. "He was there to deliver the voice of the customer," says Taylor.
"And they asked him some very difficult questions." The M-Class
debuted in 1998 to fanfare, with the ML320 winning Truck of the
Year honors from both *Motor Trend* and the North American International Auto Show,[25] but it also suffered from quality concerns.

It was an era of industry consolidations, and in 1998 Mercedes's parent company, Daimler-Benz, announced the purchase
of Chrysler, which further distracted management from its core
values. Meanwhile, the company's status in the J.D. Power and
Associates ratings continued to slip. When their quality issues
were taken up by the press, some in the company got touchy and
fired back disparaging comments about Dave's company and the
relevance of its ratings for their brand. They bristled at being compared on a list to much less luxurious, lower-cost cars.

As he had done so many times before, Dave took his concerns
to upper management, but this time he wanted to address more
than just internal roadblocks. In a letter to COO Jürgen Hubbert,
Dave suggested taking the bickering out of the press and instead

having the two companies work together. He had met Hubbert years before, when the executive had come to the U.S. to open the company's Alabama manufacturing facility. It was not J.D. Power's mission to condemn Mercedes and thwart its success, Dave wrote; it was to help. Hubbert warmly accepted the suggestion and invited Dave to Stuttgart to make a presentation to the company's operating board.

Dave and "the two Davids"—David Sargent and David Letson (head of the quality consulting group)—traveled to Germany, loaded down with survey data. In his presentation, Dave differentiated quality and perceived quality. "What J.D. Power and Associates measures is the difference between what the consumer perceives they require and what they perceive they received," he told the Mercedes-Benz executives. "These quality measures are relative. If we keep raising their expectations, it's tougher to meet their expectations."

Dave recalls, "As we pointed out a problem area, Jürgen Hubbert would point to the man in charge of engineering, or production, or marketing, and he'd say 'That's your problem.' It was not that he didn't want anything to do with it. He was putting them on notice."

"It was a breakthrough moment for Mercedes," Taylor says. "For the first time, the executive committee created a team to inject voice-of-the-customer information into the design process. It really turned what was an engineering-centric organization into a VOC-centric organization. It was an aha moment for the company when the customer satisfaction rankings of Mercedes immediately started to rise."

That first presentation, over Labor Day weekend in 2000, led to a multiyear, multifaceted consulting relationship with Mercedes-Benz. Dave and key associates began advising the carmaker confidentially, improving their systems to take into account the voice of the customer. Soon the quality efforts became a point of public pride for the company.

"We have organized the company in a new way to make quality the top priority," Hubbert told *Automotive News* in 2004. The article noted, "Mercedes wants to be tops in the J.D. Power and Associates Initial Quality Study by 2006. In the 2004 survey, Mercedes improved its ranking but still placed behind nine other brands, including Buick, Mercury, and Hyundai." The article detailed the close attention Hubbert and his team were paying to J.D. Power studies in the U.S. market.[26]

Following the merger with Chrysler, Hubbert's successor, Dieter Zetsche, who at the time was in charge of Chrysler, was an outspoken company proponent of J.D. Power's work, and he pushed both companies to focus on quality results.

Dave's insight also helped identify a problem that amounted to a turf war between Mercedes and the other top German brand, BMW. "They were introducing new technologies too fast," he explains. "They weren't proven enough. We pointed out that we felt there was a race between BMW and Mercedes to beat each other out in terms of being the first with new technology. Therefore, both of them, when a new model was introduced, would have unanticipated problems." The J.D. Power team was given access to prototypes of forthcoming models and took a look at potential problems—"from the point of view of customers," Dave points out, not that of engineers. He had to remind the German designers, as he had done with reluctant U.S. companies, that his information came from surveys: "It's the customer saying this, not J.D. Power."

Dave's acceptance by Mercedes-Benz worked to make J.D. Power and Associates more mainstream among European carmakers. Dave helped Mercedes-Benz and other European car engineers finally understand that in some important respects, drivers on either side of the Atlantic legitimately desire different driving experiences. For example, European drivers tend to prefer stiff seats. Dave explained that Americans, who tend to spend more time in their cars than Europeans, prefer softer seats. He went through the market research, from vehicle handling to interior accessories.

"Dave had to find his place in Europe before he was listened to," Bill Taylor recalls. "It was a matter of credibility. He wasn't the enemy, but it was a tough road for Dave." Once Mercedes embraced J.D. Power and Associates' research and analysis, the customer satisfaction rankings began to rise, and ever since Mercedes-Benz has been one of the most improved brands in the IQS. For efforts like the turnaround at Mercedes, Taylor says, "The consumer owes Dave Power a tremendous debt."

CHAPTER FIVE

REVOLUTIONIZING RETAIL

J.D. Power has long been a champion of the dealer, recognizing that the car-buying experience has a profound impact on customer satisfaction. The best-designed and best-engineered cars in the world could not succeed if the buyer's experience at the dealer was not equally focused on customer satisfaction. This was the basis for Dave's commitment to creating dialogues—both among dealers and between dealers and manufacturers—that would result in a better customer experience.

Some of Dave's greatest influence has been through the relationships he cultivated with auto retailers. In a sense, he approached their needs and ideas as he did those of the end user, recognizing dealers as the intermediary customer of manufacturers that they are.

"Dave is very invested in the relationships between the manufacturer and the retailer," says John Bergstrom, chairman and CEO of Bergstrom Corporation in Neenah, Wisconsin, which operates twenty-five dealerships that sell more than thirty-five brands. "He is an amazingly insightful collector of information, and he is always looking for ways to leverage what worked for some people to help others learn." Many J.D. Power and Associates products have enabled savvy dealers to gain insights into customer needs, build their reputations, and be more successful. But in Dave's experience working with dealers, manufacturers, and the trove of data his company generated, he found that dealership retailing was one of the greatest challenges facing the industry. He came to see it as a fundamentally flawed system where change would not come fast enough to keep up with an evolving marketplace.

In retrospect, that evolution tracked with cultural changes and greater marketplace sophistication. "If you dial back the time machine to the early 1970s, the auto-buying and -servicing experience was not always a pleasant one for consumers," observes Jamey Power. "The salespeople and the managers didn't have the best reputations, generally, and car buyers often felt that they had to be on guard so as not to be taken advantage of. It's not to say that there weren't dealerships that were reputable and considerate of customers, and legitimate in terms of their business practices, but it was 'the Wild West,' or pretty inconsistent in terms of how customers were treated. The industry was male-dominated, and salespeople didn't often acknowledge that women in the household were part of—if not primary in—the car-buying decisions. And it was very inconsistent in terms of the cleanliness, appearance, and even safety of dealer facilities."

"In the automotive world, historically, the customer had no information when it came to buying a car," says Chris Denove, who oversaw J.D. Power and Associates' Sales Satisfaction Index studies before developing divisions on Internet car sales and mystery shopping, among others. "It wasn't that long ago that you didn't even have a window sticker with the manufacturer's list price. It took federal law to require a window sticker. So the dealer could just size up that customer's experience when they walked in the door and price that car at anything they wanted.

"A window sticker is just a baby step toward information. Dave saw that this transparency was going to shift the balance toward the customer, especially with the advent of the Internet, and Dave helped manufacturers and dealers navigate—even thrive—in an age when the customer was becoming more powerful. What Dave always believed was that to get the dealers to change, they've got to see the link between satisfaction and profits. And that link is really the key to getting dealers, or any business for that matter, to change their focus on customer satisfaction."

The Franchise System

When Dave began working with the automotive industry in the 1960s, the complex arrangement between manufacturers and dealers was a deeply entrenched one, born of both shared and conflicting interests between the entities that make cars and those that sell them.

"Vehicle distribution evolved fairly quickly in the industry's first few decades," described an *Automotive News* article on early dealers. "The earliest inventors sold directly to consumers, starting with one-of-a-kind models that went to wealthy friends. To reach more customers, though, carmakers started using third-party retailers. That practice gradually developed into the franchised dealer system."[1] Soon after automobiles began being mass-produced, automakers realized that to reach customers throughout the country, they needed to rely on outside retailers rather than sell directly to customers. Because most manufacturers were concentrated in the Northeast but wanted to reach customers spread throughout the United States, it was not practical to attempt to sell directly to customers, though Ford briefly tried. Plus, salespeople who drew their salaries from a manufacturer were paid the same whether they sold few cars or many, and manufacturers needed capital to keep their assembly lines humming, not to invest in a network of retail operations.

Early dealers were usually businessmen who had established retail operations, sometimes selling hardware or wagons, many times selling—and servicing—bicycles. These proprietors secured the rights to sell to a wide geographic territory and were so eager to have the opportunity to sell to a clamoring public that they signed agreements to represent only a single manufacturer. They not only paid a hefty deposit on each vehicle when ordering but also the balance when the car was delivered, regardless of whether or not they could actually sell it. But the risk was worth it to thousands of dealers, who signed mostly yearlong franchise agreements to sell and service an automaker's vehicle line under terms that increasingly favored the manufacturer.

By 1920, dealers were crying foul over the way manufacturers were leveraging the agreements to pressure them to order more cars than the market would bear, and sometimes under threat of canceling a contract or having a competing dealer set up right across the street. In 1956, Congress prohibited these sorts of pressures placed on dealers, and GM and other automakers redrafted their agreements accordingly. States strengthened the laws protecting dealers in the 1960s and 1970s. The model, however, was still one in which dealers were tasked with somehow selling all the cars a manufacturer could produce, rather than the manufacturer responding to the needs of the market.[2]

It was in this climate that Dave first started working with the auto industry, and he almost immediately began to identify the flaws in the retailing system. One of the ways in which he learned that the problems plaguing the industry were of concern to manufacturers as well as dealers was through his participation in the late 1970s and early 1980s as a guest speaker for regional dealer associations and what were known as Dealer 20 groups—so called because a typical network encompassed twenty geographically dispersed dealerships organized by franchises. Dealer 20 groups were made up of non-competing dealers who would agree to share experiences, ideas, strategies—even financial information. The collaboration was designed to help all dealers do better. The dealers within any single Dealer 20 group couldn't be geographically near each other because the federal government made it illegal, under restraint-of-trade laws, for dealers in one marketplace to cooperate.

The Dealer 20 groups were often organized by accounting firms that specialized in serving car dealers or consulting firms, such as NCM Associates, and served the larger brands, such as Chevrolet and Oldsmobile, as well as all the smaller brands, such as Mercedes, Volvo, and Audi. The Dealer 20 groups proliferated because dealers found them so useful. The sponsoring firm gave each dealership its unique statistics on key metrics, such as sales, costs, and profits. These were private. In addition, it provided the average of those same metrics so each dealer could compare its own results with the group average. The results were immediately eye opening. If, for example, the profits on used car sales at one dealer were significantly lower than the group average, the dealer was alerted that something was out of whack. From the group discussions, best practices emerged, and dealers learned from each other in an environment of trust. The quality and profitability of many dealerships improved.

Charting Dealer Attitudes

While he often has an opinion—one he considers backed by data—Dave more often is the one to sit back and listen to the conversation of others. And perhaps there is no topic more rife with dealer opinions than the policies and performance of the manufacturers. In this arena, Dave also planned a service that would break new ground. Long before he invited the dealers together to discuss issues, he built a study that would give the manufacturers objective insight into dealer concerns. He simply asked dealers in the study to share their attitudes, independently and privately, about manufacturers.

"The dealers loved rating the manufacturers," Dave learned when he pioneered the Dealer Attitude Survey in the mid-1970s. Because of his dealer interactions—attending their meetings and events, often as an invited speaker—he heard many common dealer frustrations and began to think about how manufacturers could benefit from access to issues the dealer groups seemed to share.

"The origination of the Dealer Attitude Survey was the result of hearing the frustrations expressed by the majority of dealers when they got together," explains Dave. "As individuals, they could not be effective in changing the policies or behaviors of their manufacturers. The manufacturers would meet with dealer councils, but the automakers had the upper hand and directly and indirectly controlled the meetings. At least this was the impression the dealers gave me back in the 1960s and 1970s." At this time, the vast majority of dealers had only one franchise with a single manufacturer.

To launch the survey, Dave obtained the names of dealership principals from a standard business directory offered by Dun & Bradstreet and sent out a survey to each of them, asking them to record their thoughts, opinions, and attitudes about all the major manufacturers serving the U.S. market, whether the dealer owned a franchise of that maker or not. The first year about two thousand dealers responded. "We had the dealers rate all the manufacturers, and then we analyzed it by competitive manufacturers and the franchise dealers for that make." The study, Dave says, showed "differences between the general dealer population and what the manufacturers' own dealers were saying," and the results could be analyzed by small, medium, and large dealerships.

The clients of the survey were the manufacturers, who "wanted to know how they were viewed by their current franchisees and, if they were being downgraded by the other dealers, what they had to do" to encourage new dealers to acquire a franchise. The manufacturer would also learn if a dealer was considering dropping a particular franchise, which, as Dave says, "was important if they wanted to replace dealers or add new franchisees." The first year just two or three automakers subscribed to the study—a single domestic and a Japanese maker or two. Understanding the thinking of dealers was especially vital to the Japanese carmakers, which were quickly expanding across the United States. But by the 1980s, 80 percent of the manufacturers were subscribers.

The survey, initially run in conjunction with *Auto Age* magazine and operated solely by J.D. Power and Associates over the next two decades, covered many manufacturer-dealer topics. Perhaps the most provocative one was the quality of the carmakers' sales reps, which came to light a few years into the study. "We had dealers rate the sales and service representatives who were calling on them," Dave says. Dealers were asked about competency, availability, and the level of trust they had in the rep.

One of the surveys showed the reps for Lincoln-Mercury scored the lowest among all manufacturers in the trustworthiness category. That concerned the automaker, which insisted its representatives were not dishonest. Lincoln-Mercury was not aware of having a reputation of lying to dealers or engaging in unsavory retail practices, so the first reaction by their staff was that there was a problem with the data. The executive in charge, General Manager Robert Rewey, asked Dave to take a closer look at the data.

Dave was confident about his results but he, too, was surprised by them. In true Dave Power fashion of playing fair and letting the facts speak for themselves, he agreed to do a follow-up survey to test the results. In that one, he discovered the problem of the "green peas."

"Ford did well recruiting young men, and a few women, to become local field staff," Dave recalls, "but they did not let the new reps make decisions." Instead, the reps reported to district managers, who in turn reported to regional managers. It was at this regional level that decisions were made, and often if a program changed, the news didn't make it down to the sales rep level. "The reps would call on the dealers and promise them this or that, and then their managers would go back to the regional office and the boss would say, 'Oh, we can't do that.'" This led to the dealers calling the new recruits "green peas" and ultimately dismissing them for not being ripe enough to command authority. The lack of trustworthiness was not a reflection of any lack of honesty on the part of the rep; instead it was a training issue within Lincoln-Mercury, one the automaker did not know was affecting its reputation until Dave's data brought it to light.

Rewey was relieved to learn about the further results, Dave recalls. "They started looking into giving the reps better training and educating the regional managers who oversaw those people and have them understand that it worked against them to have an inexperienced representative."

Another audience for the survey results was the dealers themselves. "Dealers were delighted to have further insight into what their dealer friends or compatriots were all about," Dave says. "We gave them feedback that showed there were several dealers throughout the country that felt the same way they did." Some dealers, like Shau-wai Lam, even commissioned spin-off studies of their own. Lam, who owned Pontiac franchises in Southern California and New Jersey, asked Dave to find out whether any other Pontiac dealers were having the same excessive warranty problems that Lam was, a problem that Lam feared would result in a loss of customers as drivers gravitated to more reliable makes. Dave looked at the data from the Dealer Attitude Survey and found that, indeed, Pontiac dealers across the board were complaining about the number of warranty repairs they were having to field. The data helped Lam make the decision to get out of his Pontiac franchises and focus on building his Honda and Acura franchises.

The strong interest dealers had in the study ultimately led to its demise, however. As the National Automobile Dealers Association (NADA) board tracked interest in the survey, it saw the potential for a logical extension of their own interactions with its dealer members. The association started a competing survey of its own, which polled only NADA members and provided access to the results at a fraction of the cost J.D. Power and Associates' efforts required. Dave discontinued the survey in 2005 as J.D. Power staff found it harder and harder to compete against the NADA's less expensive survey.

Over the years, Dave was an invited speaker at dozens of dealer meetings. He generally talked about trends in automobile quality and other subjects of interests to dealers. Dave also emphasized the difficulties dealers faced in the "push" model of automobile manufacturing. "The assembly plants were designed to build, say, 200,000 cars a year, and it was only the last 10 percent of those sales that made a model profitable," explains Dave. "Once the manufacturer had a car designed and pushed the product out, it would need to have sales events and so forth to ensure that those last 10 percent got sold, and sometimes dealers resorted to deceptive practices to confuse the buyer. The whole situation was built on production of vehicles and pushing them out the door to the dealers, who then had to push them on the consumer." Dave knew the dealers would have much preferred a system that could be more responsive to consumer demand, and the sympathy he expressed—as well as his ideas for alternatives—kept dealers interested in what he had to say.

The invitations kept rolling in. "One month I might be talking to a Toyota Dealer 20 group," Dave recalls. "The next month, it might be Mercedes dealers." By regular attendance at their meetings, he came to understand their issues very well and developed many friendships and personal connections. These dealers became subscribers to monthly communications, such as the *Automotive Consumers Profile* and the *Power Report,* Dave generated on industry trends, and they became the basis for a dealer networking program J.D. Power and Associates itself would facilitate.

A Superdealer's Concerns

In 1984, Dave was the keynote speaker at a Dealer 20 group meeting at the Hotel Del Coronado in San Diego, California. One of the dealers took Dave aside and told him he owned a dozen or so car dealerships; he was one of the first "superdealers," car retailers who expanded their traditional Chevrolet or Chrysler dealerships by opening franchises to sell other makes of cars. Franchise restrictions kept most of them from selling other domestic cars, so many of them opened dealerships selling Mercedes, Hondas, Toyotas, Volvos, or Volkswagens. Even this was technically against the dealers' franchise contracts with the Big Three, but the dealers would find ways around the restriction and just not report that they also had a Toyota or Honda dealership. Sometimes the other dealership would be a hundred miles or more from their first one. This superdealer from the Bay Area said that Dave's message about the revolution in retailing was even more relevant for the dealers who had multiple franchises. He told Dave, "I have different problems than the average dealer, because I own several franchises and I can't get them to work together. If you come talk to us, I'll pull together a dozen dealers at my facility." This was a topic that couldn't be broached at the Dealer 20 meetings, and Dave was intrigued.

The man who took Dave aside was Donald Lucas, founder of the Lucas Dealership Group. Lucas was a pioneer in getting multiple brands under one umbrella company. His firm, which he sold in 2000, grew to operate more than forty dealerships in California and Hawaii, which together sold vehicles from more than thirty-three manufacturers. The Lucas Dealership Group was one of the top twenty-five automobile companies in the country, with nine hundred employees and $500 million in annual sales.

Dave was delighted by the invitation and quickly accepted. He was always ready to speak to a receptive audience, but he was particularly excited to address this group. He understood the challenges that these superdealers, joined under a single ownership umbrella, had in propagating best practices in sales and marketing across their various entities. He saw that economies of scale could quickly revolutionize the consumer buying experience as well as strengthen the dealers' demands for fundamental changes in quality from the automakers. He felt there was a big opportunity here, if only he could key into their most pressing concerns. The superdealer was a brand-new constituency, with a unique set of issues. He pondered how he could make a lasting impact.

Dave's first exposure to superdealers would presage one of the most influential projects his company ever produced for dealers. It would take the interest of a new friend to give the project wings.

Just a few months earlier, Dave had received a call from the head of national market representation for Toyota Motor Sales

U.S.A., Don Keithley, the executive in charge of building Toyota's North American dealer network. Keithley had long admired Dave and asked him for a meeting. "Having worked in the automobile industry, I was very aware of J.D. Power and Associates," Keithley says, "and I was particularly impressed with Dave Power's irreverent take on the auto industry. I was working for Ford early in my career, and Dave's reports were not always well received by the establishment. But I thought he had some very good insights about the entire industry, and especially the auto industry in California. I was impressed by Dave's reputation as a trendsetter and leader of a forward-thinking organization." Keithley had a feeling that he and Dave had something to offer each other.

Dave was enthusiastic about meeting with Keithley, too. Keithley had an excellent reputation among the car dealer community. After an exceptional career in sales and marketing with Ford and then Toyota, Keithley knew every significant car dealer in America. He had the contacts and the credibility to help make Dave's vision for the superdealers a reality.

Their initial meeting took place at the J.D. Power headquarters in October 1984. "Dave was a maverick, which is what I expected," Keithley says. "I was impressed by the sophistication in how he thought about research and analysis. Mostly, I was impressed by his integrity. Dave owned the research he conducted, which was a game changer, and he didn't care where the chips happened to fall. He never pulled his punches. For my money, Dave Power reinvented the concept of market research in the auto industry."

Keithley said he was looking for a new challenge after Toyota. Later that day, Dave was scheduled to meet with Don Lucas's dealers in San Jose, California, and he told Keithley about the event. He planned to present the dealers with information from J.D. Power and Associates' Dealer Attitude Survey, but mostly he wanted to listen to their issues and learn how they dealt with different manufacturers. He wanted to see what he could do for them.

In short order, Dave ended up sitting next to Keithley on a flight to San Jose. They used the meeting with the California superdealer to test their chemistry. As it turned out, they worked seamlessly as a team and left the multiple-franchise holders wanting more. By the end of their initial meeting, it was clear that Keithley's thoughts about the auto industry and organizing car dealers were perfectly aligned with Dave's. They agreed that the superdealers had ongoing information needs that J.D. Power and Associates could uniquely serve. On the flight back to Los Angeles Dave and Keithley shook hands on a working relationship. Before they landed, Dave came up with a name for the new project: Superdealer Roundtable.

Forming an Influential Roundtable

The Superdealer Roundtable program, headed by Keithley, quickly ramped up and went into action as the newest initiative by J.D. Power and Associates. The idea represented a logical evolution for the company. Before the introduction of the roundtables, J.D. Power had focused on the deployment of original market research information to clients who wanted to know consumers' opinions of their products and services, but the roundtables codified the strong relationship that Dave had forged with dealers.

Many dealers cite Dave's influence on a personal level, relating it to their own business practices. Wisconsin car dealer Bergstrom, in fact, credits Dave's influence as second only to his mother's—high praise from a successful dealer who has frequently named his mother as the inspiration for his dealerships' corporate culture. Bergstrom had learned at home how important it was to treat guests well, and he applied those lessons to customer service, treating customers as he would guests in his home. Dave, he says, "took that philosophy of delivering care to people and measured it," so a dealer could chart how he was doing. That was vital, Bergstrom says, because as the dealer grew, it became harder and harder to track it.

Dave was always delighted to see what the clients using his company's research actually did about the problems the research revealed. Since founding J.D. Power and Associates in 1968, Dave had witnessed a revolution in the quality of cars rolling off the assembly lines, and he could take some measure of credit for spurring many changes. But there was always an element of frustration in not being able to directly create meaningful change on an industry level. The Superdealer Roundtables afforded J.D. Power an opportunity to do just that. By bringing together the superdealers with other industry leaders, Dave saw that the roundtables could become a force that would give J.D. Power the type of grassroots credibility it needed to earn a seat at the table of the global automobile industry.

The company moved quickly. In January 1985, J.D. Power and Associates hosted the first Superdealer Roundtable in San Francisco, just days before the annual convention of the NADA. Don Lucas and many of his dealers were in attendance, as well as dozens of others. The events were invitation-only and closed to the press. Dave wanted it to be a place for unvarnished dialogue. "The roundtables existed to allow the dealers to speak their minds," he explains, "and since we kept the press and the factory people out of it, they were able to openly give their views." He and Keithley couldn't have been more pleased with the credibility and contacts, in addition to the revenues, that the roundtables generated for the company. Each participant in the roundtables paid a one-time membership fee, which covered four meetings a year, plus a registration fee for each meeting. "We had a very good start," Keithley notes.

The annual member meeting was always scheduled immediately before the NADA convention, to make it more convenient for the dealers. The roundtables usually kicked off with a keynote address from an industry leader. The rest of the conference was organized into a series of speakers, panels, and breakout sessions. "Dealers were acutely interested in what their peers were accomplishing and how they did it," Keithley says. At those early meetings, there was a lot of concern among the Honda dealers about issues that would later explode into the full-blown conspiracy scandal involving kickbacks to grant dealerships and car deliveries. Another big issue was the introduction of a new import from the South Korean automaker Hyundai. Dave astutely invited a senior executive from Hyundai to address the group. Many of the dealers had missed out on representing the Japanese imports and they were not about to lose out on this new opportunity. The roundtables delivered, but J.D. Power "learned as much as we gave," Dave says. His company reported on survey results and received instant feedback from the assemblage as to their research.

After just two years of the program, J.D. Power and Associates had more than 250 of the best multiple franchise holders in the U.S. signed up. In the fall of 1987, the Superdealer Roundtable program expanded to become the International Automotive Roundtable. "The concept," Keithley explains, "was to bring all interested parties into the discussion, not just dealers."

"It seemed to me that if we wanted real change in the auto industry, we had to expand the conversation by bringing as many voices into the mix as possible," Dave says. Dealers were key players, but manufacturers, finance units of the automakers, consultants, service providers, and, later, investment bankers all had a stake in the industry, too. Dave's vision was to expand the table, create a new mix, and raise the stakes by making the roundtable exclusive.

The first International Automotive Roundtable got off to an awkward start. It was scheduled for November 11, 1987, in Washington, D.C.—the same day Mother Nature delivered one of the biggest snowstorms of the decade.[3] The snowstorm created a lot of inconvenience as National Airport closed and roads became impassable, and only twenty or so dealers showed up for the first night's keynote. The keynote speaker was Paul Volcker, the recently retired chairman of the Federal Reserve Board of Governors. Bob Rosenthal, a very influential superdealer with multiple franchises in the D.C. area, contributed one of his four-wheel-drive cars to ferry registrants from their hotels to the conference site. Volcker, not about to miss his second speech as a private individual, actually walked. The other keynoter, Bob Lutz, who at the time was vice chairman of Chrysler Motors, flew in on the corporate jet.

The late 1980s were a turbulent time for auto dealers—dealers were trying to figure out how to remain competitive in the face of energy crises and the rise of popular imports—and the dealer roundtables were reflecting the turmoil. Dealers had always been "very much beholden" to the manufacturers, Dave explains, but now, more dealers were getting larger, and their power in the relationship with the manufacturers was growing. Since a superdealer did not have all its eggs in one basket, it could just concentrate its efforts on whichever brand was selling well. In 1989, Dave published his thoughts on the future of the dealer in the year-end issue of his monthly *Power Report,* and his outlook was not rosy. He predicted that as the quality of cars increased across the industry, buyers would be less concerned about which brand of car they chose or where they got it, and price competition would make it increasingly difficult for dealers to make money. Indeed, some dealers found in the late 1980s they could have made more money selling their car lot's land than they could selling the cars on it. Some were turning to imports and away from Detroit in a bid to make a better profit under a new system.

As the roundtables evolved with more involvement from super-dealers and foreign car companies, Keithley retired and Tom Shaver came on board in 1995 to further boost the roundtables' visibility and impact. Shaver was a former zone manager for Chevrolet in Los Angeles, had served as the first marketing director at Saturn, and had held a high-level marketing position at Volkswagen, a job Dave had actually helped him land. It was natural to have another old colleague join the team. "One of my objectives was to get the most outstanding and influential speakers to address the roundtables," Shaver recalls. Dave mentioned names such as the U.S. ambassador to Japan, former Senator Howard Baker; the CEOs of Toyota (Hiroshi Okuda), Ford (Bill Ford), and GM (Roger Smith); and the CEOs of Mitsubishi, Volvo, Mazda, Rolls-Royce, Firestone, and other luminaries from the worlds of business, education, and politics. Shaver was skeptical. "You'll never get those people," Shaver told him. Dave, the eternal optimist, countered, "You'll never know until you try." All of them agreed to address the roundtables.

Shaver helped increase the attendance, visibility, and impact of the roundtables. Dave and Shaver encouraged speakers to use the roundtables as forums to make major announcements within the automotive industry. For example, shortly after he joined GM, Lutz used a roundtable to announce that his primary objective as a leader was to reward employees who best served the customer and to give dealers great products they could sell at a profit. Shaver says, "It was the first time I had seen the audience give anyone a standing ovation."

Okuda, appointed chairman of Toyota in 1999, used the roundtable forum to present a vision of Toyota that would be even more relevant when Toyota faced the biggest quality crisis in its history. In 1999, Okuda spoke about the need to destroy today's Toyota to build tomorrow's successful Toyota. It was a good example of the concept of creative destruction, the notion that to make room for new products or ways of thinking, old systems must be eliminated. To further the impact of his address, Okuda invited the leaders of all of Toyota's key suppliers to the roundtable, an invitation that was considered more of a command than a request. That year the roundtable was overrepresented by attendees from dozens of Toyota suppliers.

While the popularity of the International Automotive Roundtables increased, there was constant pressure to make the tent bigger. One insight was that buying a new car for most consumers was a complex financial transaction. It just made sense to include the financing players, such as General Motors Acceptance Corporation (GMAC) and the financial arms of the other automakers, in these retailer discussions. The roundtables invited lawyers who specialized in automotive franchise law to debate the pros and cons of various arrangements. Investment bankers, sensing an opportunity to take some of the larger and more successful superdealers public, also applied for admission and were made welcome.

Building a Network

It was primarily through the roundtables that Dave became acquainted with several dealers he considered smart, forward-thinking business owners, many of whom were founders of the superdealer group. For Dave, the dealers he connected with the most were individuals who thought bigger and deserved one of his highest accolades: "entrepreneur."

Bergstrom from Wisconsin was certainly in that group, as was Russ Darrow of Russ Darrow Group, in the Milwaukee area. In Michigan, so were the strategic Bloomfield Hills dealer Roger Penske of Penske Automotive Group, Irma Elder of Elder Automotive Group in Troy, and Al Serra of Serra Automotive in Grand Blanc.

The network also reached up and down the East Coast: Herb Chambers of Herb Chambers Companies in the Boston area; Tom Nemet of the Nemet Auto Group in New York City; and the Potamkin Group, whose founder, Victor Potamkin, had a Manhattan Cadillac dealership and was the first member of the roundtable before handing over the reins to his sons, Alan and Robert. There were also Ronald Ertley of Wilkes-Barre, Pennsylvania's Ertley MotorWorld; Jack Pohanka of Pohanka Automotive Group in Maryland; Robert Rosenthal of Rosenthal Automotive Organization in Arlington, Virginia; Jim Hudson of Jim Hudson Group in Columbia, South Carolina; and Rick and Rita Case of Rick Case Automotive Group in Fort Lauderdale, Florida.

On the West Coast, the entrepreneurs included Bert Boeckmann of Southern California's Galpin Ford, the late Martin Swig of the San Francisco Autocenter, and Bob Baker of the Bob Baker Auto Group in San Diego, as well as Mike and Sully Sullivan of the LACarGuy family of dealerships in the Los Angeles area. Also, Bob Nesen of Nesen Oldsmobile-Cadillac of Thousand Oaks, Tom Price of Price Family Dealerships in San Francisco, and Frederick "Fritz" Hitchcock of Hitchcock Automotive Resources in City of Industry, California.

All these roundtable dealers, and many more, used the services of Dave and the interactions and information he made available to them to help build their businesses in a strategic, expansion-focused manner. Often, they have been vocal about his support and value to them. "Dave is like the Rosetta Stone. He had the information and could explain it to any audience," says Ernie Boch Jr., CEO of Boch Enterprises, a billion-dollar business of automobile dealerships in Norwood, Massachusetts. "I don't think there's a manufacturer selling cars in the U.S. that hasn't been influenced—and for the better—by J.D. Power."

Many retailers respected Dave's point of view and sought his advice. He served as the only non-dealer board member for Driver's Mart, an early attempt by a group of savvy, mostly younger dealers to create a nationwide network of used car stores. Although Dave's director role was unpaid, "he received some heat from the automotive industry" for perceived impropriety, Jamey recalls. "But he saw it as an opportunity to be on the inside of a grand experiment. Eventually the Driver's Mart concept failed, but it spurred ideas used today by CarMax and AutoNation, among others."

Mark F. O'Neil first met Dave after O'Neil had become president of one of the first auto malls, a large dealer complex where many makes were represented by one dealer, each with its own showroom. O'Neil went on to be part of the start-up team that conceived and launched CarMax Inc., a publicly held used-automobile retailer. "Dave is a visionary in that he predicted two things years before they happened," O'Neil says. "The first is the degree of consolidation the dealers would see; the second is the rise of publicly owned dealerships." A third prediction has yet to come true, but O'Neil doesn't advise anyone to bet against Dave's expectation that when Chinese automakers eventually come to the U.S., they will succeed in half the time the Japanese carmakers required. O'Neil adds, "I suspect that in the next few years we'll see that prediction come to pass."

O'Neil is currently the chairman and chief executive officer of Dealertrack Technologies, a service that provides more than

19,000 automotive dealers with real-time access to about 1,300 lenders in the Dealertrack Technologies credit application network. In 2001, O'Neil invited Dave to join Dealertrack Technologies' board of directors. "Dave is always the quietest person at our board meetings, but he only has to clear his throat to get the attention of everyone at the table."

Helping Manufacturers Encourage Dealers

Although Dave was a strong supporter of helping dealers exchange information with each other and provide feedback to the automakers that improved matters for them and bolstered their position within the industry, he was equally supportive of manufacturers having access to information that would improve the car-buying experience for their customers. Early in the company's history, J.D. Power and Associates was already studying the way the retail experience worked, and that research eventually evolved into one of the company's most popular indexes.

In the mid-1970s, Honda asked J.D. Power and Associates to conduct a proprietary dealer-by-dealer study of its retail network. The dealers often objected to being measured, but Yoshihide Munekuni wanted to hold the dealers accountable for quality as much as he insisted that manufacturing be accountable. Dave repeated the Honda dealer study in 1979, and soon Honda replaced Toyota as J.D. Power's biggest client.

At the time, the dealer-by-dealer study taxed every function of J.D. Power and Associates. It was a huge study, by the standards of the company and all available technology, as it required the company to tabulate the results of surveys sent to 400 customers from each of Honda's more than 750 automotive dealers throughout the country. As Tom Gauer, who served as senior director of automotive retail research, explains, the Honda Dealer Image

Study, begun in 1977, was a mailed survey that questioned customers about their satisfaction with the purchase process, vehicle delivery, service department, and parts availability, as well as the car buyer's likelihood of recommending the dealer for either sales or service. Dave and his associates were forced to develop sophisticated manual processes to handle such tasks as the printing, mailing, sorting, data processing, and analysis of such a large number of documents.

Along with massive amounts of hand processing, the fundamental challenge for J.D. Power and Associates was to develop an intuitive way to compare the performance of the Honda dealers as evaluated by their customers. "The whole point of statistics is data reduction," explains Gauer. "It was only when we suddenly saw this wealth of data, we had to figure out, 'How can we concisely convey this information in a readily understood format?'"

The result was the development of a customer satisfaction scale that weighed the customers' satisfaction levels with the various areas of interaction with the dealers, allowing the company to rank each of the dealers from high to low on every aspect. "We developed this point system based on the interaction with the sales department, the delivery of their vehicle, the service department, parts availability, and their overall satisfaction with the dealership," Gauer recalls. "Rather than ten pages of tables to look through to see how they're doing in the sales department, we suddenly have a single number that tells us how they're doing."

As with many of J.D. Power's pioneering products, it opened people's eyes. When the staff presented the data at Honda's regional offices, says Gauer, "in every single meeting we did, it was uncanny how the results we got on this index matched the field organizations' perceptions of the dealers." For the first time, instead of the corporate staff going into a dealership and telling them what they had to do, "they could say, 'This is what your customers are saying about your dealership. Why do you think they're saying this?'" It started a dialogue toward powerful change.

Often, the rankings would also spark competition among the dealers, Gauer recalls. "The field reps could show the dealers the data and tell them why those top performers were getting awards from the manufacturer. But they also could talk to a well-performing dealer and say 'You're only five points behind! If you improved in this area, you could be number one.'" Gauer says, "Suddenly there was this competitive environment among the dealers to start becoming responsive to the customers" to build satisfaction levels. The argument for following up on their shortcomings was strong: "You're going to have more repeat business, you'll have more word-of-mouth referral, [and] you'll be more successful as an organization."

The results were so positively received by Honda that Dave and Gauer discussed scaling up the study to measure trends across the entire auto industry instead of just dealer by dealer for one manufacturer. Dave proceeded with the industry-wide undertaking, naming the new study the Customer Satisfaction Index (CSI).

Accolades for Dave and the research also came from Munekuni, who in an address to NADA in 1994 revealed the influence of Dave's philosophy on his vision of customer satisfaction at Honda and the critical role dealers play:

> The role of the dealer is more important than ever. I would argue that the dealer may be the most important factor in the industry right now, but that is not just praise; it is also a tremendous responsibility.
>
> I do not believe the current definition of customer satisfaction is enough by itself to gain the true satisfaction of

our customers. Over a decade ago, I worked closely with David Power on the creation of the Customer Satisfaction Index, CSI. Honda wanted this index to help distinguish us from our competitors and to help our dealers sell more cars.

The CSI approach is still important, but dealers who haven't done so already must consider the creation of a new approach to establish close relationships with their customers. While we are all in the auto business, it is important to understand that we are actually in the "people business." Providing the highest level of satisfaction is a people issue. Everyone in the industry—automakers and dealers alike—must put quality people in the sales and service area. If we all do our job—listening to our customer and serving their needs—we can assure our continued success into the next century.

Munekuni's public support of the concept spurred the CSI's acceptance in the industry. "Suddenly, the manufacturers were able to provide constructive criticism or constructive information to their dealers as to how they could improve in their customers' eyes," recalls Gauer. "That's when you suddenly saw customer satisfaction becoming a real goal for organizations." But success often breeds imitators, and many automakers also saw this new survey as something they should try to do themselves. However, without the stringent, objective approach of J.D. Power, and coupled with many of the manufacturers offering financial incentives for good performance, the internal programs bred their own problems, with dealers finding ways to boost their scores. "Now, the problem with all of this is that many dealers are essentially gaming the system," Gauer says, especially on manufacturer-run surveys, coaxing their customers to give them high marks or even helping them fill out the satisfaction survey so all the dealers would appear "like God walking on earth. Unbelievable satisfaction levels came out. And then the annual J.D. Power study would come out and the automaker would often rank below the industry average."

Helping Acura After a Slip from the Top

Americans first encountered the Acura Legend and Integra, the first luxury vehicles of Honda Motor Company, in 1986. Following a decade of research, Honda opened sixty new dealerships to support its Acura automobile division. "It was Honda's goal to design products and a dealer system that focused on the customer," explains Jamey Power.

Acura's initial success was spectacular, and it led the industry in after-sales service satisfaction for four consecutive years. Acura came in at number one on J.D. Power's Customer Satisfaction Index the first year it was eligible and held that ranking for the next few years—an achievement that was highlighted in its advertising. But in the early 1990s, sales started to sag, a sign that customers were losing confidence in the brand. Having a brand in such hot demand, with customers literally lining up to buy an Acura, had made dealers so cocky that attention to product knowledge was all but lost. Despite its early-mover advantage, Acura fell behind Lexus in customer satisfaction.

Koichi Amemiya, president of American Honda at the time, suspected that the main problem resided in the retail experience. Through analysis of the Sales Satisfaction Index (SSI), Dave helped him confirm that the root cause of Acura's sales downturn was the lack of product knowledge on the part of the sales consultants. As a result, Acura salespeople were coming across as lacking credibility and confidence. Amemiya commissioned J.D. Power and Associates to design and implement a program of sales training driven by the specific activities Acura buyers had identified as having the most impact on customer satisfaction. The Acura Satisfaction Action Plan (ASAP) represented an inflection point for J.D. Power. "Market research surveys are like prisms: they refract the light from customers," says J Ferron, a J.D. Power vice president who designed and supervised the Acura project. Ferron was the number-two executive at the National Automobile Dealers Association (NADA) when Dave hired him specifically to develop, along with Glenn Pincus, the Acura sales training program. "What comes out of such a prism is a spectrum of customer opinion. The training side was to take that data to make it actionable so that decisions at Acura became motivated to anticipate a customer issue or problem."

At a time when many such programs featured "fun" events designed to psych up the dealer sales staff, Dave elected to use a data-driven approach that separated the measurement from the training. This was vital because effective training is impossible without precise data on what customers regard as important. "We were able to track the sales satisfaction scores by customers who had been served by a salesperson who had gone through the training, and a salesperson who had not," recalls Jamey. "With the data, we were able to prove that it improved their performance." The multimillion-dollar contract from Acura fueled the development of this service from J.D. Power.

The new training department was also transformative for J.D. Power, Jamey says. It went beyond Dave's company's core competence but also utilized an angle only available to his market research firm. Although there is a well-established training industry focused just on automakers, those training companies were knocking at J.D. Power's door, asking for survey insight that would help them understand what Honda and Acura could do.

"In my father's entrepreneurial way," Jamey recalls, "he said, 'We could be doing this. We could be doing the training.'" Not only did J.D. Power seek out training specialists, but also "we were able to combine the analytical background and insight with more progressive adult education techniques, beyond just lectures. We hired a team of people who brought a different type of skill set as well as creativity." Along with Ferron and Pincus, Doris Ehlers played a significant role, and Charles Mills served as curriculum writer and developer.

The training program had a measurable impact on Acura, but it also helped many other companies. At its height, the department had twenty trainers in the field and another ten to fifteen office-based staff. It expanded to work for Ford and Lincoln-Mercury, General Motors, and even the Ritz-Carlton Hotels.

Learning from Rejection

While manufacturers often found dealer satisfaction measurements like the SSI to be helpful tools to encourage improvements within their dealer ranks, dealers were less enamored of being measured, especially if they were not already performing at the top. "Dealers that tended to do a very good job of satisfying customers didn't have a problem with the SSI; they loved the recognition that came from it," explains former longtime associate Chris Denove. Even then, though, dealers generally bristled against tracking studies.

Denove thinks the dealers' resistance was understandable. "As important as customer satisfaction is, you can't take it to the bank. A dealer can't go to the bank and get a capital loan on their customer satisfaction score. And this was especially true with dealers, because the link between customer satisfaction and profit isn't clear to them. It's a lot clearer to manufacturers that see the logic of that if I make the owner of a Chevrolet happy this time he or she is going to be likely to buy a Chevrolet three or four years later." For dealers, who don't have the perception that there is as great a loyalty tie to particular dealerships as there is to a brand, the belief is that "no matter how happy they make the customer in the buying experience, even if they're going to buy the same brand of car again, they're going to shop all of the local dealers for the best price the next time around. That tends to give dealers compared to manufacturers a much shorter-term mentality in dealing with the customer, which in turn tends to lower customer satisfaction and create all of those jokes about how someone would rather go to the dentist than buy a car."

Tracking studies like the SSI, which served more as a "thermometer of whether the dealer was doing a good job or bad job with satisfaction of customers who bought a car," Denove says, "didn't really give the dealer much in the way of diagnostics to understand what mattered or how to correct it." One solution, Dave and Denove realized, was to develop a study that shifted the emphasis from the concept of customer satisfaction to the tangible: profits. Although the name was far from cheery, the proprietary Rejecter Study focused on a dealership's rate of closing sales and provided specific diagnostics for improvement. "When you're talking about close rates, dealers embrace it a little more because it's easier for them to connect the dots and see how it affects the bottom line," says Denove. "Those studies became very popular, and in some cases that concept is starting to take over the pure buyer satisfaction studies.

"Instead of focusing on the people who bought a car from a dealership," explains Denove, "we would survey the people who went in a dealership and ended up buying a car somewhere else. Those surveys would measure what a dealer's close rate was, and of the ones that got away, specifically why—what happened to make them go away."

One of the biggest users of the Rejecter Study, Denove says, was Toyota. "Toyota really embraced the Rejecter Study. They would hire us to go to every major city in the country, rent a hotel conference room, and bring in every two hours a different dealership so that we could go over its results." The meetings were well received by dealers. "Dealers would regularly say things to the manufacturer, such as 'You've been having meetings and showing data for ten years and this is the best stuff you've ever done because I can actually use it.'"

Blue Oval Certification

In 1998, a new program was proposed at Ford Motor Company that sought to address issues with franchise retailers. Ford wanted to not only improve its service; it wanted to utterly transform it, creating standards and certification inspired by the ISO/QS-9000 quality standard the Big Three had established in 1994.[4] Jac Nasser, a global business executive who had joined Ford's North American Truck Operations thirty years earlier, was about to become Ford's new CEO. Nasser's arguably more open leadership heralded new opportunities for J.D. Power and Associates. It didn't hurt that Nasser, who had begun at Ford in Australia the same year Dave started his company, felt a kinship with Dave over their shared career trajectories. "I always had a bit of a soft spot for Dave," Nasser says. As CEO, Nasser was known for his sharp cost-efficiency initiatives and a metrics-driven approach to strategic brand and product positioning that was externally focused. "Nasser was tasked with shaking things up at Ford and to set ambitious global targets," says Jamey.

Nasser acknowledged the value of Dave's approach to measuring customer satisfaction. "Unfiltered information from J.D. Power and Associates was very important," he says. "It gave us a benchmark that not only had independence but a sense of good comparability from one manufacturer to another, one dealer body over another, as we shifted from an internally focused system that measured defects toward an integrated model of customer satisfaction." A direct outgrowth of Nasser's confidence in Dave was the Blue Oval Certification program, which became a very large engagement for J.D. Power.

Nasser understood that a quality focus limited to vehicle design, engineering, and manufacturing was suboptimal if it did not consider quality improvements in the retail end of the business, particularly sales and service. In response, Nasser put together a team that asked J.D. Power to establish best-of-class dealer sales, service, and facility standards. Thus, the Blue Oval Certification program was launched.

The goal of the Blue Oval campaign was to improve customer satisfaction by improving the standards of Ford dealers. Internal surveys showed that many Ford customers were generally satisfied by the quality of Ford vehicles but were increasingly dissatisfied with their interactions with—and the variability of—the dealers, especially in the area of service.

In charge of Ford's Blue Oval program was Jim O'Conner, who had been recently named group vice president of sales and service. O'Conner was certainly aware of the tension between Ford's in-house market research and Dave's rankings. But instead of ignoring Dave, he was willing to take the risk of being an outlier and go against the party line at Ford that claimed Dave's methodology was hurtful to the company. "We may not always agree with [J.D. Power and Associates], but we should be under the tent with

Dave," O'Conner recalls telling Ford leadership. "He's expressing a customer satisfaction methodology, and whether we agree or not, his are the benchmarks that are being published and acted on." O'Conner wanted J.D. Power to implement the administration, training, and measurement for the Blue Oval program.

The program had been created by a committee composed of Nasser and half a dozen other change-oriented executives from different departments. Dave presented a proposal for training that included tracking the dealers and presenting an award to the top qualifiers. The basic concept was that trainers from J.D. Power and Associates would visit each Ford dealer to conduct standards reviews and training sessions to improve performance where Ford in-house survey results revealed problems. Then J.D. Power would conduct extensive surveys of each dealer's customers to track improvement. "They bought off on what we were proposing to do," Dave explains, "I told them they should keep the qualifiers to maybe 10 to 15 percent in the first year, and the next year up to 25 percent, then grow it that way over a three- to four-year period."

Unfortunately, Ford then disbanded its executive committee and turned the program over to its marketing department, which had long been skeptical of J.D. Power's services. However, Dave was soon surprised to receive an invitation from Bob Rewey, who had moved from Lincoln-Mercury to become Ford's group vice president of sales and marketing, to meet at his Detroit office. "The marketing department wanted to build in an incentive" that would be in addition to the performance awards, Dave recalls. To fund the incentive, Ford decided to take one percentage point of the dealer's margin and put it into a Blue Oval fund. Dealers that qualified for the award would get two percentage points back. But those who did not qualify would see their shares of profit from each car sold reduced, a prospect sure to invoke ire instead of eagerness to improve.

"There was a lot of pressure on dealers to comply with the program," recalls Herb Williams-Dalgart, senior director of certification and performance improvement at J.D. Power. The percentage difference for being Blue Oval certified could make the difference between being profitable or not at the end of the year, he says. "For those that did comply, the benefits were obvious; for those that did not comply, they faced going out of business."

The way the program was altered by Ford to include a financial incentive did not go down well with Dave. "We didn't know about this until well into our involvement," Dave explains, "but when we did find out, I said that's not going to work." Because of Ford's funding the program through a hold-back of dealer margins, J.D. Power staff saw clearly that "the only way the program could fund itself was if people continued to be noncompliant. It certainly was not our intent to see anyone be noncompliant," Williams-Dalgart says. "Our hope—if we had one as a disinterested third party— would be that everybody had the means and will to comply."

Dave could not put his imprimatur on such a plan, believing it was not the way to motivate dealers to excellence. "I said we don't want to have our name associated with it," Dave recalls, "because this kind of arrangement is going to be tough for the dealers to swallow." Rewey agreed to leave J.D. Power and Associates' name off the program but insisted that the financial incentive be included.

Another problem appeared to Dave, which he brought to the attention of Ford executives. He had advocated for tough quality standards that only a small percentage of the dealers would qualify for in the first year. As the program went on, more would rise to meet the quality measures. Ford marketers, however, wanting buy-in from more dealers to soften the blow of the one percentage point margin loss, pushed to have the standards lowered. "We didn't have much to say about it," Dave explains. "It wasn't a good measure of what the dealers were doing or not doing, and that was a key problem for us."

The program started off in Ford's operations in Canada, with the sponsorship of a very supportive executive, Ford of Canada's President and CEO Bobbie Gaunt. The certification criteria were rolled out to the dealers, says Darren Slind, who was hired from Nissan to be the director of J.D. Power's Blue Oval Certification program in Canada, and many found the particulars of the program to be fair. "To become certified in Canada, Ford dealers actually had to look at their operation from a holistic perspective," Slind says. "There were specific criteria across the purchase experience, the service experience, and in some additional categories, such as facilities. And it was not a question of does this dealer have a marble floor versus this one only has tile. . . . The Blue Oval facilities criteria related to things like clean, comfortable, well maintained, and safe. The intent was, if you were a Ford dealer that had an older facility, you had just as much of an opportunity to demonstrate compliance to the criteria as the guy who just put up the $3 million building." Simple things like clear signage, parking, daily maintenance, and cleanliness were to be inspected.

The program, which was also rolled out for Lincoln and Mercury dealerships in the United States, measured other things, such as employee satisfaction, training, and development, "the theory being, quite simply," says Slind, "it's hard to imagine the delivery of a great customer experience by employees who don't feel valued and empowered and trained."

"Concern resolution" was a key criterion. No dealer was expected to be perfect, Slind says, but how a dealership dealt with problems was measured. Also key was how dealers captured customer complaints, how they responded to them, and how they acted on problems to ensure they didn't continue to happen. "The Japanese would call this *kaizen,* continuous improvement," explains Slind. "That was not the term used at Ford, but the theory was similar. Which is, can we get better and reduce the number of issues the customers might have?"

J.D. Power and Associates used various evaluation techniques to confirm such a system was in place. They looked for evidence of a written, documented process. They interviewed employees at random and asked them to describe the concern-resolution process. And they inspected the concern-resolution documentation to see if the concerns were being logged and to determine if trends, when they appeared, were being dealt with at the root-cause level. "The idea was that they had to identify at least one common trend and then show us evidence that the trend had been substantiated," says Slind. Then the evaluators would ask, "What was the action plan that you implemented to address those underlying root causes? The idea was to help the dealer get good at avoiding problems, not fixing them."

Among the Canadian dealers, the feedback was generally positive, Slind recalls, and there was a recognition that the program was needed. Dealers knew the competitive landscape was shifting, and they had to protect their market share from aggressive Asian carmakers like Toyota, Honda, and even Hyundai. "I think they recognized that this was an opportunity to hopefully solidify their competitive position in the marketplace."

And the results seen for Ford of Canada just a few years after the Blue Oval program launched were astounding. Although the Canadian Customer Satisfaction Index rankings for Ford were never made public, they represented a marked improvement. "I'm tempted to use the word 'unprecedented,'" says Slind. Between

2000 and 2003, in the category of purchase experience, Ford went from the bottom half of the rankings to the highest-ranked full-line manufacturer, bested only by luxury brands. "At J.D. Power we're very proud of the role that we played and the impact that we had, but we cannot and will not take full credit for that, because there were a lot of people involved and the dealers did the heavy lifting."

But when Blue Oval rolled out in the U.S., dealers balked. Forms of the program were instituted for Ford, Mercury, and Lincoln brands. Not only did some Ford dealers not see the value in being held to customer service standards they felt were appropriate for a luxury line, but they strongly resented how Blue Oval was to be funded.

"Blue Oval could be interpreted as punitive," says Wisconsin dealer John Bergstrom, "so it wasn't enthusiastically received, and the way it was funded out of the margins made them [upset]."

This reaction was not present north of the border. "I don't recall anywhere near the kind of resistance that I was observing with the U.S. dealers," says Slind. "Financially the structure was similar, but the Ford of Canada leadership team had the ability to make some adjustments, and they did so."

Despite the negative reactions to the way Blue Oval was funded, the ultimate impact of the program was positive, says Bergstrom. It was a "wake-up call for everyone that if we're going to be successful, we need to take care of [customers]." He credits Dave for such an "insightful" approach and says the foresighted dealers who followed that concept were ahead of their time as well.

Although Blue Oval did not sit well with Ford dealers, the program, as instituted for the other lines—called Lincoln Premier Experience and Mercury Advantage—met with a much better reception.

"Blue Oval was a mile wide and an inch deep," says Loretta Seymour, a former senior director at J.D. Power and Associates, but the Lincoln-Mercury program went much deeper. "It didn't go as wide in number of issues to handle, but it was much more successful and better received by dealer management. [Dealers] acknowledged improvement, even in terms of employee reaction." In fact, the program raised the Lincoln rankings in all measures in J.D. Power's Customer Satisfaction Index, bringing Lincoln to the number-one spot for two years running, and causing other related metrics to see measurable advances.

Blue Oval and its affiliated programs held some benefits for J.D. Power and Associates as well. In addition to it being a financially rewarding program for the company, it expanded J.D. Power's capabilities and stature, says Williams-Dalgart. "We did this program for five years across one of the largest auto manufacturer's franchises in the world—in North America in particular—so we got a lot of street cred for having had a prominent role in that way."

It also showed new ways that J.D. Power could help its clients. "This was a very large and very public initiative where we got involved with the operations, where we actually had a presence in the dealership, where we really got a chance to review the inner workings," recalls Williams-Dalgart.

And it brought in more business: a similar program was designed for the insurance industry, for instance, and the Nissan Edge program was instituted with J.D. Power and Associates operating on a consultative basis. Mazda employed the firm to handle in-dealer assessment of its performance improvement program. Although Blue Oval will be remembered tartly by Ford dealers in the U.S., who were caught in the misfire of an ill-conceived funding plan, the concept was proven to be useful, and J.D. Power and Associates provided yet another way to use research for the ultimate betterment of customers.

GM Shoots for the Moon with Saturn

It became clear that GM had deepened its commitment to Dave's philosophy of customer satisfaction when it unveiled what was billed as a "Different Kind of Car Company." That company was called Saturn. In 1982, in an initiative approved by GM Chairman Roger Smith, the Saturn experiment was launched. To create a car company truly organized around customer satisfaction, GM enthusiastically engaged J.D. Power and Associates to conduct a round of early studies to help it frame the quality issues, develop customer-centric processes, and build a unique retail experience.

"In response to the success of the Japanese imports, GM attempted a bold experiment," Dave explains. It would establish a new car company that built small cars in a separate manufacturing plant in the U.S. and sold them via a separate dealer network in an innovative way. GM hoped Saturn would engender a new corporate culture not bound by the history and traditions of GM. "It was designed to be separate and independent of the GM bureaucracy," Dave says. "It would use Japanese manufacturing techniques and design products to compete against them."

Dave's influence permeated the planning and implementation of Saturn. As they developed the cars and their marketing plan, Saturn and its ad agency, Hal Riney Partners,[5] brought Dave in almost monthly, briefing him on their actions and discussing what they were worried about or debating. Meanwhile, they pored over J.D. Power data on quality, dealer service, dealer satisfaction, and sales process satisfaction, "tearing it apart and finding opportunities to exploit and shore up areas where they could do better," explains Jamey. Dave was a key behind-the-scenes adviser. In fact, Saturn incorporated four core insights rooted in philosophies derived from the data and analysis of Dave and J.D. Power and Associates. First, Saturn cars would be small and fuel-efficient.

Second, Saturn retailers would be carefully selected, trained, and given large geographic territories, so they would compete with other brands, not with other Saturn retailers. Third, the Saturn cars would be offered at a fixed price, like most consumer products. Saturn salespeople would not engage in haggling and other high-pressure sales tactics, which J.D. Power studies showed car buyers disdained. This policy would be especially attractive to a growing class of car buyers: women. Finally, Saturn dealerships would focus on specific details that all consumers, but especially women, identified as important to a quality retail experience: well-lighted showrooms and waiting areas, clean restrooms, and convenient service hours.

Dave knew many thought-leading dealers and worked with some of them to come up with recommendations for Saturn retailing, consulting with Al Serra in Detroit, Mike Maroone in South Florida, and Don Flow in Winston-Salem, among others. The company set up three hundred individual franchised "retailers." Saturn took to heart Dave's recommendation that they shouldn't be called dealers. The number of retailers was far fewer than franchises for most other brands. Where there might be dozens of Chevy dealers in a major metropolitan area, Saturn would have just a handful. In this way, each Saturn dealership had a bigger piece of the pie in its individual market; landing a franchise quickly became desirable.

Saturn would work with these three hundred retailers to develop franchisee staff who were well trained and reliable. They believed also that they could build a more consistent experience for the customer, from sales to service. Because the cars would be sold in a fixed-price, low-pressure environment, the company advised retailers to pay salaries rather than commissions. While critics argued that Saturn's no-haggling policy would erode retailer profits, in fact Saturn retailers earned an average of 17 percent profit. Non-Saturn dealers averaged 12 percent profit.

J.D. Power and Associates also recommended the no-haggling idea. Saturn let retailers set and revise prices, even on a daily basis. "But each morning when they turned the lights on, they had to set a price and stick to it," recalls Tom Shaver, who was Saturn's marketing chief from 1987 to 1992. Most retailers stuck with the sticker price, a predictable tactic to which consumers responded. Dave's research showed that the one thing customers hated more than anything was the thought that they were paying more than the next customer for the same vehicle. "Saturn's pricing policy eliminated that concern," Dave says.

Karen Radley was one of the first superdealers. (She owns dealerships, which she founded with her husband, that represent Volkswagen, Acura, Chevrolet, and Cadillac.) She was also a Saturn retailer in the Washington, D.C., area. "Dave's fingerprints were all over the Saturn experiment," she notes. "The customer focus, the one-price philosophy—it was all plucked from Dave's writings and philosophy of customer service."

The training of floor personnel was critical to Saturn's early success, according to Dave. "We did a number of studies on common attitudes about shopping, including one on the dealer selection process, a survey of customers who had gone to more than one dealership of a given brand and how they selected the dealership they chose to buy from." Dave showed that while price matters, the biggest factor influencing whether a customer buys or not was the salesperson. Saturn compensation policies helped keep salespeople focused on the customer instead of their commissions. Saturn compensated salespeople based on the number of units sold. This worked to focus the salespeople on volume, which was good for the franchise owner.

J.D. Power also conducted a special study on female car buyers. The study found that half of all new car sales were influenced by wives and female partners. "Most female car buyers detested the fact that when they walked into a dealership with a man, the salesperson would ignore them," says Dave. "We were sensitive to that insight well before Saturn started and, to Saturn's credit, retailer training made a point of welcoming and involving women buyers, whether they were unaccompanied or with a man."

Saturn's tactics were affirmed in J.D. Power and Associates' surveys. With the motto "A Different Kind of Car Company," Saturn was ranked third by new car owners in customer satisfaction and sales satisfaction. Lexus and Infiniti, which at the time were expensive new luxury lines from Japanese automakers Toyota and Nissan, respectively, were the only brands to rank higher. Saturn continued to score highly in these two measures on Power surveys over the next decade. Clearly, guided by Dave's research, the young automaker had hit on an effective formula.

That first year, the Spring Hill, Tennessee, factory produced 50,000 cars,[6] and dealers sold out. In June 1993, Saturn sold nearly 25,000 cars in a single month.[7] A "homecoming" event in 1994 saw thousands of owners drive to Tennessee, "showing the sort of loyalty that few vehicles other than Harley-Davidson motorcycles commanded in America," noted *Automotive News*.[8]

Although some dealers of other brands mimicked the Saturn model for a time, not everyone in the industry was a fan, with competitors asserting that the cars weren't that special, even if the marketing tactics were. As time went on and Saturn's sales did not meet expectations, many industry observers—especially within General Motors—speculated whether the parent company had shot itself in the foot by investing so heavily in the new enterprise. "The first Saturns went on sale in October 1990 after nearly $5 billion had been spent on vehicle development, factory construction, and retail planning at the insistence of GM Chairman Roger Smith," explained the 2011 *Automotive News* piece. "Within a year, GM was in financial straits. Within two years, GM's management was shuffled in an October board coup."[9]

Dave sees Saturn as a victim of overly ambitious complexity: "Everything at Saturn had to be developed from scratch: the car design, the plant, the workforce, and the dealer network. It also didn't help that some of the standard brands under the GM umbrella, particularly the Chevrolet division, resented the huge budget that Roger Smith had endowed to Saturn." Within a decade, Saturn's glow had begun to fade, and the auto industry's plight in the recession of the late 2000s spelled doom for the brand, which was discontinued in late 2010.

The Future of Retail

One of the biggest developments to alter the landscape of retailing was the Internet, and the auto industry has not been exempt from those changes. In general, dealers viewed the prospect of online retailing with suspicion, if not outright terror. "Dealers were afraid of the Internet because they thought that the Internet would be used for car sales like Amazon.com was for books," says Chris Denove, who headed up J.D. Power and Associates' Internet division. "In other words, the brick-and-mortar dealership goes away in favor of buying the car online. Well, Dave realized that wasn't going to happen. Dave didn't see that as a short-term threat. Instead, he felt that dealers needed to embrace the Internet."

Most dealers were not so ready to relax. "If we go back to right around 2000, most dealers would like to have put a bounty on the head of whoever invented the Internet," says Denove. "They didn't like the transparency, because just as Dave had correctly predicted, it was shifting the power to the consumer. By doing that it was squeezing their profit margins."

Dave's team felt it was important to help automakers understand how customers were using the Internet so they could proactively respond to changes and benefit from them. In 1998, Denove worked with Dave to establish the NewAutoShopper.com study, which looked at two thousand car buyers who reportedly used the Internet in some fashion to aid in their purchase. "It was measuring not only what percentage of people are going online but then, more important, what are they doing online," says Denove. The percentage of buyers using the Internet in their purchases grew rapidly each year the study was conducted. "Back in 1998 I believe that number was 16 percent—less than one in five. And that was a huge, important number that we would track as it grew to 25 percent then 33 percent." Eventually, the Internet became such a dominant source of information for auto buyers that the figure approached 100 percent. "I don't think they're measuring that number anymore. That's like someone making a living counting what percentage of households own at least one television."

What the study quickly bore out was Dave's belief that Internet sales were not an immediate threat to brick-and-mortar dealerships. The majority of shoppers were using the Internet for informational purposes rather than to make sales transactions. Despite providing clear understanding, the syndicated study geared to manufacturers was slow to gather subscribers. "It wasn't until I employed what Dave taught me, which was use the media," Denove says. "I started going to the press and giving tidbits and facts about how the Internet was going to impact the auto industry. Once that got into the press, all of a sudden clients started calling for the study."

An early and enthusiastic subscriber of the NewAutoShopper. com study was Shau-wai Lam, chairman of DCH Auto Group, a superdealer with twenty-five dealerships in California, New Jersey, New York, and Connecticut. "At the time when most dealers were fighting the Internet, Shau-wai felt it was an opportunity to connect to dealers," says Denove. "It seems like a no-brainer today but it was almost heresy back then."

Lam purchased the NewAutoShopper.com study for his dealership, and featured its findings at a meeting of his general managers at the dealership's home office. "He brought me in personally because he felt his managers needed to understand the importance of the Internet and the shift that was taking place for the customer," says Denove. "He believed that if they could make the customer love him as a dealer, it was the key to their long-term success. As he introduced me he said, 'Please pay attention. This information is going to be the way we do business with our customers in the future.' It's taken for granted today but back then it was very revolutionary."

CHAPTER SIX

MARKETPLACE INSIGHTS

Although consumers most readily associate J.D. Power and Associates with automotive quality, and the company has had a high-profile role in the evolution of retailing within the auto industry, Dave and his team have also had significant impact in providing automakers with thoughtful, in-depth information about what the customer wants.

"Anyone could collect data, and we were not the only group who were interested in the voice of the customer," explains Linda Hirneise, who retired from J.D. Power and Associates as a partner after working for the firm for twenty-six years. "The difference is how we use the data to help the client improve. We became our clients' trusted adviser. This was a key differentiator."

The impetus for researching trends in the automotive market usually came from an inspiration that Dave or one of his staff members had in studying the findings of an existing study. "I'd pick out something that was unique and had not been touched upon," Dave explains. The company's front-wheel-drive study was a prime example. Here was a new, as-yet-unpopular type of vehicle, but Dave was intrigued. An early partner in the business, Barry Robertson, was from England, and "he had a perspective on front-wheel drive that I didn't have," Dave says. "So, putting our heads together, we designed the front-wheel-drive owners survey."

The process happened again with four-wheel-drive vehicles, minicars, and minivans. The result was that the industry heard about, and considered, these ideas and was provided valuable customer attitudes, whether favorable or unfavorable.

Dave was sometimes unsure whether a new study would be financially feasible. "If something caught his fancy in terms of concept, then the potential profit-making ability of that study was not necessarily important in Dave's mind," former J.D. Power Executive Vice President John Uhles said to a writer for *Brill's Content* in 1999.[1] Some of the studies were not successful on their own, meaning they did not generate enough buyers to break even or become profitable, but that did not stop Dave from finding them useful.

The front-wheel-drive study, for instance, "wasn't successful in terms of a syndicated study financially," explains Dave, "but it gave us a ton of information that we used over the next ten years." The study data, which could be parsed out in many ways, provided fodder for other innovation. The successful syndicated studies were profitable because they tracked trend data from year to year. "Customers had to keep buying it, because their competitors were."

Coupled with observations of industry and societal trends, even unprofitable studies fed ideas for new studies. "In the early '80s, we showed the importance of women in choosing the car," Dave explains. Previously, carmakers had assumed that women were only involved in smaller decisions, like car color. As a result, "when the companies recruited for surveys, they chose 75 percent men," which skewed the results. "We showed that women had an influence on two-thirds of car sales."

Auto Styling Clinics

One of the useful tools that Dave adapted early was the automotive styling clinic. Sometimes conducted under conditions of tight secrecy, the J.D. Power clinics were structured to let targeted prospects examine a new model so the company could get actionable information about design and other elements of the car. Years earlier, while Dave worked at Marplan, he had gained firsthand experience running a product styling clinic in support of the Buick Riviera. Marplan worked hard to keep the clinic secret, but somehow word of the clinic leaked and a Chicago newspaper reporter tried to get in. The reporter, denied entry, later wrote a story about the car industry's cloak-and-dagger activities. Dave wondered if all that secrecy was really necessary.

He soon had the opportunity to conduct his own styling clinics. Within two years of founding J.D. Power and Associates, Dave received a commission from Toyota to oversee a clinic for the Carina model it hoped to introduce to the U.S. market. Product styling clinics can be logistically complex and expensive. J.D. Power ran the clinic at the Anaheim Convention Center in Southern California. The methodology involved recruiting qualified people by telephone and offering an incentive for them to examine the car. The clinic data indicated that the Carina would meet with significant consumer resistance in the U.S., and Toyota accepted this data. The model was not introduced to the United States.

Dave's method of putting on a high-profile clinic garnered notice, sometimes from the most unusual subjects. For instance, the late John Marin, a former Time Inc. executive and a founding member of the *Sports Illustrated* magazine staff, first met Dave when he saw a J.D. Power clinic taking place. "I was making a business call on Adidas, then an unknown sports equipment company, in Calabasas," recalls Marin. On his return, Marin took a wrong turn and, as he was driving around searching for the freeway, he drove past a small shopping center. He was intrigued by the sight of a tall man standing beside a group of cars and about thirty women. "When there was a break in the activity, I went up to introduce myself." Dave was conducting a clinic on the new Honda Accord.

Years later, Time Inc. commissioned J.D. Power and Associates to conduct a number of media studies for one of its prime properties, *Sports Illustrated*, at the urging of Marin.

Over the next ten years, J.D. Power conducted styling clinics for Honda, Nissan, Jaguar, GM, Ford, and American Motors, and sometimes they were done just as a car company was introducing new models. Because the design of these models was usually final, the clinics were used to generate consumer information that could sharpen marketing and promotion efforts. In some cases, the information was useful for styling the next model.

In 1980, J.D. Power pioneered a twist on the methodology for auto clinics when it studied the concept of what minicar-size vehicles would be attractive to American consumers. After the energy crisis, there was substantial interest in small, fuel-efficient minicars, which were already on sale in Japan and Europe, and Dave decided to conduct an independent, syndicated study of them. The clinic eventually involved a small car from Subaru only available in Japan, a Suzuki, an Innocenti minicar made in Italy, a Yugo, a Volkswagen, and a car from Daihatsu Motors. A total of nine minicars were featured.

This clinic was unique in that it was not being conducted for an exclusive automaker client. Just as he had done with mailed surveys, Dave was now turning automotive customer research on its head by creating a syndicated product-styling clinic. "We invited all the car companies to observe," Dave recalls, "and of course this was when the second energy crisis was in full swing, so the interest was there because we had soaring gas prices, and the auto companies were trying to figure out how to react."

The minicar clinic was first conducted at a Thousand Oaks shopping center near the company's headquarters. The cars were displayed among the shops, and J.D. Power staffers invited shoppers to stop, express their opinions, and compare the features of three vehicles at a time. J.D. Power wanted to determine the reactions of American consumers to these small vehicles, some of which they had never seen before, according to Dave. Periodically, the models were moved around the mall, so each model appeared in every possible combination relative to two others. In addition to the static clinic, qualified respondents were invited to take a test-drive, and an interviewer recorded the test-driver's responses to questions about the car before, during, and after the test-drive. Each test-driver was again asked to compare three vehicles. An identical clinic was conducted in Cleveland, Ohio, to get a Midwestern point of view.

The minicar clinic was a huge success for J.D. Power; more than ten car companies subscribed to the resulting study. Dave also invited all potential study subscribers to the North Ranch Country Club in Westlake Village after the clinic to inspect the models and test-drive the minicars. This invitation proved irresistible. "Most of these cars were not certified in the U.S., so it was a novelty," explains Jamey Power. "The engineers, especially from Detroit, had never seen a car this size. They were won over." Several GM engineers showed up for the brunch event and became intensely interested in the Suzuki minicar, dominating the test-driving of it. The next day, Dave got a call from an executive at GM requesting that the Suzuki be shipped to Detroit so that GM chairman, Roger Smith, could look at it. Dave got authorization from Suzuki and prepared to ship the car to Detroit that Sunday.

The night before it was to be shipped, Dave had the Suzuki minicar parked across the street from his home. A neighbor backing out of her driveway in a large SUV failed to see the little car and backed right into it. Dave was embarrassed to ship the car with a big dent in the door, but there was nothing to be done. The GM executive was upset, too, but he called a crew to fix the dent before Roger Smith examined it. Smith must have been impressed on some level because in 1981 GM took a 17 percent stake in Suzuki.[2] "It was a shortcut," Jamey surmises, "because they knew they couldn't engineer and build a fuel-efficient car of this size in such short order." GM maintained a good relationship with Suzuki for two decades, but in 2006 the cash-strapped GM sold all but 3 percent of its ownership.[3]

Transforming Subaru

In the early 1970s, Subaru was not a well-known brand in America. Its first foray into the U.S., the Subaru 360, was not auspicious. "It had a 360 cubic centimeter engine and couldn't get out of its own way," Dave says. "It couldn't maintain 50 miles per hour. The California Highway Patrol banned it on freeways."

In the early years of his company, Dave observed the auto market and searched for unique inroads he could make by studying new or evolving trends. For instance, in the early 1970s he realized that oil shortages were causing people to talk about alternatives to large, gas-guzzling family cars. Through the success of the imported Volkswagen Beetle, Dave saw the possibility of other small cars being brought to the U.S., which led him to his first market research study on their viability. That, in turn, steered him to a study on front-wheel drive, which was an innovation not yet being used in American cars. Subaru had a front-wheel-drive car that was a copy of the Beetle, and the company was aiming for the Beetle's market, Dave recalls. "Subaru was included in the front-wheel-drive study, and I took the study to them." He made contact with Harvey Lamm who, with his partner Malcolm Bricklin, had set up Subaru of North America.

Dave commenced a series of studies for Lamm, which included an outlook for the small-car market, studies on automatic transmissions and air-conditioning installation, and a summary of Subaru owner evaluations. They later studied the Brat, Subaru's attempt to get around the import restrictions of the Voluntary Restraint Agreement of the 1980s. "They had a pickup designed, so what Harvey and his engineers did was design the Brat, which had two seats in the bed of the pickup, against the cab, facing backwards," Dave recalls. "They were considered dangerous, so it had limited potential." But it helped brand Subaru as a company with vehicles for people with an active lifestyle, a concept that was further cemented once Subaru understood the interest in its four-wheel-drive vehicles. It was marketing to that demographic that really helped the automaker take off. "What we had to do," Dave recalls, "is convince the Japanese that these products would work."

In Japan, Subaru became so respectful of Dave's input that the company requested a statement for use in its 1985 Fuji Heavy Industries annual report. Dave obliged as follows:

> The automobile industry neglected the consumer in the 1960s and 1970s. Subaru, however, kept the focus of their efforts on satisfying their customers with dependable and responsive product designs. They coupled this with an enthusiastic service support system at the retail level. The challenge in the 1980s, as all competitors begin to [marshal] their efforts to meet the needs and rising expectations

of automotive consumers, is for the current leaders in customer satisfaction to remain constant to those principles which gained them their success. The commitment of Subaru management tells me they will not be deterred in this endeavor.[4]

Subaru also credits Dave and J.D. Power and Associates with helping dealers understand and deliver customer satisfaction. "Dave was very effective in helping us channel our efforts," says Tom Gibson, former executive vice president of Subaru of North America. "It's rare to meet an individual who changed the course of an entire industry, and Dave did that."

Brokering Subaru to Investors

Dave's work with Subaru continued over the years. In the late 1990s, he was on a trip to Japan, one of dozens of trips he made to work with automakers in the country that had first kept the lights on at his company. By this time, J.D. Power and Associates was operating out of a bustling Japanese office, and Dave heard from the president of J.D. Power's Asia-Pacific operations, Tak Fujita, that there was trouble with Subaru's owner, Fuji Heavy Industries. The largest stockholder of Subaru was Nissan, who was nearing a financial meltdown. The Japanese economy had hit hard times, and Nissan had been looking for investors who could take a share of the company and keep it from collapsing. Subaru wanted out from under Nissan as quickly as possible, and they wanted Dave to intercede on their behalf.

Dave asked Fujita who Subaru's first choice for an investor would be, and the answer was BMW. By this time, Dave had also made it a practice to meet regularly with the heads of all major automobile companies worldwide, so it was not a problem for him to approach

Bernd Pischetsrieder, the CEO of BMW (who would eventually go on to become the CEO of Volkswagen), about the prospect. However, Pischetsrieder had just led the purchase of Rover and Mini Cooper from British Leyland. "Dave, I can't do it," Dave recalls Pischetsrieder telling him. "I'm up to my ears in Rover." An investment in Fuji Heavy Industries was out of the question.

The Japanese company indicated that their next choice would be Mercedes, so again Dave went to the leadership, discussing the prospect with the head of Mercedes Car Group, Jürgen Hubbert, at an auto show. He was interested, but the executive said he'd need two months to work it out.

Shortly thereafter, Dave was on another trip to Japan, making the rounds with Jamey to see executives at all the major companies. At Nissan headquarters, the chairman "seemed nervous as hell," Dave recalls. "We knew he was in trouble." Later in the day, Dave learned why. Mercedes CEO Jürgen Schrempp had been visiting Nissan the same day, and a news report announced that Schrempp had publicly declined to participate in a partnership to save Nissan.

Finally, Dave had a talk with Jack Smith at General Motors, and Smith—whom Dave calls a friend and a straightforward business leader—listened. The world's largest automaker did the buy-in. Dave had thus played a key role in giving Subaru a chance at surviving.

Despite several attempts, the relationship between Fuji and General Motors never really clicked. Eventually GM sold its interest in Fuji; subsequently Toyota became a substantial investor in Fuji, and today there are numerous joint development projects and assembly activities between the two companies.

Nissan looked to leaders like Jed Connelly to help it recover from its financial difficulties. Connelly was appointed to run Nissan's luxury line, Infiniti. Dave had gotten to know Connelly while working for Bill Young at Volkswagen, "and he was always very cordial and respectful to us," recalls Dave, who worked with Connelly primarily on studies covering Infiniti's competition with Lexus and Acura once Connelly moved over to Nissan. After Connelly decided to retire instead of move with Nissan's headquarters to Tennessee, Dave invited him to work for J.D. Power and Associates. That didn't pan out, though Dave continued to socialize with him at an annual Fourth of July party hosted by Young.

Honda Sees the Sense in Simple

Cars made by another Japanese company, Honda, later to become an international powerhouse, were still a novelty on American roads when Dave first encountered the brand.

Honda was established in 1948 by Soichiro Honda as a motorcycle manufacturer.[5] But it wasn't until 1969 that the company sold its first automobile, the N600, in the United States.[6] In July 1972, as the U.S. entered an energy crisis, Honda debuted the fuel-efficient Civic.[7]

That same year Honda introduced the compound vortex controlled combustion (CVCC) engine, which met clean air standards without the use of a catalytic converter. When the EPA issued its first list of America's most fuel-efficient autos in 1977, the Civic CVCC topped all cars.[8] The popular and reliable Accord debuted in 1976,[9] and in 1982, Honda started producing the Accord in Marysville, Ohio. The wildly popular Accord was the best-selling car in America from 1990 to 1992.[10]

Dave had been conducting small studies for Honda since 1971, starting with a study on the motorcycle market and eventually looking at the Honda N600. Dave looked closely at the N600 as part of the front-wheel-drive owner study. Honda also asked Dave to do some proprietary research in support of the introduction of the Civic.

During Honda's early successes, Dave met and became allies with Yoshihide Munekuni, executive vice president and director of American Honda. In time, Munekuni would rise even further, to become chairman of the entire Honda corporation. He and Dave spent a lot of time together and even bonded by walking away from a minor car crash.

On the occasion of one meeting in 1973, Munekuni invited Dave to lunch, and they drove there in a brand-new Civic. Also in the car was Honda's executive vice president of sales, Cliff Schmillen. As they were driving to lunch, a motorist in a big Chevy van was so astounded by the sight of this neat little car, Dave recalls, that he did a double take and accidentally accelerated into the right rear of the Civic. Luckily, no one was hurt, and after a short wait, Honda dispatched another car to take the party to lunch.

Dave provided useful marketing advice—and backed it up with research—early in his association with Munekuni. The company was testing an ad slogan, "We make it simple,"[11] which seemed appropriate to Dave but did not translate well from American to Japanese culture. If not for Dave's intervention, it might have been scuttled. To Munekuni's ears, "simple" had a negative connotation, as in simplistic or unsophisticated. Dave understood that, to American ears, the slogan would suggest trouble-free. After conducting a number of focus groups to test various advertising slogans, Munekuni accepted the ad agency's recommendation and "We make it simple" became an effective and long-running advertising theme for Honda.

Sobering Advice for Mazda and Isuzu

In the early 1990s Mazda planned to release its first entrant in the North American luxury car segment to challenge the Lexus, Acura, and Infiniti marques, manufactured by Toyota, Honda, and Nissan respectively. Mazda announced that the initial Amati models would include the Amati 500 and the Amati 1000 (a rear-wheel drive with a V12 engine). The cars, to be delivered in 1994, would be built at a newly constructed manufacturing plant in Hofu, Japan, dedicated to producing luxury vehicles.

Under the direction of Dick Colliver, group vice president and general manager of Amati, Mazda assembled a task force to consider all the issues related to establishing a new Mazda car division and launching a new line of cars in the United States. Mazda embarked on an unprecedented effort of market research that involved J.D. Power and Associates under Dave's personal supervision.

"Customer satisfaction is the keynote in all aspects of the operation from the sales experience to service and parts to eventual resale,"[12] Mazda stated in a 1991 news release, clearly echoing the lessons of J.D. Power. Colliver was quoted in the release as saying, "Our research tells us that for the luxury car buyer, the buying and servicing experiences influence long-term customer satisfaction almost as much as the vehicle itself."[13]

As requested, J.D. Power conducted research to explore the prospects for the Amati in a field saturated with luxury vehicles not only from Japan but also from a crowded field of European carmakers, such as BMW, Mercedes, Audi, and Jaguar. Dave's conclusions, shared with Kazuo Sonoguchi, president and CEO of Mazda Motors of America, were pointed: "The bottom line is that I didn't feel that the U.S. needed another luxury car line, and I wasn't confident that Mazda could meet its aggressive timetable given the resources it was prepared to devote to the effort." There are always other factors at play in such complicated decisions, but Dave's opinion played a significant part in Mazda's judgment to scrap the Amati marque before any cars hit the North American market.

Car companies often gave Dave's opinion more weight than their own. Earlier in his career, Colliver had been a regional executive for a Mazda distributor when an opportunity presented itself. Mazda had been manufacturing a light truck that Ford imported and sold as the Courier pickup truck. When 150,000 units of production were freed up, Mazda considered using those units as the platform for a Mazda-branded light truck. Colliver was excited but unsure whether it was better for the truck to compete at the high end or the low end of the market. "My intuition and reading of the market suggested that there was more opportunity at the high end," Colliver recalls.

Colliver's adviser from Foote, Cone & Belding advertising, Welton Mansfield, felt a sportier truck would reach a wider audience and encouraged Colliver to engage J.D. Power and Associates to get a better sense of the market. "After Dave presented the latest research that showed the numbers of younger buyers that were coming into the market, I was persuaded that we should go with a low-end product," he says. From that research and a market test in Southern California, Mazda developed the SE5 pickup truck and targeted it to young buyers. It was a phenomenal success. Within two years, Mazda had put more than 280,000 pickups on the market.

A similar dynamic played out at Isuzu Motors. Although the company's roots date back to 1916, Isuzu entered the U.S. market in 1981[14] and saw quiet success with the Trooper, an SUV introduced in 1983.[15] In a partnership with GM, Isuzu also supplied the popular Geo Storm passenger car model distributed by Chevrolet dealers.[16]

Despite its initial successes, in the face of relentless competition Isuzu sales in North America were declining. Customer satisfaction and product quality were low. When Isuzu considered introducing yet another passenger car into the North American market, company executives sought Dave's opinion. It was at an NADA convention in New Orleans that Dave and Yoshito Mochizuki, president of American Isuzu Motors, had a frank talk. Never one to pull his punches, Dave suggested that success for Isuzu in the crowded passenger car and light truck market was improbable and that the better strategy was to specialize in building small diesel engines for sale to GM and other car manufacturers.

"What Dave did for us at Isuzu is to emphasize the importance of the issues we were failing to deal with," says Bob Reilly, who was chief operating officer at American Isuzu Motors Inc. before being named executive vice president for the automotive group at J.D. Power and Associates. "Helping communicate our position that we needed to distinguish the Isuzu brand on quality and customer service was probably Dave's greatest contribution to my tenure at Isuzu," he says. At the Tokyo Auto Show in 1988, Reilly arranged a meeting between Dave and the then-president of Isuzu of Japan, Kazuo Tobiyama. That led to ongoing consultation work between J.D. Power and Isuzu Motors, Japan, which ceased its North American passenger vehicle sales in 2009.[17]

VW Aims Beyond the Beetle

Asian companies were not alone in getting insight from J.D. Power and Associates in their uphill battle to win over American consumers. Volkswagen, which had gotten into the U.S. market earlier than most foreign automakers but had lost market share to the Japanese in the 1970s, was a company teetering back and forth on success.

Headquartered at the time in Englewood Cliffs, New Jersey,[18] Volkswagen Group of America wasn't as convenient for Dave to call on as the Japanese companies, which tended to base their North American operations in Dave's Californian backyard. But Volkswagen couldn't be ignored. After the company's incorporation in the U.S. in 1955, it marketed the Beetle and sales of the ungainly but beloved "Bug" took off, remaining strong throughout the 1960s. "In the 1960s," says Dave, "Volkswagen garnered 88 percent of the import market with volumes of well over a half million units."

Dave predicted that Volkswagen would lose market share to the Japanese imports, and that's exactly what happened. Bill Young, former president and CEO of Volkswagen of North America and later an executive of J.D. Power and Associates, recalls that the company called on Dave to help it figure out what it could do to reverse the erosion of market share. "We at VW were very threatened by the Toyota Corona, which was designed to compete directly with the Beetle," Young recalls. "Dave showed us studies which demonstrated that American consumers were looking for cars with more design features." Volkswagen responded by introducing the Dasher and the Rabbit.

In 1979, Dave and his staff designed a syndicated study to determine what consumers thought of these new VW cars. In both cases, the syndicated studies distinguished between vehicles manufactured in the U.S. (the so-called Westmoreland VWs, built in Pennsylvania)[19] versus those manufactured in Germany and imported. Dave wanted to determine if the quality of the U.S.-manufactured vehicles would hold up to the German-manufactured vehicles. No one else had that information. Dave's ingenuity made it relatively inexpensive to conduct the survey. He knew that the headlights on the American-made vehicles were rectangular; round headlights identified German-made vehicles. So, instead of going through the expense of getting manufacturing information, Dave simply asked respondents to indicate on the surveys if the headlights on their cars were rectangular or round. The results showed that the quality of the vehicles built in U.S. and Germany was identical. Although that might have been a difficult statistic for Volkswagen's German workers to swallow, it was a huge boost for the brand's image in the U.S., and for the morale of its American employees.

Unfortunately for Volkswagen, the longer-term quality of the Dasher and Rabbit from both the German and U.S. plants did not meet American consumers' expectations. Sales dropped and warranty costs skyrocketed in the face of serious engine problems, such as valve-stem seal failures. "The interesting findings that all the plants had the same engine failures indicated that the majority of the serious problems were product design in origin," says Dave, "not due to manufacturing and assembly operations." Such failures at Volkswagen paved the way for the Japanese imports to grow their market share in the 1970s and early 1980s.

A Cautionary Voice for Saab

As Dave's reputation for having his finger on the pulse of the American car market expanded, a number of car companies sought his advice about whether they should introduce a particular model into the U.S. market. If, after doing research, Dave wasn't enthusiastic about a company's prospects, the company more often than not declined to introduce the model or pulled out of the U.S. market.

One such company was the Swedish automaker Saab. Unfortunately, Dave's guidance, although enthusiastically received, was not enough to turn around the company's U.S. efforts. Although Saab had earned a small base of fanatically loyal enthusiasts, and Saab dealers took first place in the 1986 Dealer Attitude Study, the brand had never been very successful in the U.S. market. One reason was perhaps peculiarities such as the unusual placement of the ignition switch. It was mounted on the floor, conveniently and safely—Saab's engineers thought—near the parking brake, gearshift, and seatbelt release. Although an ergonomic innovation, it was different than all the other cars in the market.

Dave knew that Saab paid particular attention to the Dealer Attitude Study. Following the 1985 survey, in which Saab finished first, Robert Sinclair, president of Saab of America, sent out a congratulatory memo to all Saab of America employees:

> Each year J.D. Power and Associates of Westlake Village, California, conducts a Dealer Attitude Survey in which all automobile dealers in the United States are asked to rate their current dealer-factory relations. The Power organization has just released the results of their 1985 survey.
>
> Dealers were asked to rate their franchises on a variety of attributes, including key issues such as sales outlook and franchise desirability. As the July issue of the Power Newsletter puts it: "Saab tops the entire list, with 66 percent of its own dealers terming the franchise relationship 'excellent' (or a mean rating of 3.61)."
>
> The top five franchises in terms of "excellent" ratings were:
>
> | | |
> |---|---|
> | Saab | 66% |
> | Honda | 62 |
> | Mercedes-Benz | 55 |
> | Mazda | 53 |
> | Volvo | 52 |
>
> The overall ratings of other key import competitors were: Audi, 14th; BMW, 15th; with Peugeot far behind the pack in 27th position. . . .

One of our corporate objectives has been to treat our dealers as Number One. *They* are the ones we rely on for outstanding customer service and, of course, they are the ones who actually sell our cars to the public. In short, "That's where the money comes from."

The results are now clear. Our dealers have ranked Saab as Number One. . . . I know you share my pride in this. It's great to be winners![20]

Dave's persistent efforts for more than a decade failed to put too much of a dent into Saab's lackluster fortunes. That didn't keep Dave from trying, occasionally using its competition with archrival Volvo to spur Saab into using more of J.D. Power's services. For example, in a January 27, 1989, letter Dave gently challenged Sinclair:

As I am sure you are aware, the results of the 1988 Dealer Attitude Survey have been released, and Saab ranks fifth out of 37 nameplates. While fifth place is a respectable finish, it represents a steady decline since its first-place finish in the 1986 study, indicating dealer relations with the factory are somewhat weakening. In fact, since 1986, the number of dealers who rate their dealer-manufacturer relationship excellent has declined nearly 50%.

In addition to a decline in the dealer-manufacturer relationship, current Saab dealers are also less optimistic about their Saab franchise as a financial investment, view their reputation for product quality sinking, are less likely to rate factory policies toward dealers excellent, and are less likely to rate the desirability to own a Saab franchise over the next five years excellent. These evaluations, coupled with a host of others, concern me as well as they should you. That is why I wanted you to have this information.

Finishing 10th in this year's survey, your Swedish counterpart, Volvo, takes the results of the survey to heart. They have put together a special task force who will be calling on dealers to learn what Volvo can do to improve their dealer-manufacturer relationship. With the complete results of the survey, Saab, too, can look at its strengths and weaknesses relative to their relationship with their dealers and design a program to once again put you ahead of the remaining competition.[21]

Saab continued to struggle. General Motors took control of Saab in 2000 but, with GM's bankruptcy in 2009, Saab was thrown into turmoil. Saab was acquired by the Netherlands-based premium sports carmaker Spyker Cars in February 2010, but then subsequently filed for bankruptcy in December 2011; the Saab bankruptcy resulted in a lawsuit against GM by Spyker.[22] In summer 2012, Saab was purchased out of bankruptcy by National Electric Vehicle Sweden AB.[23]

Unsuccessful Entrants

Saab was not the only manufacturer unable to overcome its reversal of fortune in the U.S. market. J.D. Power and Associates played an advisory role for a number of other lesser-known carmakers that, despite their best efforts, did not find success in the United States. "We did our level best to help these companies by giving them a more specific understanding of the demands of the U.S. auto market," Dave says. "I found that all of the executives were genuine in their desire to build a quality product and earn good customer satisfaction, but their ability to deliver on these goals was not equal to their good intentions. We were always willing to help carmakers do the hard work of forecasting demand for a particular car model and developing a sustainable distribution strategy." But the nature of competition is that sometimes even an organization's best efforts are insufficient.

There are any number of reasons for the failure of a car company in the complex U.S. market, but some commonalities stood out for Dave. Some of the companies tried to cut corners, either by failing to invest in the quality management of their North American operations or by not giving their teams enough time or resources to prepare for the launch. Some of the companies simply didn't offer vehicles designed for the American driver. Many of the companies didn't understand the complexities of establishing a retail and service network in a country as large as the United States. Several car companies, many of them successful in their home countries, were advised by Dave that either their strategies or their products were insufficient to penetrate the U.S. market. As a result, their efforts to enter the U.S. all failed, some more spectacularly than others.

Yugo, for example, is still the punch line for jokes about poor car quality. *Time* magazine counted it among the fifty worst cars in history, dubbing the Yugo GV the "Mona Lisa of bad cars."[24] Manufactured in the Socialist Federal Republic of Yugoslavia, the Yugo left the distinct impression of something assembled at knifepoint. Its only merit was that it carried the unheard of price tag of $3,990.[25] The downsides were an unreliable electrical system and such shoddy construction that parts would literally fall off. The joke was it had a rear-window defroster—reportedly to keep your hands warm while you pushed it.

Through Dave's engagement with Yugo, he encountered two of the more interesting individuals in American business history.

Dave first saw the Yugo in the mid-1980s at the Los Angeles Auto Show, where an enterprising young man had obtained the rights to sell Yugos in the United States. At the time, Dave was studying minicars for a product clinic he was preparing, so he requested permission to include the Yugo vehicle in the J.D. Power and Associates minicar study. Permission was granted and Dave was allowed to borrow a Yugo for the product clinic. After the study, the Yugo found itself parked outside Dave's house in Westlake Village.

One night the phone rang. On the other end was Malcolm Bricklin, who had introduced Subaru to the U.S. in the late 1960s.[26] Bricklin, who had purchased the franchise from a Czechoslovakian man who had the American rights to the Yugo, said that a notable individual in Los Angeles was interested in making an investment in bringing the Yugo into the U.S. market. Could Dave possibly get the Yugo that was sitting in front of his house to the Occidental Petroleum headquarters building in Los Angeles? And do it by eight the next morning?

Bricklin didn't have to use the investor's name. Dave immediately suspected it was Dr. Armand Hammer, a business tycoon who had run Occidental Petroleum for decades. He was famous for his art and business ventures—both before and after his involvement with Occidental began—as well as his work in the Soviet Union. "He was virtually the only one who could tell Mikhail Gorbachev firsthand what Lenin was like," an energy research consultant told the *New York Times* for Hammer's 1990 obituary. Hammer had a medical degree, had owned a New York art gallery as a young man, and contributed large amounts to charities as well as to politicians.[27] Dave was interested in meeting the fabled Dr. Hammer and, perhaps because he didn't want to risk any of his employees' lives by asking them to drive the undependable Yugo, he decided to deliver the car himself.

The inspection was to take place in the Occidental Building's parking garage. In due course Hammer came down to take a look. Bricklin improbably invited Hammer—in his eighties and a large man—to take a test-drive in the little four-seat Yugo. Hammer demurred. Bricklin was insistent. Eventually a compromise was reached. Hammer's chauffeur would test the car. Dave didn't stick around for the end of the meeting, but Hammer's company was reported to have assisted Bricklin with trade talks.[28] Bricklin eventually formed Global Motors Corp.,[29] and at first he saw some success. The Yugo broke sales records for the launch of a European import. However, its lack of quality caught up with it, and its reputation plummeted. Bricklin divested himself of the company in 1988, filing for personal bankruptcy in 1991.[30] Global Motors filed for bankruptcy protection in 1989.[31]

Daewoo was the second largest South Korean conglomerate,[32] with electronics, textiles, securities, and other corporations under its umbrella. It entered the automobile industry in 1978, manufacturing vehicles in the Korean market through a partnership with GM that lasted until 1992.[33]

After watching the early successes and stumbles of Hyundai Motors, Daewoo approached J.D. Power and Associates in 1995 with the intent to enter the U.S. market, giving Dave a chance to work closely with one of the most enigmatic executives he has ever met: Kim Woo Choong. Kim had built the company from scratch, and he was a powerful force. "He was a supremely confident, engaged, and demanding chairman," Dave notes. Four J.D. Power associates worked with a small Daewoo staff to prepare the company for its launch strategy. Kim would come to Los Angeles and, holding court in a downtown hotel, ask Dave to make progress reports. Kim referred to Dave as "Godfather."

From the beginning, Dave questioned Daewoo's business model in the United States. When the company publicly announced in June 1996 that Daewoo would launch in the U.S. in October 1997, Dave struggled to make Kim accept that its launch date was unrealistic. Dave was candid in a June 26, 1996, letter to C.S. Lee, the chief operating officer of Daewoo Motors of North America:

> I would be remiss if I did not communicate to you at this point our belief that Daewoo has put itself in a virtually impossible situation. You are allowing your six-person North American team just 16 months to carry out tasks which require 30–50 months to be properly executed, as described in the U.S. Market Entry Plan. We believe that such a compressed timetable will inevitably result in insufficient planning and poor execution.[34]

Later, Dave personally communicated his concerns directly to Kim. The chairman listened carefully to Dave's advice but in this instance went against his recommendation. Daewoo never did get its U.S. launch off the ground. It attempted to speed entry by not using traditional dealerships. Instead, Daewoo owned and operated its own retail network. In the U.S., Daewoo's retail strategy was to use college student advisers to market the cars to their classmates, faculty, and parents using an early form of "buzz" marketing. Student advisers would earn commissions for each car they sold. Prices would be fixed, following the no-haggling policy pioneered by GM's Saturn unit. The cars would actually be sold by a national network of company-owned retail stores.[35] In 1998, Kim ran into deep financial trouble when the Asian financial system collapsed; within a year, Daewoo was bankrupt. In 2002,

Daewoo was forced to sell off its automotive arm to GM. Kim was charged by Korean authorities with accounting fraud and money smuggling and was wanted by Interpol from 2001 until he returned to Korea in 2005. Upon his return to Korea, Kim was sentenced to ten years in prison but was pardoned less than two years after his sentencing.[36]

French-based carmaker Peugeot entered the U.S. market in 1958.[37] By the time Peugeot engaged J.D. Power in the 1970s, its division in the U.S. was operating on fumes. Its difficulties stemmed from the same product-driven mentality that plagued the Big Three, Jamey explains: "Peugeot cared more about listening to its engineers than to the market." In America, Peugeot appealed to higher-income consumers who were enamored with European engineering and handling. In addition to a small but enthusiastic customer base, the company had a small but energetic sales force and dealer network. However, Dave advised that to blossom into a major player in the American market, significant changes were needed: Peugeot's design and sales organizations had to adapt their cars to the desires of American consumers. Despite Dave's persistent counsel, those modifications never materialized.

Dave concluded that the problem was not so much the quality of the cars as the quality of Peugeot management, both in France and in the United States. The company's French management was guilty of both ignorance and arrogance; ignorance because it didn't have a clue about what American car buyers wanted in a car, and arrogance because it felt that Americans should adapt to the car instead of the other way around. For example, J.D. Power and Associates reported that U.S. Peugeot owners, especially those living in the Snow Belt, reported difficulty starting their vehicles. The reason for this difficulty was easy to understand; its solution was rather more complicated.

Everyone understood that the source of the difficulty was that American car buyers, used to driving carbureted cars, were in the 1970s still accustomed to pumping the accelerator one or two times before turning the ignition on. "Though most drivers didn't know why they did it, the action released fuel into the combustion chamber and helped the engine turn over," Dave says. "With the Peugeot, however, when drivers pumped the accelerator, they were unwittingly flooding the engine, making it impossible to start," because the cars had fuel-injection systems. The real issue was what to do about this mismatch between consumer behavior and vehicle behavior.

The French response was self-defeating. In a meeting with Dave, the chief engineer of Peugeot angrily rejected Dave's market research. "Peugeot has the best-starting car in Europe," he said, pounding his first on the conference room table for emphasis. He said the problem was with the American driver. "We need to educate these customers," he said.

Dave's response was measured. Yes, the chief engineer was correct about having the best-starting car in Europe but wrong about the U.S. drivers. Dave advised him that Peugeot could spend every cent it had on advertising and promotion to educate American drivers on how to start the car, but that it would be futile. "If you want to do better," he said, "you have to build the ignition and fuel system so that it operates the way American drivers expect it to work."

Peugeot's management issues created even more problems than its engineering problems. The North American operation was in shambles, Dave recalls, with constant turnover among managers, who for a variety of reasons were resistant to engaging with the hard facts presented by J.D. Power and Associates. In any case, the culture of Peugeot made it almost impossible for managers in the U.S. to be honest with their superiors in Paris. Dave's response, as always, was to bypass the local managers and create relationships with corporate executives who were presumably more open-minded. In this quest, Dave met with qualified success. In due course, he was invited to give a comprehensive presentation at Peugeot's North American headquarters in New Jersey. Most of the company's American staff were present as well as three Peugeot officials from France and the executive who handled the Peugeot account for the ad agency Ogilvy & Mather Worldwide. Dave's role as an adviser to the industry was never more tested.

Dave began in his usual way, by quietly reviewing pertinent data from the most recent J.D. Power studies, including the CSI, the IQS, and the Dealer Attitude Study. He pulled no punches laying out the facts that Peugeot's situation in North America was desperate. He was surprised when, after the presentation, there was none of the defensiveness or bombast he had earlier experienced from the French executives. He thanked the group for its attention and then excused himself to fly back home to California. It was a Friday.

The following Monday, Dave received a call from Graham Phillips, president of Ogilvy & Mather. Phillips asked Dave to fly back East as soon as possible to repeat the same presentation. He was frustrated representing Peugeot. "We purchased Peugeot cars for our senior executives and, without exception, all the cars had serious quality problems," Phillips told Dave. Phillips focused intently on the data as Dave repeated his presentation to Ogilvy & Mather executives. Partly based on this presentation, the agency resigned from the Peugeot account. Peugeot left the U.S. market in 1991,[38] but maintains a good relationship with Dave and J.D. Power and Associates.

Providing a New Perspective on Media Studies

Dave felt that the insights he could offer automakers should extend to understanding how best to reach potential customers. In the mid-1970s, Dave pioneered a new way to study the media habits of vehicle buyers, but he didn't do it by starting with automobiles. Instead, he studied motorcycles.

Dave knew that motorcycles represent a small portion of the automotive market. But in the early 1970s, in the wake of the first energy crisis, the American motorcycle industry took off as consumers sought a fuel-efficient alternative to cars. So, Dave decided to look into the shopping habits of motorcycle owners through a study of the media, particularly magazines, to which motorcycle riders were exposed.

Media research was very specialized, so Dave knew he would be playing ball on someone else's home field. The standard media research approach was to survey readers of a particular magazine about their buying habits. In the case of the motorcycle markets, affinity magazines for motorcycle riders provided data to media buyers indicating that since a high percentage of their readership owned or were in the market for motorcycles, their publications were a good avenue to reach potential buyers. Dave saw another angle. He decided to survey motorcycle buyers and ask them what publications they read. In that way, he could provide a list to the manufacturers that would more accurately guide their media buys.

J.D. Power's motorcycle media study premiered in 1975, examining the dozen or so specialized publications geared for motorcycle and off-road bike riders. The study was complicated by the fact that, unlike automobile drivers, not all motorcycle and dirt-bike drivers are registered. Thus, it was more difficult to identify and qualify drivers. Nevertheless, the motorcycle and off-road dirt bike media studies succeeded and had a big impact on how advertising dollars were allocated in the motorcycle segment.

Not every publisher was pleased with Dave's results. For example, *Cycle* magazine represented itself as the leading magazine for all motorcycle enthusiasts, pointing to survey data showing that nine out of ten motorcycle owners read *Cycle* regularly. The J.D. Power data did not substantiate this claim. "Our research revealed that a large number of motorcycle owners and enthusiasts did not read *Cycle* or any other specialized publication." Instead, Dave's market research showed these readers favored general interest publications, such as *Time*, *Popular Science*, and *People*. These conclusions led to a shift in advertising spending, away from specialized publications such as *Cycle*.

At that time, automobile manufacturers were the largest media advertisers, especially in magazines, and Dave perceived a greater business opportunity in syndicating media studies that tied magazine readership to car- and truck-buying habits, providing data on the most effective magazines for the manufacturers to reach their potential buyers.

"Media research people were very academic in their thinking," he recalls. "They would end up with a ten- or twenty-thousand sample" from a big national survey, but only a fraction of those people would be buying a new car. What's more, many specialized auto marques or models carried only a tiny fraction of the overall market, making the data from a traditional study less appropriate for them. The traditional media research method, Dave says, "was fine for grocery items or soap, which had large acceptance across a population, but not for something as critical as a Porsche 911 purchase."

But Dave didn't jump into studying the reading habits of sports-car drivers just yet. Instead, he hit upon a market that was developing due to his Japanese clients: the small pickup truck. Until the mid-1970s, the pickup had been mostly a commercial-use vehicle; purchasing decisions were not made in the same way as with cars, Dave explains. "But when the Japanese came in, they had cheaper, small trucks that became personal-use vehicles." In 1980, J.D. Power created a media study of potential pickup-truck buyers.

With his first study of the media habits of truck buyers, Dave quickly discovered that automakers had been spending a lot of money in the wrong place. People might read car-enthusiast or outdoor-sports magazines to shop for cars and trucks, but—just like motorcycle buyers—far more of them read general-interest magazines, so those were the publications where ad purchases would be much more effective. "The cost was tremendous for the automobile industry," he says. "It supported a lot of magazines."

That study got the attention of one future client (and future J.D. Power employee), a Detroit-based executive at the giant J. Walter Thompson advertising agency, which at the time managed the national advertising account for Ford. The agency was participating in the rollout of Ford's new small pickup truck, the Ranger. Tom Healey, the agency's media director, was looking for a way to find potential buyers and he wasn't happy with the methods or results of the agency's existing media research, the omnibus study by W.R. Simmons and Associates. Concurrent to J.D. Power's media studies, Healey developed a similar research project at the agency. "I came across a J.D. Power questionnaire . . . of truck buyers," Healey recalls. "They asked about eight or ten magazines . . . but that was not a large enough net to cast. We wanted to ask about any magazines that had any claim to the

Ford business. We wanted to go for over a hundred magazines." So, Healey convinced his boss to fund a truck study, which they did twice in the mid-1980s.

Concurrently, J.D. Power was producing its first automobile media study. Again, Healey thought that Ford also could use a car study, but "the study that Power had done was preliminary and it really didn't meet many of the criteria we needed." He began discussions with Dave about taking over their studies for Ford. "We were looking at J.D. Power doing it to see if they could do it effectively," Healey recalls. "Of course, they were in it to make money. We were in it basically to save money, to be more efficient in our advertising. But the goals were not totally inconsistent." But first Dave and Healey had to come to a meeting of the minds.

"We got criticized by the media researchers," Dave recalls, and not just because "we were treading on their territory." They looked at his study methodology and said it would not get a great enough rate of return; in the media world, a 50 percent response rate was expected, and media researchers got that through person-to-person interviews. Plus, the survey was a whopping sixteen pages.

In typical fashion, Dave studied the problem and decided the solution was to get advice from those who were offering up the criticism. Coincidentally, they would also be the customers for this new product, so Dave was returning to his own mantra: listen to the voice of the customer. He convened an advisory committee, which included Healey, representing Ford, as well as researchers representing General Motors, Chrysler, and Toyota, and the chairman of the Magazine Publishers of America's research council. Over a weekend, they debated the methodology. Healey recalls they changed the questions to be more specific so "we could develop a statistic called the average issue audience for a given type of prospect, based on the vehicle they had bought the year before." With that, J.D. Power had a legitimate hit on its hands. The first passenger car study was released in 1985; by 1986, J. Walter Thompson had shut down its study for Ford and Healey had convinced Ford to purchase the J.D. Power study.

With its success, Dave needed someone to take the new product to its next level. He saw that Healey's department was being cut back, and Dave offered him a job, saying, "You criticized our media study. I need somebody in house who can run the media study the way it should be run." To get to the industry-standard 50 percent return rate in a mailed study would be possible, they determined, but it cost more because you had to boost the incentive and re-mail to target lists. "Tom did a marvelous job," Dave says. "It was because of his expertise that we could improve tremendously." The studies could effectively drill down to very specific results. Healey recalls that they identified "the BMW gene" by getting people to respond to the statement "I like to drive on challenging roads with hills and curves." Through another correlation, they found that people who had bought Jaguars tended to read the U.K.-based *Economist* magazine, Healey explains, because they were Anglophiles.

In the end, not only did the carmakers subscribe to the media study, but it also became must-have market knowledge for the media companies and their ad agencies.

Expanding Media Services

Over the next decade, the product grew and the services expanded to help advertising agencies select the best publications in which to advertise and land automotive accounts. In 1989, Healey started a yearly J.D. Power conference, called the Automotive

Advertising Strategy Conference, which "increased our credibility in the advertising community," he says. It led to brand analysis and consulting services as well. The conference brought together the best minds in that industry to develop and share demographic information and ideas in media strategy.

Publishers and ad agencies responded positively. Publishers such as Time Inc. (*Time, Fortune, People,* and *Sports Illustrated*) demand up-to-the-minute demographic information about their readership and used the data to justify their ability to reach target audiences and advertising rates. Dave could see that publishers wanted the same thing as automakers: a sense of who was consuming their product and what they thought about it. Ad agencies began to use J.D. Power research data to help them measure the effectiveness of publications in reaching targeted demographics.

J.D. Power and Associates was commissioned by Time Inc. to conduct a number of media studies for one of its prime properties, *Sports Illustrated.* Time Inc.'s John Marin wanted actionable information the magazine's sales team could use to get more automobile advertising. "At the time, Time did a lot of market research studies on its own properties, but the studies tended to be self-serving, and potential advertisers knew it, so they tended to be skeptical of our numbers," Marin said. "What I wanted was a study from an independent source that would enable my sales team to be more credible and effective in selling ads." Marin recalled, "it was quite a success. Dave made market research useful for someone like me."

Seeking an Overall Consumer Profile

While studying media habits was useful, J.D. Power's study—called the Automotive Consumer Profile (ACP)—was one of

Dave's most pioneering efforts. Nothing like this study had ever been attempted before. J.D. Power and Associates created the ACP in 1979 to fill a void in the syndicated market research field. "Our objective was to generate very specific and actionable information on consumer driving habits, future purchase intentions, and consumer attitudes about automotive transportation," Dave says. The study would cover the total U.S. market of homes that had vehicles.

The ACP was a continuation of a national profile of car and light-duty truck owners that J.D. Power and Associates first published in the 1970s. The purpose of the study was to collect broad-based information on the attitudes and opinions households have about all aspects of owning and operating their motor vehicles. "There was no study available at that time that analyzed the household dynamics of vehicle usage," says Dave. "If a household had four licensed drivers and only two vehicles, we wanted to know how and when the drivers used the vehicles." The second energy crisis of 1979 had a profound but little-understood influence on consumer driving behavior that, Dave believed, the ACP could reveal.

It was a huge undertaking that taxed all the resources of the company. Starting with a list of registered vehicles segmented by type (passenger car, pickup truck, etc.), model, and geographic location, J.D. Power and Associates engaged National Family Opinion to send out surveys to more than five thousand car owners nationwide. "A separate questionnaire was sent to each licensed driver in the household," explains Dave, "which allowed us to individually analyze the behavior of all drivers associated with each vehicle." The surveys captured such information as driver-owner characteristics, driving habits, consumer opinions, actual and projected behavior patterns, vehicle purchase intentions, desired vehicle attributes, service information, and even lifestyle changes, discretionary spending patterns, and other metrics that showed an impact on industries beyond the car manufacturers.

It was critically important for the study to include the consumer's broader wants and needs beyond the vehicle purchase, Dave felt. He understood that for a syndicated study of this size and cost, the company would have to broaden the ACP's appeal to potential customers such as makers of audio systems (every car needed a music system), oil companies (every car consumes gasoline and petroleum products), tire manufacturers, the travel industry, auto publications, and other industries that share an interdependence with the auto industry. Dave's insight was to recognize the degree to which the mobility of consumers affects myriad decisions, from the purchase of new and used vehicles, car accessories, and discretionary spending to such items as meals and lodging. The ACP attempted to capture the interrelated effects of energy costs, inflation, and government regulation upon the automotive consumer. "Dave was very confident in what he was doing," says former J.D. Power statistician Mark Rees. "Dave lost money on that study every year, but he believed in it and thought it offered valuable insights."

But few of the insights were interesting to automakers. Car manufacturers were fixated on selling new cars. From a marketing point of view, they had almost no interest in the used car market, even though, as the ACP noted, among those planning to acquire another car within the next year, 41 percent would buy a used one. "I hoped the ACP would give subscribers a deeper perspective on the car market, especially after the second energy crisis when consumers wanted more efficient cars," Dave says. "Nobody knew how used cars were being handled and passed on. We showed, among other things, what percentage of used car owners would upgrade to a new car versus how many would replace a used car with another used car."

Like some of Dave's initiatives, even though it was ground-breaking, it became a victim of the recessionary cycles that buffeted the America auto industry. The ACP never caught on and it was discontinued, after sixteen quarterly waves, in 1984.

Dave was not about to abandon the rich data generated by the ACP. "We lived in the data generated by the ACP for ten years," he says. The company parceled out the data over the next decade in a subscription publication called the *Automotive Consumer Profile Newsletter*. The first issue was dated August 1979 with the gas-crisis-era headline, "Consumer Fuel Fears Give Government, Industry Multi-Headed Serpent to Slay—But Which to Attack First?" The story focused on the implications to the entire travel industry if gasoline prices approached the improbable level of one dollar per gallon.

Publishing with Impact: the Power Report

Advertising and consumer awareness were vitally important for Dave and his team in order to get in the doors of potential customers, but it was the value of the information that always kept those clients coming back. Dave's viewpoint on the auto industry came to be highly valued as well, and that, too, was based on the information generated by his firm.

So, it was only natural that in 1981 Dave evolved the ACP monthly newsletter into a report that offered his personal perspective on the auto industry. This was a powerful tool and one Dave used to great effect. It highlighted interesting information gleaned from the research that J.D. Power and Associates was conducting and carried a monthly editorial from Dave himself. The company called it the *Power Report on Automotive Retailing*, and much of the content came from Dave, says John Rettie, who managed publications for the company at the time. "It was one of his hobbies."

It also gave Dave another outlet for sharing his enthusiasm for his work. "Dave is incredibly passionate about the business, customer information, and trying to organize that information in a way that the people who needed it would understand and actually take action on," observes Charles Mills, a writer and editor who worked with Dave on the *Power Report*.

The company hired journalists and associates with communications backgrounds to work on the *Power Report*, and the publication became a respected, useful element of J.D. Power's services that complemented the study reports. Mills recalls that he was first hired to write sales and service training programs that would communicate the company's valuable customer data to the auto manufacturer clients in an actionable way. "That's why I got tapped to work on the *Power Report*, so the dealer-reader could understand and make sense of that data."

Mills became editor in 1995, which meant he worked very closely with Dave on the content, sometimes causing a bit of angst for the young associate. "Every month I would send him a draft," Mills recalls, "and the next day he would sit me down in the office and we would walk through the articles that he had redlined up. He would joke to me that he had an English degree and it was clear that I was not writing in English." It wasn't always a lighthearted conversation, however. "Sometimes he would be very direct on his commentary on an article or the way I interpreted the data. He had a very strong opinion."

Although the publication was resonant with Dave's voice, other analysts, both from inside and outside the company, helped round out the monthly offerings. Mills recalls one guest contributor,

Stephen Girsky, who became vice chairman of the board at General Motors in 2010. Back then, he was an analyst at Morgan Stanley and provided industry forecasts. "He was quite kind with his time and incredibly informative for the readers," Mills recalls. "I'd do interviews, or he'd send me some articles."

Such analysis went beyond the company's research studies, but it contributed to the overall knowledge of the subscribers, whether they were powerful industry leaders purchasing J.D. Power research services, or rank-and-file people who wanted to get the big picture. Perhaps the latter audience was its true target, says Mills.

"I think the *Power Report* was a powerful tool for J.D. Power to communicate its information to a broader audience than just the auto executives that may have bought the large studies." The publication staff, Mills explains, would analyze information from J.D. Power studies and aim for an article "that would be interesting to the dealerships and the department- and function-level personnel at the automakers." The articles would aim to "either give them insights or provoke questioning along the lines of, is the current approach appropriate given what we're seeing in the data?"

The *Power Report* staff saw results in circulation, which peaked at about 1,200 subscribers—a significant reach given the $399 yearly price tag—and in responses from readers. Dealers wrote back. The media occasionally reprinted *Power Report* articles. Industry leaders commented. Some passed the publication around, while others got a bit more testy when their company was mentioned in print.

"We knew we were making an impact," recalls Mills, "when one of the articles I'd written about the importance of initial quality came back to me Xeroxed with a bunch of Post-It notes from Bob

Lutz." Lutz was head of automotive at Chrysler and an intimidating presence for the J.D. Power associate. Mills recalls serious trepidation when he first saw Lutz's critique. "Here I was, fairly young and receiving such strong and assertive feedback from one of the industry giants. When Dave Power called me into his office and showed me this and told me who these comments were from, I thought he was going to fire me. Instead he embraced me and said, 'This is great. We're making an impact! They may not agree, but at least they're listening to what the customers are saying and they're taking it seriously enough to push back.'" Mills breathed a sigh of relief after that show of support.

The value of these reports to automakers was brought home to Dave in one memorable instance. He was visiting Tom Shaver, the Detroit-based director of merchandising for Chevrolet, who had first begun reading the *Power Report* when he was a zone manager for Chevrolet in Cleveland. He would highlight key points in the report and circulate it among his colleagues. Dave had become a frequent visitor to Shaver's office and this time, as the two men were meeting, Shaver's secretary came in with a tall stack of photocopied and highlighted *Power Reports* to ask Shaver a question about distributing them to GM executives. Dave burst into laughter. "I knew people made illegal copies," he told the executive, "but this is the first time I've ever caught them red-handed."

From the early days of J.D. Power and Associates, when Dave's advice often needed to be accompanied by a lesson on the importance of the voice of the customer, the firm's data-driven insights were key to a carmaker's success. As studies and consultations proliferated, and those insights became widely circulated intelligence through the *Power Report*, the company's impact reverberated through the industry like radio waves from a transmitter. By the 1990s, it was a rare executive who didn't understand the term "voice of the customer" or associate it with Dave and his team. And it was through the unwavering integrity of the data and its presenters that Dave achieved a lasting impact in the quality and retailing of automobiles, as well as a deeper understanding of what the consumer looked for in a vehicle.

SECTION THREE
INTEGRITY

Just as J.D. Power and Associates provided tools for the auto industry to measure various standards of success, Dave and his leadership team were constantly evaluating the success of their own company at meeting its objectives of independence, impact, and integrity. As the company built its reputation and international clientele, it grew in number of employees, and number of offices around the world. With its rapid growth, it faced some of the same quality and satisfaction issues that challenged many of its automaker clients, specifically the emphasis on production rather than quality. After all, J.D. Power and Associates was a business whose success depended on exceeding the expectations of its customers. When market research reports lacked the depth of analysis that an industry relied on, customers complained and Dave heard about it. His response could be immediate and unsparing. For example, in a May 4, 1993, memo to a J.D. Power manager, he wrote:

> Exceeding "our" customers' expectations, especially our largest client, is what we must do. We appear to be too production-focused, like our automotive brethren. The concerns I have are based upon the feeling that in the Market Research Department our mode of operation has

been to get the report out the door just like the car manufacturers pushing the product out. Time and cost pressures rule the decisions, and our client customer ends up with the bare minimum. I know that we have 1,001 reasons why this goes on, but we need to change our focus and do it immediately. The junior staff has no idea of the importance of this. When they do, we will see an immediate pickup in morale. Please show the leadership enthusiasm that is necessary to get there. We need to focus on our clients' needs, wants, and expectations. Do I make my point?

Along with internal quality control, Dave wanted his company to be objectively credible, in much the same way as he counseled his clients. Thus, he was not afraid of turning the spotlight of the voice of the customer and independent scrutiny on the firm itself. As far back as the 1980s, carmakers in Detroit and, to a lesser extent, Europe were critical of the company's analytical and business methods, calling them flawed, biased, and unfair. Dave was open to knowing what his customers really thought of the company, and he was not afraid of putting his own firm under the microscope.

In November 1985, Dave asked Bill Young, the national sales manager of Volkswagen of North America and then an automotive consultant in Manhattan Beach, California, to conduct an independent study to determine the extent to which J.D. Power was satisfying its own customers. Young (who a few years later would go on to become the president and CEO of Volkswagen of America) was given complete independence to interview the customers of J.D. Power, from the automakers' market research personnel to the dealers. Young took more than three months to conduct the marketing audit. Much of his time was spent interviewing the market research professionals representing the Detroit manufacturers, though he talked with European and Japanese automakers as well. These were the people who, by and large, purchased the syndicated studies produced by J.D. Power. Young's audit surfaced a number of objections.

As Dave suspected, the most common objection was that J.D. Power and Associates was biased in favor of Japanese cars. The survey also revealed that the executives at the very top of the manufacturing organizations often felt powerless to enact the change needed to rank higher in J.D. Power's ratings and therefore did not see Dave's illumination of satisfaction problems as being the helpful information he intended it to be.

All of the U.S. and European carmakers that Young spoke with hated that the IQS and CSI results were made public. "When I talked to the market research people," recalls Young, "they didn't like the fact that they were a client paying for this research, and it was ending up in the public venue." Young didn't expect J.D. Power and Associates' business model to change because of this criticism. "Dave's view was that he'd never get any pressure on the system to change the behavior of the manufacturers if there isn't some public pressure."

Dave did not just refute the study findings, though. As he would advise any client, he took action on the data. He acknowledged that perceptions were effectively reality, and he responded by doubling down on his relationships with automobile executives. "He became more sensitive to the challenges that our individual client leaders were experiencing," explains Jamey Power. Dave also took notice of complaints about some associates who rubbed clients the wrong way, and he worked with those individuals to improve service.

The marketing audit prompted Dave to move forward with opening the Detroit office, recalls Young. "If you open an office in Detroit, you can start to work to break that perception that you fly in from the West Coast, you do your work, and you fly back," to an office with greater proximity to the Japanese automakers.

But plenty of objective evidence of the firm's integrity—coupled with its ongoing client support and growth—lays to rest the majority of such criticisms. An article that dealt with the question in the magazine *Brill's Content* in June 1999 quoted none other than a *Consumer Reports* executive, who remarked on the challenging "balancing act" Dave had to play between serving his automaker clients and the consumers who answer his surveys and rely on the results. "'His money depends on his credibility,' said David Champion, then director of automobile testing for *Consumer Reports*. 'If the data were not credible, the manufacturers wouldn't pay what amounts to an absolute fortune for his studies.'" He said later in the article, about the company's integrity, "They can't be bought."

"I can't think of any other company that did a marketing audit like the one I did for J.D. Power and Associates," says Young. "Part of the reason is that no one wants that kind of honest feedback. Not really. But Dave Power, being in the research business, really wanted straightforward, honest feedback."

CHAPTER SEVEN

MANAGING THE BRAND

The breadth of influence of J.D. Power and Associates grew with the firm, and with every study performed for an automaker, Dave's counsel became more valuable. As the value of the J.D. Power services strengthened, Dave and his staff sought more ways to build brand awareness, which would translate into selling more studies and consulting services. One clear route was through the media. Dave had learned the power of public relations when that early controversy involving Mazda's rotary engine had gotten him into the *Wall Street Journal* and greatly boosted the firm's stature. The company soon began to publicize its studies regularly. Every time syndicated studies were completed, the top-performing brands were listed in a press release. Dave regularly chatted with auto-industry journalists, and the company's analysts became sought-after sources. In typical fashion, J.D. Power and Associates had surveys done to track that brand awareness, and the broad reach of the brand became clear.

"We hired a separate company [Lou Harris & Associates] to go out and survey consumers and ask them about their awareness, use, value, and the image of ourselves," recalls Steve Goodall, former J.D. Power president. "Of those that had heard of J.D. Power, almost everyone had a pretty positive image of us." They associated the company with the concepts of independence and objectivity. Other than *Consumer Reports*, "there was no other company that had that sort of awareness."

In 2008, four decades after Dave's kids had taped quarters to survey forms at his family's kitchen table, a survey showed that 80 percent of consumers were aware of the J.D. Power brand. The brand even extended into the young minds of the family's next generation. In a situation that provided an anecdote he may never live down, Dave's grandson, James David Power V, was asked his name by his kindergarten teacher on the first day of school, and he proudly blurted, "J.D. Power and Associates!"

Though their brand awareness probably didn't extend to other kindergartners, Goodall says that level of recognition might be the firm's greatest asset. "It would have taken other brands millions and millions to build, and Power built it through basically its work, its publishing of that work, and the press coverage that comes from that and from the licensing that companies who ended up winning awards did to build the brand name."

"I see a great brand as a promise wrapped in an experience," says Charles Hughes, founder and CEO of Land Rover North America (formerly Range Rover) and author of *Branding Iron: Branding Lessons from the Meltdown of the U.S. Auto Industry.* "Building a stand-out brand requires not only the market perspective to recognize that you can do something better, but also the courage to declare it and the ability to make it happen," Hughes says. "J.D. Power and Associates has delivered on all those counts."

Scoring with a Football Ad

J.D. Power and Associates was one of the first companies to see its brand awareness catch fire through the efforts of other entities rather than through a traditional marketing campaign. It all started in early 1984 when a new automobile commercial began to run during the college and professional football seasons. The spot started with a black screen. Then text appeared: "According to J.D. Power and Associates, Subaru is second only to Mercedes in customer satisfaction." The commercial surprised and astounded Dave and his wife Julie, who saw it for the first time while quietly watching a televised game. They had no idea that such a commercial had been made. Other J.D. Power associates, many of whom were sports fans watching TV on a weekend, reported being similarly stunned.

Subaru was destined to have a key role in transforming J.D. Power and Associates into a national brand, but Tom Gibson, then executive vice president of operations for Subaru of America, says it started innocently enough. "We were astounded to see that the CSI reported that Subaru came in first in quality among all Asian imports and second to Mercedes-Benz among all vehicles." Gibson thought the results would make for a good TV commercial. "It never occurred to me to get permission or notify Dave that we were doing this." After an internal debate about whether it was more effective to compare Subaru to Asian imports or to the leading symbol of German quality, Gibson commissioned a TV spot that opened with the Mercedes-Benz comparison.

The ad didn't impress any of the television executives who reviewed the spot. They had never heard of J.D. Power and Associates, so all three initially rejected the commercial. Subaru had to threaten to sue before they allowed the spot to air. "The results were immediate," Gibson laughs. "Up to that point, Subaru had a small cult following in the Northeast. The ad gave us instant credibility with the public and the rest of industry. The ad was successful for us. It helped us break out from the group, including Isuzu and Mitsubishi, and showcased Subaru as a quality, reliable, rugged choice. But it was even more successful for Dave."

In the days after the commercial aired, Dave came to understand that this new development was both an opportunity and a headache. An opportunity because, in a world where brands are king, the holy grail of marketing is to get others to do your marketing for you. Why pay for a branding campaign when others will spread your message around at no cost to you? Dave realized that automakers, in their need for third-party validation, would promote the J.D. Power brand around the world and he could even charge them for the privilege. The headache came from figuring out how a company committed to integrity and independence can control its message in an unruly world where brands often get twisted out of shape. Moreover, there was the immediate difficulty of existing clients, all of whom were competitors in one way or another, objecting to the use of J.D. Power and Associates' brand in a way that might hurt rather than help their own brand. Dave anticipated that, come Monday morning, he would have to deal with the fallout from the Subaru commercial.

He was not wrong. The first call Dave fielded was from a furious executive at Mercedes, asking how dare he authorize a company making economy cars to mention Subaru and Mercedes-Benz in the same sentence? Perplexed calls from Toyota, Ford, and GM soon followed.

"The truth was," Dave says, "I did not authorize anything." The only person in the company to know anything about the Subaru ad was Mark Rees, who some weeks earlier had received notification from CBS that Subaru wanted to run a commercial using the J.D. Power company name. Rees informally reviewed the ad and found it consistent with the recent rankings. He sent a confirmation to the network without realizing he was handling something that would blast the J.D. Power brand across the world and eventually generate substantial fees for the company.

The Growing Power of the Brand

When Mark Rees approved the Subaru ad for CBS, he did not immediately consider the ethical thicket running such ads created for the company. But as Dave fielded angry phone calls from clients after the ad ran, he soon realized that the company with his name on it couldn't allow its data to be hijacked by one automaker attempting to make another automaker look bad. He soon saw many ways in which marketers tried to twist the survey results. "Advertising agencies drove us absolutely crazy with their ideas," Dave says. "Our goals were always well intended. We were trying to uncover the truth. Ad agencies were trying to promote a product. So, if our data suggested that a certain car manufacturer had the 'best door handle,' the next thing we knew there was an advertisement saying that J.D. Power and Associates says car X is the 'best car.'"

The agencies always pushed the limits. For example, one agency proposed an ad that showed its client's car on top of a junk heap made up of competitors' cars. J.D. Power was constantly assailed to lend its name to advertising campaigns and occasionally offered large sums to do so. Dave put his foot down. "We told the ad agencies that we were not going to allow J.D. Power and Associates to be part of denigrating the competition. We are about celebrating excellence in customer satisfaction." To formulate advertising policies, Dave turned to J Ferron, whom he had recruited from the National Automobile Dealers Association (NADA). A lawyer by training, Ferron created enforceable policies to deal with advertising making claims about J.D. Power data.

"I found a metaphor helpful in formulating our advertising policies," says Ferron. "If you are on a life raft in the middle of the ocean and a bright, colorful fish jumps into your boat, don't eat it. It's probably poisonous. Instead, bait your hook and do the hard work of fishing for a sustainable meal." The moral: these revenue-generating ads came to the company at no effort, but unless they were resisted, or at least regulated, they would quickly compromise the integrity of the J.D. Power brand. The resulting rules were strict and zealously enforced.

Ferron drafted a license agreement for all syndicated studies that all clients had to sign. The license established that J.D. Power and Associates owned the data; for a fee, clients were entitled to use the data in limited ways. One right they did not have was to use J.D. Power data to validate advertising claims without prior review and written permission. J.D. Power had the right to vet and approve all ads that mentioned the company in any way. In its fervor to protect its brand, the company turned down a number of ads, weathering the loss of revenue and even the occasional threat.

No Data Mining

The first rule: no data mining. Marketers were not permitted to sift through the J.D. Power database and extract selective data to make particular advertising claims. The company designated in advance of the syndicated study publication the limited categories that ad agencies could work with. It was like the Academy Awards. The Academy of Motion Picture Arts and Sciences has nominations such as Best Actor in a Leading Role or Best Original Score. It doesn't allow others to make up their own categories. Ferron says the company announced, "Here are the categories permitted in ads that reference J.D. Power research. Don't go beyond that!" Other rules rejected the use of such terms as "winner." Advertisers could claim their companies were "top-ranked" or "most reliable" but not "better" or "superior." "We created 'words of art' that were then repeated over and over, further reinforcing the J.D. Power brand," explains Ferron.

Predictably, J.D. Power clients who had their ads rejected were furious, and some pushed back. For example, in an October 14, 1988, letter the advertising manager of Toyota Motor Sales U.S.A. complained:

> Our advertising agency has advised us that Mazda is using the claim of "most reliable," based on your recent CSI survey. We requested to use "most reliable" for our compact van and full size SUV which were CSI winners in their respective categories. Our request was denied by your company. Please explain why Mazda can use this claim and Toyota cannot. Documents detailing our concern are attached for your review.

The document prepared by the staff of Saatchi & Saatchi, Toyota Motor Sales U.S.A.'s advertising agency, attempted the very data mining the J.D. Power advertising policy rejected. For instance, the document noted, the Toyota Land Cruiser was "Rated #1 in 'Vehicle Repair and Reliability Measure' with a score of 109 vs. the segment average of 86." The Mazda pickup, the document noted, was "Rated #1 in 'Vehicle Repair and Reliability Measure' with a score of 135 versus the industry segment average of 113." By setting up this equivalency, Saatchi & Saatchi felt that its claim to "most reliable" was justified.

In another example, Chrysler's ad agency sought to run a full-page newspaper ad that said one of its cars was better than five other models it supposedly "beat." The ad was rejected. Chrysler responded that it paid for the data, the campaign was factually accurate, and that J.D. Power had no say in the matter. Dave responded that if Chrysler ran the ad in question, he would run an ad that put the satisfaction scores of Chrysler in the context of all the cars, not just the five the ad agency had cherry-picked. Chrysler backed down.

Enforcement of the company's advertising policies became a major department within the company. Linda Hirneise, a twenty-six-year veteran of the company, worked closely with Dave, Ferron, and fifteen other people to control the use of the J.D. Power brand and logo in advertising. "We wanted to make sure we were not diluting the brand," Hirneise says. "We went through excruciating pain to protect the validity of information."

Since 2001, Cindy Jewett has managed the team responsible for the licensing of the J.D. Power and Associates brand for use by clients in promotional programs, including the J.D. Power award program. Her team reviews and approves all advertisements—both print and broadcast. Companies wanting to use the J.D. Power brand must adhere to guidelines controlling how the logo and trophy could appear. "Our goal is to be consistent, apply our rules fairly, and treat all clients similarly," Jewett says. Usually, the rules are pretty obvious. When a client requested an exception to the rules, many times Dave was consulted. "He would always do what advanced the integrity, independence, and influence of the company."

It was Graham Phillips, head of Ogilvy & Mather from 1989 to 1992, who first suggested there was a revenue stream to be had in licensing the J.D. Power brand for use in client advertising. The initial fee was a modest $350 for the rights to advertise for ten months. The company wisely insisted on a quiet period so as not to dilute the value of the award to the forthcoming awardees; Dave understood that one year's top rankers might be next year's runners-up.

The company incurred substantial costs in managing the advertising program. In addition to the internal staff, the company retained a media monitoring service to police advertisements in print, broadcast, and the web for unapproved uses of the J.D. Power brand. Unauthorized claims from parties in the auto industry were rare. Sometimes a car dealer ran a local ad with an unauthorized reference to J.D. Power and Associates. A cease-and-desist letter usually put a stop to such uses. Over the years, the company has found peculiar uses of its brand in ads by gunsmiths, closet organizers, and mom-and-pop businesses in industries J.D. Power has never ranked. After a time, the policing of ads became so labor-intensive that Dave suggested that $350 per ad was insufficient. "Double it," he suggested. Hirneise said the carmakers would never go for $700. "Fine," Dave said. "Make it $750." In fact, the carmakers didn't complain. By 2005, this part of the business contributed substantially to the bottom line.

The results of these brand-protecting policies were grander than Dave predicted. At one point, the company calculated that the advertising program generated annually more than ten billion print impressions while television commercials referencing the brand exceeded a hundred and fifty thousand.

"Dave used the J.D. Power awards to drive the interest in the research at the senior executive level on down, with a focus on positive change," says Pete Marlow, the company's vice president of corporate communications. "The awards provided transparency of results, established something to strive for, and gave the carmakers and dealers something to talk about when they achieved their goals." Moreover, the awards created opportunities for J.D. Power to sell its consulting services to both carmakers that did well and won awards and those who didn't. "The carmakers that were ranked highest wanted to stay ahead and would engage us for best practices and continuous improvement to stay ahead of the competition," Marlow says. "Carmakers who did not do well would hire us to better understand how to drive their performance forward."

Dave understood perfectly the ethical challenges this business model created. "You can't be both the referee and the coach at the same time," he notes. "We had to create and maintain very strong firewalls between the brand licensing side of the business and the proprietary consultative side." Just as they had created a barrier between the survey teams and the trainers, the advising side could in no way benefit, or even be perceived to benefit, from the licensing side.

"It's not a perfect solution," says Marlow, whose job included creating those firewalls and enforcing the separation of the business units involved in these tasks, "but as long as we are disciplined, it has served us well."

Thanks to all the advertising with the tagline "According to J.D. Power and Associates . . . " the J.D. Power brand quickly became internationally associated with the consistent and accurate expression of excellence as defined by the customer. It became as trusted as *Consumer Reports*, and even more credible because its conclusions represented more than the opinions of a few editors or testers. J.D Power and Associates, alone and unchallenged, stood for the independent voice of the customer.

Developing a Meaningful Award

In 1992, Dave decided to create the emblem to honor the winners of the various J.D. Power and Associates studies. The idea emerged from an advertisement that the advertising agency representing Acura submitted for review. Acura had recently been ranked first in sales satisfaction, and to graphically represent that achievement, the art director had framed the achievement in a trophy format. The ad agency told Dave that if he approved the ad, it would turn over the rights to the trophy design. Ogilvy & Mather's Phillips encouraged Dave to create a physical award and, what's more, to have a formal awards ceremony, like the Oscars, where excellence in automobiles could be formally recognized. An industry-wide awards ceremony did not work out, but the advertising community embraced the idea of having a physical representation of a good showing on the J.D. Power rankings.

Dave turned to his daughter-in-law, Julie McCracken Power, an art director formerly with the advertising agency Foote, Cone & Belding, to design the trophy. Dave sent her the Acura design and asked her to create something with classic lines. As a possible model, he also included a tombstone-like trophy with a clock in it that he had lying around the house. Julie teamed up with J.D. Power associate Patty Patano and created the well-known crystal slab trophy with the J.D. Power and Associates seal. The tagline on the trophy was "The Voice of the Customer." To manufacture the trophy, the company went to the same firm that produced the famed Oscar statuettes for the Academy of Motion Picture Arts and Sciences.

Dave decided he would announce only one award for each category; there would be no runners-up. "In this way," he says, "everybody knows who's on top." The Saturn division of GM was one of the first carmakers to use the J.D. Power awards in a strategic fashion to promote its brand. Saturn purchased trophies for every single one of its dealerships.

"What's great about the J.D. Power award is that it was not Dave's personal opinion," says brand licensing director Jewett. "It's the carmaker's customers, the people who own and use the product every day, who decide. The study drives the awards. The awards don't drive the studies." The company also organizes award presentations for the individual manufacturers, with a representative of the company—often Dave or Jamey in the early years—on hand at the event. "After a company receives an award, they might want an event to celebrate with employees and leverage with the media."

Opening Up to 20/20

Dave's confidence in his company's integrity and transparent methodology was tested in 1991 when the ABC investigative television newsmagazine *20/20* approached J.D. Power and Associates to do a segment on the business of ranking automobiles in terms of customer satisfaction. On the air since 1978, *20/20* had developed a reputation for hard-hitting exposés in the style of CBS's *60 Minutes*. Hugh Downs and Barbara Walters co-anchored the show; John Stossel was to be the segment's correspondent. Stossel's "Give Me a Break" segments usually featured a skeptical look at subjects, such as unethical business practices, government regulations, and junk science.

The overture from *20/20* represented a benefit as well as a risk for J.D. Power and Associates. A positive piece would further cement Dave and J.D. Power as the foremost independent exponent of the voice of the customer in the automobile and other industries. The risk for the company was that the message would be out of Dave's control. It was the era of "ambush journalism." Dave understood that TV programs such as *20/20* thrived on conflict and, in their quest for ratings, fairness sometimes went out the window. To make this decision, Dave reached out to senior managers, including J Ferron and John Hammond.

"'What questions do we not want to get asked?' we asked ourselves," Dave recalls. "The answer was, there are no questions about our process that we could not respond to accurately." Ferron agreed that "opening the kimono" was the best course, noting that the strongest media relations strategy is always to be open if a company has nothing to hide. With Hammond's coaching,

Dave considered the questions the *20/20* producers were likely to raise and practiced his responses. They had ten days to prepare. Associates, if they were approached, were encouraged to remember what they could say to *20/20* producers (they could describe their responsibilities) and what they could not say (revealing proprietary processes or private client information). Although the company at the time employed two hundred coders, many of them part-time, it had a solid survey system in place, and excellent supervisors. "We did a marvelous job of being open but remaining confidential on the surveys," Dave recalls.

In the spring of 1991, a *20/20* camera crew descended on the Agoura Hills office and over the course of three days taped interviews with Dave and dozens of associates. As Dave suspected, the producers wanted to determine if J.D. Power and Associates' surveys were truly an unbiased and independent expression of customer satisfaction, or if the company was pandering to the car manufacturers. This went to the heart of the values of independence and integrity that Dave fought so dearly to establish. The *20/20* program would be the test of whether he succeeded.

The news program broadcast the segment, called "Car of the Year," on May 31, 1991. The segment opened with John Stossel noting that, next to the purchase of one's home, for most people the purchase of a car is the most expensive financial transaction. With so many cars to choose from, how can consumers know which are the most dependable? To answer this question, Stossel went through a series of vignettes. First, he fanned out a pile of automotive industry magazines, each of which ranked cars and bestowed awards for their "Car of the Year." Yes, the editors tested cars, but the tests were conducted by professional race-car drivers and the test cars were submitted by the carmakers. Stossel suggested that the cars were probably pretty carefully selected and maybe professional drivers rate cars differently than average motorists. He then undermined the independence of these magazines by revealing that many of them had cozy relationships with the carmakers, and that their reporters accepted paid junkets and even moonlighted for the carmakers. Could such reporters be unbiased?

Stossel then turned his attention to another potential resource of objective advice: *Consumer Reports*, which also tested and rated cars. Unlike the magazines, *Consumer Reports* purchased the vehicles it tested anonymously, and it did not accept advertising or allow its ratings to be publicized by advertisers. All that was encouraging, Stossel said, but *Consumer Reports* ratings still had two limitations: the ratings were based on a single, or possibly two, test vehicles; and the testing was done by a handful of automobile experts. Maybe it would be more effective to rate cars based on hundreds or thousands of evaluations by regular drivers. "People in the know," Stossel suggested, "turn to J.D. Power and Associates."

"The picture the world got of J.D. Power and Associates was that of a consistent, ethical, open organization," Ferron says. "Viewers took away the impression that everything at J.D. Power and Associates was above board, that the next time they saw a J.D. Power rating, they could be confident that it's a reliable expression of the voice of the customer."

Protecting the Integrity of the Research

Dave went to extraordinary lengths to ensure the integrity of both the process and the results of market research attached to his name. Over the years, his deep knowledge of the auto industry kept the company from making inadvertent mistakes. Before he allowed something suspicious to be published, he scrupulously established its accuracy. For example, for one of its car tire satisfaction surveys, a critical response about Michelin tires caught his eye. The questionnaires went to recent purchasers of Chevrolet pickup trucks. Dave knew that Chevrolet pickups were not equipped with Michelin tires. Yet a response from a Chevrolet pickup truck owner was very critical of Michelin tires. The response was so negative (and the sample so small) that it threatened to lower the ratings on Michelin. If this was the fair assessment of customer satisfaction with the tires, so be it. But Dave wanted to avoid a mistake. He took it upon himself to call the respondent. When he got the truck owner on the phone, Dave asked, "Are you sure there are Michelin tires on the truck?" The man answered yes, he was sure. Dave said, "Would you mind doing me a favor and go out to just make sure?" A few minutes later, the man came back on the line and apologized; the tires were in fact made by another manufacturer. Dave adjusted the tire satisfaction survey.

Even when Dave played an infrequent practical joke, he looked to ensure the accuracy of J.D. Power research results data. Dave Sargent recalls a conversation he had with Dave over an upcoming research study that included cars from Renault as well as a number of other carmakers. Dave asked Sargent how he expected Renault would do on the rankings. "I thought about it and said that Renault would probably end up a little below average in the rankings," Sargent says. "I'll bet you a dinner that Renault will rank much higher than average," Dave responded. Sargent accepted the bet.

In due course, one department within J.D. Power and Associates calculated the raw scores. Another department, working independently from the first, then used the raw data to generate the rankings. Sargent had seen the raw scores and it seemed to him that he'd won the bet, but when the rankings were circulated internally, Renault came out very high. "It struck me that the raw data didn't really support the ranking," he recalls. "I asked that the calculations be re-analyzed. Same results. I spent two days fretting over the data." Eventually, Dave cracked and confessed that he made the department provide just Sargent with temporarily incorrect rankings for Renault. Sargent was right and eventually he got a free dinner out of it. It was a practical joke, but Dave was reassured that if any mistakes crept into the results, his people had enough expertise and sense to question the numbers.

Dave had zero tolerance for staff who cut corners or compromised the integrity of the company. At one point, he received a phone call from a Honda dealer in Oxnard, California, thanking him for rating this particular dealership as the number-one dealer on the strength of its showing on the latest J.D. Power dealer survey. There was just one problem: the results the dealer quoted hadn't been publicly released yet. The only explanation could be that J.D. Power and Associates had a leak. Dave conducted a little detective work and determined that one of his employees in the data processing area had a friend working at the Oxnard dealership. Dave fired the offending staffer on the spot. He wanted to send the unmistakable message that such behavior would not be tolerated.

The Five O'Clock Shadow

Great ideas, such as the way the brand was marketed, were not often born as agenda items of a team meeting held around a conference table. As the owner of the company, Dave had a brainstorming style that was decidedly more casual.

"Dave was not a person who set up meetings or rigorously followed a calendar," says longtime company leader Steve Goodall. "He would check in. He wanted to know how things were going."

Often, he practiced management by walking around, which many key team members found comfortable and useful.

"If you were working late in the office and he'd come walking down the hall and see you there, he'd always come in and talk about whatever was going on," recalls Tom Gauer, who served as senior director of automotive retail research. "The idea of normal bureaucratic channels, that would be in an organization, was not the way he lived or ruled the company." Gauer, who started at J.D. Power while he was still in college, saw Dave as a father figure and "a stately gentleman who knew everything."

"His passion for the business was infectious," recalls Charles Mills, who served as publications editor and also came to the company very young. He says the "incredibly informative and educative time" with the company's chief was made possible by Dave's willingness to interact in a collaborative manner rarely granted to junior staff at more traditional firms.

Dave's stature with the staff made the casual interactions all the more powerful. "It was that personal contact, with him walking down the hall at the end of the day, where you'd get these gems and insights," Gauer says, adding that Dave continued to do this even after the company had hundreds of employees and he presided in an imposing corner office.

Jamey Power connected his father's leadership style to his family's educational background. "The staff interacted with him almost like they would a favorite college professor. He could really light the creative spark and inspire people. And he would challenge them, in that kind of Jesuit education way. Sometimes he would ask questions just to provoke a more inspired and creative thought process."

Goodall recalls that attitude stretching back to when he was hired as well. During the interview process, "I was struck by how relaxed he seemed to be." Goodall was meeting with different firms as part of his job search, and Dave was his third and final interview. "He didn't actually put his feet up on his desk, but I almost had a feeling he could have. It was more kick-back, and we just talked."

"He'd come to my office late in the afternoon and bullshit," recalls John Rettie, editorial director through most of the 1990s, who says he always found the discussions pleasant. "Other people in the office would be looking for Dave, and they couldn't find him. They'd come by my office and say, 'Oh, there you are.'"

Goodall had the same experience, often at the same time of day. "Dave would come into my office, typically about five o'clock, after the business day was done, so there weren't interruptions." What began as chitchat could turn strategic. "A lot of the discussions struck me more as brainstorming sessions," he says. Then, "time would kind of get away from both of us, and you'd look at your watch and it was eight o'clock."

While those evening sessions were fruitful, they frustrated some staffers, who came in early and wanted to knock off at five. But, says Rettie, with Dave the practice went deeper than just a quirky management style. "Do you want the honest truth? J.D. Power was Dave Power's total life, his hobby, everything else. If you were going to play with him in his sandbox, you had to play when he was in the sandbox."

But if Dave's style was a bit obsessive, his method was nothing but collegial. He was widely regarded as generous with credit for good ideas and willing to give his people the space and power to generate their own projects. "Often, it was five o'clock on a Friday," recalls Loretta Seymour, a senior director at J.D. Power and Associates, when his "outside-the-box exploration" would come to light. Dave would have dug into the data and found something that interested him. "And he would bring that nugget and would say, 'Did you know that?' and follow it up with, 'Isn't there something we could do with this?'"

"He was the visionary," Seymour explains. "Our job was to get from here to that vision. You always felt that entrepreneurial spirit at every level and every dimension." The result was a steady progression of "organic, new ideas," and "Dave's mode was, if you came up with an idea, then you owned it. Then you had to create it, produce it, and sell it."

Dave's ability to surround himself with the right type of people played a key part in the success of such an organic operation, and he and his wife, Julie Power, fostered a family-like attitude, even as the company grew. When Dave moved the company headquarters to new, larger offices in Agoura Hills, California, in the late 1980s, he took steps to establish one of the area's first nonsmoking workplaces. And in characteristic fashion, he led by example. First, he cut out his practice of smoking cigars in his office. Then, taking a page from successful process-improvement practices, he incentivized the staff to follow suit. He offered a bonus to employees who quit smoking and another bonus if they were still not smoking six months later. Eighteen associates accepted the company's offer, and the nonsmoking environment actually became a draw for prospective employees.

The policy had a far-reaching effect, which Dave would only learn years later. He was in a supermarket, and a man saw the J.D. Power logo on his shirt. The man approached Dave and asked if he worked for the company. When Dave said yes, the man responded, "You know, Mr. Power was a great person, because he got my wife to give up smoking and saved her life." Recalling the incident with a smile, Dave says he then told the man who he was.

That attitude about the Powers was widely shared among associates, recalls Linda Hirneise, who had been with the firm for a decade when plans were made to celebrate its twenty-fifth anniversary in 1992. She was asked to say a few words, so she gathered some thoughts from colleagues, and she asked Dave what he had hoped to get out of the founding of the firm. "Dave said, 'I'd always hoped to be able to build a house for my wife on Kauai on Hawaii,'" Hirneise recalls. She realized the associates felt so strongly about this family-run firm, "that's what the employees of J.D. Power at the twenty-fifth anniversary of the firm wanted to do—they wanted to build a house for Dave and Julie Power on Kauai. We didn't get that opportunity, but we would have hand-built that house."

Late in Dave's career, with the company regularly reaching new heights, Dave and Julie's life together hit rocky times. Julie's multiple sclerosis, which had manifested in the early 1980s, had grown more debilitating by the year 2000. She had been Dave's constant companion on the road, and even though those trips tapered off, she still accompanied him when she could, even wheelchair-bound. But without her by his side, Dave's passion for getting out into the field also waned. Julie Power passed away in April 2002; it was a personal turning point for Dave and signaled his eventual exit from the business. He turned it over to a larger operation, the McGraw-Hill Companies (now McGraw Hill Financial), a group that he and his children selected because of McGraw-Hill's own family-built roots. "I can safely say, on behalf of all associates, colleagues, and clients, that J.D Power and Associates lost a huge part of its soul and character when Julie passed away," Hirneise recalls, "and Dave lost his inspiration, too."

Continual Evolution

The sort of evolution J.D. Power and Associates had experienced by its twenty-fifth year mostly centered around serving the automobile industry, despite the firm's early work in the consumer goods and services segment. As J.D. Power's automotive business flourished in the 1990s, Dave decided to penetrate other industries. He applied his concepts to the personal computer industry, which had become a massive, demand-driven market. Dave found that the new technology was so unfamiliar that, Dave believed, consumers were functionally uninformed. "It was so driven by jargon," Dave says, "that there was no way a consumer could keep up with all the necessary information and make an effective buying decision."

As always, he faced resistance. His first hurdle was to convince computer makers that J.D. Power and Associates could offer relevant information more economically than what they were getting from established industry market analysis companies, such as Dataquest and the Gartner Group. (Gartner purchased Dataquest in 1995.)[1] In 1990, Dave's challenge was to establish J.D. Power as a credible, independent service that had the skills to deliver sophisticated marketing information from computer buyers. The industry wasn't completely alien to them—J.D. Power had been doing work for printer manufacturer Epson for a decade. In fact, the customer satisfaction and reseller opinion surveys for Epson provided templates for other computer industry surveys that J.D. Power and Associates would offer. Its first study, in which consumers rated computer manufacturers on quality, came out in June 1991. Texas-based Dell Computer Corp. took the top spot. Just as carmakers had been doing for many years, Dell loudly touted the survey results in full-page advertising.

IBM eventually got out of the PC business, an outcome, Dave believes, that could have been avoided had IBM been more willing to listen to outside voices. The irony is that IBM actually had a robust commitment to customer satisfaction. The company had implemented a customer satisfaction tracking program associated with a bonus system; bonuses were awarded every year IBM's PCs improved in customer satisfaction. Based on their internal measures, IBM quality was good and there was little reason to believe its customers were not satisfied. IBM wasn't a subscriber to the J.D. Power and Associates PC study. As was its practice, Dave published only the top ten manufacturers to the media; only subscribing companies could see all the detailed rankings. Nevertheless, the whole report was leaked and ended up being covered on NBC's *Today* show in 1992. Apple Computer occupied the top spot, followed by Dell and Compaq. Dave says, "I was told that IBM Chairman John Akers was in a hotel room shaving when he heard the report and immediately got on the phone with his staff, demanding to know how IBM's PCs could be rated so low."

IBM refused to comment on the survey and dismissed the results as not relevant for corporate buyers. Although it could choose to publicly ignore the J.D. Power Personal Computer Report, privately IBM executives had to be worried. In the weeks following the report, Dell reported a dramatic increase in the volume of PC sales, even as IBM lost market share in the market it had created. Despite having four meetings with IBM, Dave failed to talk them into buying the syndicated survey. Reluctantly, he backed off from his work for the computer industry. "I believe that if IBM had access to independent VOC information, it would have known a lot more of what customers were actually thinking and could have made adjustments that might have kept the company in the PC market," he says. "They had a mindset that they were the computer experts and those other upstarts did not know how to do it."

The computer industry was just one of the many industries into which Dave and his team steered the company's services. Dave's goal of bringing his voice of the customer to the telecommunications, utilities, and financial services sectors was particularly bolstered by a new office in Connecticut, which opened in the early 1990s. At first, non-automotive clients were dubious. "You know about market research, but not in our industry," Mark Rees, who managed the Connecticut office before becoming chief research officer, recalls hearing. But Rees convinced them that there were "enough commonalities across industries" for the J.D. Power style of market research to be effective, and as prospective clients saw the objectivity and quality of the research, business grew. It was an evolution that would continue, even as the businesses became more complex and the challenges multiplied.

Succession Planning

Through much of the company's evolution, Dave was clearly at the helm, but after many years and a challenging rate of growth, even an eponymous leader must carefully distribute leadership responsibilities and eventually promote a new captain to take the rudder. Dave began to look within the company, within his own family, and externally through the ranks of available management talent for a successor who would continue the J.D. Power operation, build on its success, and make the company less dependent on the rainmaking of one man.

More than a decade of succession planning began in the early 1990s, when the company first experienced a robust growth spurt. With growth came more organizational responsibilities, such as adding structure to an expanding network of staff, services, and offices. Processes needed to be standardized, as did financial management and talent development. All these necessary functions ate into Dave's time and passion, which had always been client and study development. "Management tasks were taking up more and more of Dave's time," recalls Steve Goodall, "and I could sense a growing source of frustration." Dave began to search for the right "partner" to share some essential management duties and free him up for more client development. Former leaders of large consulting firms were brought in on trial bases and internal staff members were tested as Dave's "number two," tackling programs such as performance reviews, goal-setting, and managing the financials. But in each case, the chemistry just didn't quite work. John Hammond was, for a time, considered to be the successor in place, but Dave and Hammond "at some point diverged in their thinking," Goodall explains. J Ferron had been recruited from NADA to expand J.D. Power's dealer presence and to provide a step-up management experience. Four other outsiders were then recruited to take leading—but short-lived—roles within the company. While each of these people brought unique experiences and talents, for various reasons none proved to be the right fit with Dave. "There were important subtleties in J.D. Power's business model, strategy, and market positioning that were evolving," recalls Goodall. "It took care and open-mindedness to fully 'get' what Dave was trying to achieve." And Dave's leadership style—discussing plans rather than giving orders—often did not jibe with people who'd cut their management teeth at other firms.

After a few frustrating years, Dave realized his approach was not paying dividends, and he decided to switch course a bit. He asked Steve Goodall to return to the home office. Goodall had developed the Detroit market into a multimillion-dollar business for J.D. Power and Associates, built a staff of twenty-five associates, and led company expansion into Canada. Along with Dave, he had made breakthroughs in working with the Big Three auto-makers. Additionally, his time in Detroit had led to expanded product offerings in automotive forecasting and automotive supplier quality. With this track record, Dave saw the future in developing Goodall as the overall company leader.

With Goodall's return, Dave asked Jamey to take the helm in Detroit, providing another leadership track that would bring his son into the heart of the business while allowing him to develop his own management abilities. That Jamey would now work in Detroit represented somewhat of a circular completion for the Power family. He was returning to the city his father had moved them away from at the beginning of his own career, when Jamey was just a toddler. But Jamey, like the other Power children, had grown up in the business and well knew the value of a Detroit presence.

As the oldest, and the namesake of the firm, Jamey had the strongest connection to the company among the Power children. But all of his younger siblings, who had "taped quarters," served as consumer testers, and performed other company tasks at home as children, had also tested themselves in the family business.

Dave and Julie's second child, Mary, conducted phone surveys and did programming in high school, saying later that it was her goal to "work in every department and be well versed." After college and a stint in the Pacific Northwest, Mary returned to the firm in the mid-1990s, moving from data collection to production areas to a growing non-automotive niche for the firm: travel. She became a key project manager in J.D. Power and Associates' travel and hospitality business, doing research on customer satisfaction. She recalls her own satisfaction at seeing their surveys spurring companies to improve and once called business associates at the Westin hotel chain, after they had topped the satisfaction survey due to introducing a new bed, to jokingly congratulate them on being "Best in bed again!"

Dave and Julie's third child, Jonathan, joined the J.D. Power and Associates research staff in 1993. He worked in CSI and SSI studies and then moved into the Vehicle Quality Group, where he worked on the syndicated Initial Quality Study and Vehicle Dependability Study. When the industry needed an improved measure, he played a key role in the redesign of these studies and helped with creating the start-up of the APEAL (Automotive Performance, Execution, and Layout) Study. He also managed manufacturer-specific proprietary studies focusing on helping manufacturers improve the overall quality of their vehicles. Like his father, Jonathan focused on the motivation behind consumer choices and took pride in how the firm's work impacted the consumer. He credits his father for inspiring an interest in psychology, for which he ultimately left the firm to pursue, becoming a family therapist and clinical psychologist.

Susan, the family's youngest, also followed in her father's footsteps, but not on a path that led through the doors of the company. She attended College of the Holy Cross, the Jesuit school that Dave had attended, and while there served for several years in the Coast Guard Reserve. After college, she crossed paths with staff of J.D. Power and Associates at her first job with a firm that provided concierge benefits to auto manufacturers' warranty programs. She later went on to work in an industry that had fueled a lifelong personal passion: golf. Susan had been urged by Dave to pursue the sport in high school. "Dad taught me following the more difficult obstacle ultimately was the more rewarding path," she recalls. "That has always stuck with me as a turning point in shaping me as a person." She went on to focus her career in golf administration and association management.

Whether or not the Power children tested their business acumen at the family firm, the organization and its founder set the four youths on their paths to successful pursuits, and when those interests overlapped with Dave's work, they became valuable additions to the company.

As Jamey settled into the Detroit office, with Goodall as his supervisor, Dave did a bit more restructuring in California. First, he asked Goodall to take over all of the company's research operations, which included a wide variety of both syndicated and proprietary studies, along with analysis, data processing, and fielding personnel who supported the execution and delivery of this research. Additionally, he had Goodall oversee the regional office in Connecticut as well as the company's IT, human resources, and financial operations. Jamey would go on to expand the operations in Detroit and also open a company office in Toronto.

These moves provided a couple of key benefits. They consolidated a number of functions under one person who reported to Dave. Goodall was allowed to build his management skills and gain a deeper understanding of the firm's financial position and processes. Jamey developed his own visibility in the key American automotive market but also gained valuable international experience, which would serve him well in his next position at the helm of J.D. Power's worldwide operations. Plus, these changes freed up Dave to focus on the company's overall strategy on the Power Information Network (PIN), which was just starting to gain real momentum in the marketplace.

The partnership seemed to work. By July 1996, Dave was ready to name Goodall as president. The press was regularly bringing up "the transition question" and speculation was significant. Dave had broached the topic informally with Goodall and, in Dave's characteristic, low-key fashion, the idea moved from his head to reality without fanfare. "I came back from vacation and went to my previous office, and Tom Shaver was sitting at my desk," Goodall recalls with a laugh. "I said, 'Oh, I'm out of a job.' Tom was kind of sheepish and said, 'Well, Steve, they moved your office up next to Dave's.'" While Goodall was vacationing, Shaver told him, "Dave kind of made an announcement that you're now the president."

Goodall went to see Dave. He said *Businessweek* had come to do an interview and the question came up, so, "I kind of accelerated the process," Dave told him. "I hope that's okay." Sure enough, the weekly magazine came out with the scoop, and soon *Automotive News* and other publications were calling. "And the story was out," says Goodall.

Goodall proved to be a great fit. In his two years at the home office, he had gained a much broader understanding of the firm. He had grown up in the business, been trained, and had a deep knowledge of J.D. Power's research capabilities. He was quite familiar with the company's leading clients and had the trust of J.D. Power's two hundred associates. Most important, he possessed the right mix of skills and temperament to partner with the founder and take the company to the next level.

Staying on Course

As the company transitioned to the new leadership team in 1997, Dave wrote a long memo summarizing his thoughts about the business and its prospects for growth. The twenty-page memo, penned just after the start of the new year, outlined a number of areas of concern and revealed the depth of Dave's business acumen. Addressed to Goodall, the letter contained plenty of praise for the company's progress, but it also illustrated opportunities for the company in a number of areas.

Dave cited "major strides" in their work that would make 1996 a banner year, with a more than 30 percent increase in revenue.

He also shared his feeling that the brand awareness study commissioned by the firm had turned out "better than we expected." With more than 50 percent of U.S. adults now aware of the firm's name—an awareness that spiked to 75 to 85 percent among new-car-buying prospects—and "we have a dominant awareness and strong image" among the press and industry, Dave wrote. "This enviable positioning as the voice of the consumer allows us access to all levels of the client organizations, and our licensed advertising claims are much desired."

J.D. Power's brand equity, he said, "is our greatest asset" and "needs to be nurtured and developed in concert with the goals and objectives of the company." That meant the development of more product-information services stretching across many forms of media, from television programs to CD-ROMs. Providing these services to the consumer, Dave noted, would also increase the interest among manufacturers and service providers "in what information and counsel we are able to give them about their customers."

In a paragraph titled "Blue Chip Client Base," Dave listed the incredible array of clients the firm had amassed in recent years. While automakers still loomed large, the variety of clients beyond that sector read like a well-balanced investment portfolio:

> Our roster of clients has always included the leading automobile and truck manufacturers (i.e. GM, Ford, Toyota, Honda, Volkswagen, BMW, Mercedes-Benz, Chrysler, Navistar, Volvo, Mitsubishi, etc.) but in the past ten years, we have been adding top level OEM suppliers (i.e. TRW, Allied Signal, GE, Dow, Monsanto, Motorola, DuPont, Johnson Controls, United Technologies, Goodyear, Michelin, Pirelli, etc.) . . . Our largest annual survey in terms of revenue, the Magazine Readership Survey among

new car and truck buyers, provides an equally impressive list of clients in the publishing world, and advertising agencies such as Time Warner, Conde Nast, Hearst Corporation, Newsweek, Forbes, Business Week, McCann-Erickson, J.W. Thompson, Ogilvie, BBDO, Campbell-Ewald, etc.[2]

Dave noted, however, that although no one client accounted for more than 5 percent of company revenue, J.D. Power's goals were not just to continue to serve this diverse client base. The consumer market, he said "promises to be our most valued client base eventually."

But Dave also cited a couple of "sleeping assets" that in his estimation had not been given enough attention during the company's rapid growth period. The media study was his first target. Calling it "much more than a magazine readership survey," he noted that it included new car and truck purchasing behavior plus demographic and psychographic information, unavailable anywhere else in the industry, except perhaps at General Motors. "We now have nine years of comparable data based upon 450,000 new car and truck buyers. . . . Analysis of this database is virtually nonexistent in terms of looking at the marketing information that is available as opposed to magazine readership." He challenged staff to mine the data for insights on consideration and purchase trends among vehicle types. Without that type of effort, he said, "we have a tremendous asset that is dying of neglect."

Similarly, the annual Dealer Attitude Survey had provided the firm with the "immeasurable advantage of staying abreast of the developments in automotive distribution in the U.S.," Dave said, but was another sleeping asset. The survey created a ten-year-plus database that "provides us with an authoritative view of the industry that no other company has." However, he wrote, "We have not found time to analyze this database as a strategic tool, instead of concentrating on publishing the annual report and going on to the next project. The only time we revisit it is to use it as a tactical tool when the client raises a specific issue or question."

Finally, though, he used the example of another company product: forecasting, which had been a formal company department for a decade but only recently turned from a sleeping asset to a marketable service due to the efforts of Goodall and the Detroit office.

> Forecasting has become the best example of what can be done with an injection of aggressive and practical management to a databased asset assembled by the company to fulfill an industry need. In this activity, we have developed both information databases as well as proprietary software programs to analyze the data, and these are tremendous assets that are zero on our books. This is one of many information concepts that the company has developed that struggled for its very existence, because we were unable to execute an effective marketing program which includes the proper packaging and pricing of the products and a strong and visible commitment to current and prospective clients. Growth potential is still very bullish, especially as we expand it globally.[3]

As the company's evolution continued, Goodall inherited the strategic planning vision, putting his own spin on company growth. "My strategy was going wide and going deep," he says. "Going wide was different industries. We were going to take customer satisfaction and package that, and go into other industries." Dave was supportive. "He had a passion about the travel industry, about the home-building industry, about the banking industry," Goodall recalls. "Each of those became multimillion-dollar businesses in their own account."

The second half of his strategy concerned the long-sought success of the Power Information Network. "Going deep was my way of emphasizing and positioning PIN," says Goodall. "Okay, we do the surveying piece. But think about PIN and the detailed nature that allows us to go much deeper in automotive than just measuring customer perception about vehicles and dealers. This allows us to understand transactions and pricing points and real demand at the core level." This, of course, had long been Dave's goal, so Goodall had the founder's blessing on both strategies.

In the final four years of the 1990s, the company experienced a heady period of growth. Revenues grew at a compound annual rate of nearly 30 percent. New offices were opened in London, Tokyo, Singapore, and Orange County, California. There was a rapid expansion of customer satisfaction studies in many new industries, including financial services, utilities, telecommunications, travel, and residential construction, among others. Additionally, with Dave's strong commitment and focus, PIN was gaining wider acceptance among both U.S. and Canadian auto manufacturers, dealers, and financial providers and was beginning to move from being a large investment and start-up for Power in the early years to a successful, growing, and profitable business.

At the turn of the millennium, Dave recognized that the leadership team would benefit from external experience and counsel on the board, which up until then had consisted of him, Jamey, and Goodall. "We were growing so fast," Dave recalls, "that I felt to have outside, objective feedback was very important." In 1999, he approached Ernie Pomerantz, who was in the process of retiring from Warburg Pincus. Dave had gotten to know Pomerantz well while both of them served on the board of Cobalt Inc., an Internet start-up dealer website and traffic-management company backed by Warburg Pincus. A few years later, Dave further expanded the board by inviting Jerry Pyle to join it. Pyle was president of the Friedkin Companies, which owns Gulf States Toyota and several other automotive and non-automotive businesses. Pyle had previously held senior positions at both Ford and Chrysler.

By the late 1990s, Jamey had been moved from helming the Detroit office to expanding the company's international reach. He also stepped into a new role as ambassador for the company, representing the family and the J.D. Power brand to an expanded network of international offices and to clients and media contacts around the world. Speaking engagements and sales calls had taken too much of Dave's time in previous years; his management restructuring allowed him to step away from some of those day-to-day activities.

With the expansion of the board and restructuring of top leadership duties, J.D. Power's team continued to transition the company into a more mature and more professionally managed operation, and its leaders began to discuss making it into a public company. The extensive growth and evolution had made the J.D. Power brand more valuable than ever, with continual and expanding opportunities. It was an approach that ultimately made the company very attractive to suitors, who were lining up with their checkbooks to take over the firm. Although it would be five years into the twenty-first century before this family-run firm would make its first ownership change, J.D. Power and Associates was positioned to take on ever more vexing challenges.

CHAPTER EIGHT

TOUGH CALLS

When Dave Power took on his first professional project in the automotive industry, an audit for Ford Tractor, he became aware that there were pockets of the industry where he would encounter less than ethical behavior. That he might have interactions with individuals whose values conflicted with those established by his upbringing and Jesuit education did not deter him, but the moral failings of others also did not water down his own ethics. After he established his company, he and his staff saw troubling behavior from time to time in the field, and Dave's tendency was to do what he could to correct those problems. In the case of Honda, for instance, a disturbing situation with dealers arose out of the company's overwhelming success.

The Honda Scandal

For car manufacturers—as with any industry—moving inventory is a constant, make-or-break concern. For more than a decade, from the early 1980s to the mid-1990s, Honda enjoyed a situation most car companies could only dream of. Thanks to a combination of the genuinely high quality of Honda vehicles, glowing reviews from *Consumer Reports* and *Car and Driver*, and the Voluntary Restraint Agreement (the 1980s import quota limiting the number of automobiles Japanese automakers could export to

America), Accords, Civics, and Preludes became highly desirable. Prices shot upward, often exceeding the listed sticker price by up to $1,000. Dealers brazenly called the added assessments "additional dealer profit" or an "import tax."[1] Customers were not deterred. Owning a Honda dealership at that time was like having a license to print money.

The greed unleashed by this distortion of the market led to a series of events that offended Dave's sense of integrity and fair play. In the early 1980s Dave began hearing rumors that Honda executives were demanding under-the-table payments for granting dealers favorable allocations of Honda cars, and that business people who wanted to open Honda franchises were required to pay bribes. "After I spoke at dealer roundtables or other dealer groups, honest retailers would quietly complain about the corrupt practices," Dave recalls. In 1983, a small group of Honda dealers asked Dave for help in investigating the problem, requesting that he keep their identities in confidence. "I never got anything specific. Some were just repeating rumors and wanted to know if the gossip was true. It was always another dealer that had been shaken down."

Over the next few years, the evidence of corruption grew overwhelming. A woman at a dealership in Florida called Dave with a story of a "churn and earn" scheme whereby employees were required to use relatives' names and addresses on fake sales records so the dealership would qualify for more cars. Dave received firsthand accounts of dealers being required to fork over $60,000 in a brown paper bag if they wanted to be approved for a Honda franchise. A few years later, that figure had risen to nearly $1 million. According to Steve Lynch's *Arrogance and Accords: The Inside Story of the Honda Scandal*, Honda sales executives demanded—and got—luxury cars, Rolex watches, furnishings, and expensive suits.[2]

The dealers who reached out to Dave knew that he had influence with American Honda Motor Sales. "Many dealers implored me to speak to someone at the company about the growing problem," Dave says. Although he talked with hundreds of dealers, not one was prepared to make an accusation. "The dealers all feared retaliation from Honda," he says. "They felt they were liable to lose their franchise and the allocation of vehicles if they came forward to complain." When Dave quietly inquired with his contacts at Honda, the Honda executives said they would look into the rumors. He had the feeling he was being stonewalled.

In March 1983, with the corruption only getting more rampant, Dave decided to act. He wrote a personal letter to American Honda President Yoshihide Munekuni, mailing it to the executive's home in Rancho Palos Verdes:

> Dear Mr. Munekuni:
>
> This letter is written to you at your home because of the extreme need for confidentiality. As you probably know I have had conversations with both Mr. Fujita and Mr. Schmillen concerning a far ranging problem existing in the distribution of Honda automobiles throughout the United States. I want to discuss this matter with you in private, possibly at my office.
>
> The matter of financial irregularities and personal favors in the allocation of Honda automobiles first came to my attention three or four years ago, and I dismissed them as minor indiscretions that occur in all automotive distribution companies. However, in the past few months I have heard from a variety of sources that the Honda system is rampant with [inequitable] distribution policies inviting dealers to "pay" extra for more favorable allocations.

It is with the best wishes for Honda's continued success and my personal concern that these unethical and illegal practices be stopped, that I am approaching you with this information. I would hate to see the wonderful Honda image tarnished by a broadscale scandal attributable to a flaw in management control.[3]

Dave closed the letter by requesting a private meeting so the two could discuss the matter further. In due course, Munekuni's assistant contacted Dave and it was arranged for the two men to have breakfast at the Bel Air Sands Hotel, a neutral spot where they would not be spotted. Dave got there early and took a seat facing the door. He was surprised that the person who walked in was not Munekuni but Executive Vice President Cliff Schmillen. "Dave, what the hell is going on?" Schmillen said as he took a seat. Dave hesitated before speaking. He concluded that Munekuni wanted Schmillen to hear the allegations directly. Dave repeated the information about payoffs and bribes. He grew frustrated when Schmillen put down the rumors as sour grapes on the part of dealers who didn't receive the allocations or cars or were denied the franchise they wanted. But then Munekuni himself walked in and asked Dave to repeat the details of financial irregularities and personal favors. "Yoshihide was a good client of our studies and I considered him a friend," Dave says. "I owed him the truth, as embarrassing as it was." Munekuni ordered breakfast but didn't touch the meal. Grimly, he asked Dave for specifics, which Dave could not supply. Finally, Munekuni inhaled in consternation and said, "We'll get back to you."

His word was good. Dave was contacted by a law firm that Munekuni had hired to investigate. Dave spoke to more than fifty dealers in an attempt to gather documentation, but none were willing to make their accusations public. Dave was unable to provide the law firm with any of the documentation they needed. The investigation was shelved, with Honda taking no action. Munekuni "felt he had his hands tied," Dave recalls. In his book on the scandal, Lynch wrote, "No investigation, no meeting with the sales executives, no memos reminding employees of the conflict of interest policy, no notifying the human resources department of the alleged problems. The matter was dropped—it was all only a rumor, the officials said later. Honda's most significant opportunity of the 1980s to take action and put a stop to the payoffs was lost."[4]

Ten years went by before an FBI investigation finally revealed the scheme. By that point, the Voluntary Restraint Agreement had ended, and with Honda's factory in Marysville, Ohio, online there was finally a large enough supply of Accords to end the easy money. When a New Hampshire car dealer sued Honda, claiming it had put him out of business because he refused to pay bribes, years of under-the-table dealings became public knowledge. The federal government indicted dozens of Honda executives in one of the nation's biggest commercial bribery cases. The letter that Dave had sent Munekuni nine years earlier suddenly became an object of interest at the three-month trial in U.S. District Court in Concord, New Hampshire, where Dave was asked to read the letter to the jury.

Dave was the final witness in the case of *United States of America v. John W. Billmyer and Dennis R. Josleyn*. He had been called by the defense to present evidence—primarily the letter to Munekuni—that American Honda had been aware of the corruption for years. Twenty other defendants—fifteen American Honda sales executives, two Honda dealers, a lawyer, and two advertising executives—had previously pleaded guilty to related charges.[5] But

Billmyer, Honda's former senior vice president of sales, and Josleyn, the former West Coast zone manager, maintained their innocence. Their defense was basically that it was business as usual and tacitly approved by American Honda.

Dave's testimony "that he had warned Honda in 1983 about the corruption was splashed all over the national news," wrote Lynch in his book. "It was the most embarrassing of any statements made during the very public trial for American Honda."[6] But if the defendants believed that Dave's testimony would get them off, they were wrong. The defense did a good job of exposing American Honda as a sloppy organization but failed to demonstrate that the Japanese executives had condoned or covered up the corruption. Instead, the government showed that the defendants intentionally engaged in activities that defrauded Honda and had taken great care to conceal those activities from their superiors.

In closing arguments on May 19, 1995, the federal prosecutor took two hours to summarize for the jury what the defendants did wrong. The district court sentenced Billmyer to sixty months in prison and assessed him a fine of $125,000. Josleyn was sentenced to seventy-eight months in prison on one count and sixty months each on three other counts, to be served concurrently. Dozens of people went to jail or paid substantial fines. Virtually everyone on the American Honda sales and marketing staff was terminated.

Seeing John Billmyer sitting at the defense table reminded Dave about the one encounter he had with the former senior vice president of sales. It was in the mid-1980s, shortly after Dave had started asking questions about the bribes and payoffs. Munekuni had been withdrawn for some time but then invited Dave to Japan to be the first non-Honda person to see the new Legend, the first model to be released under Honda's new luxury division, Acura. Billmyer was invited on the trip as well, and the men ran into each other in the airport lounge. "Dave, what the hell do you think you're doing?" Billmyer whispered. Dave replied that many of the dealers were complaining. Billmyer cut him off. "It's none of your business. Just stay out of it." And then he was gone. That was the last time Dave had interacted with Billmyer until meeting in the courtroom ten years later.

Dave was pleased to play a small role in restoring a measure of justice. But his company paid a high price. As soon as the scandal started heating up in 1987, Munekuni was transferred to Japan and, in a move that Dave felt smacked of retaliation, Honda pulled the Dealer Tracking Study from J.D. Power and Associates. But two years after the trial, Honda quietly awarded the study to J.D. Power once again, and the company has it to this day.

A Redemptive Dollar Bill

The whole sordid Honda episode ended with a redemptive coda. Five years after the trial, Dave was sitting at his desk opening a letter he had received in the mail that morning and a dollar bill fell into his lap. The letter was from was S. James "Jim" Cardiges, the prosecutor's star witness against Josleyn and Billmyer. He had fought the charges up until the day the trial began but then suddenly pleaded guilty and cooperated with the U.S. attorney. He had succeeded Billmyer as Honda's top U.S. sales executive and admitted to being one of the greediest participants in the conspiracy. In colorful testimony, he described receiving cars, land, watches, vacations, and bags of cash. He provided eyewitness descriptions of similar payoffs on the part of the defendants. He was sentenced to sixty months in prison and assessed a fine of $364,000.

The dollar bill, Dave realized, had been mailed to Cardiges along with a survey J.D. Power and Associates usually sends out to new car buyers. Now out of prison, in a letter dated November 11, 1998, Cardiges was returning it:

Dear David,

The purpose of this correspondence is twofold. First, to thank you and your associates at J.D. Power for providing the customer and dealer survey information which the automotive industry, and the buying public utilizes so often to both improve their products and make more informative buying decisions, respectively.

As you may recall, I was the former Senior Vice President of the Honda Automobile Sales Division between 1988 and 1992. I was indicted, convicted, and incarcerated for receiving and conveying gifts and favors from and to numerous automobile dealers. The lack of applying basic ethical principles and the failure to disassociate with individuals that participated in illegal activities involving accepting gifts, was a character flaw on my part. I consider myself fortunate to both recognize, learn and pay for my former misjudgments.

I have now been given the opportunity to help other executives, in various fields, to avoid the same mistakes as early as possible in their careers. I anticipate two (2) decades of practicing ethical business standards in my future career. As Michael Josephson states so often, "character counts."

Secondly, please find attached the dollar bill that your corporation enclosed in a recent survey designed to assess the quality and service of a late model automobile which our family used to own, but was sold several years ago. Perhaps it can be directed toward another more useful purpose.

Last but not least, if I have embarrassed you or your company in the past, in any manner, I apologize profusely!

Thank you for taking the time to review this letter and I wish you and your associates continued success.

Sincerely,

Jim Cardiges[7]

The letter, framed, now hangs in Dave's office. "I use the letter in my business ethics lectures at Cal State University Northridge," he says. "I tell students that participating in unethical activities— even ones that appear condoned by the establishment—is like joining a street gang. Once you get in, you are hooked, and you have to live by their standards. And you have to live by what they do in an organization. Young people can get caught up in this kind of thing without realizing it."

The scandal was embarrassing, but American Honda recovered. In 1993, based on Dave's recommendation, Honda hired Dick Colliver, a twenty-year sales veteran with Mazda Motors of America, to rebuild Honda's ruined sales infrastructure. Just days after he was hired, Colliver was in meetings with the ten zone managers and their assistants from across the country who had been brought together. He learned about the organization and the issues, and evaluated which people he could keep on staff and "build around." But because nearly every executive at American Honda had been tainted by the scandal, "Sixty days later eight of them were gone," he recalls. "They had to be fired."

Personally Testing Audi's Safety

Dave's faith in market research and his deep knowledge of the auto industry led him to take personal chances that reflected his beliefs. In one instance, when Dave felt Audi was being unfairly maligned by both the press and public opinion, he personally tested the safety of the brand in question.

Audi, which traces its origins to 1909[8] and is headquartered in Ingolstadt, Germany, is a subsidiary of Volkswagen Group.[9] Volkswagen introduced the Audi brand to the United States in 1969.[10] Audi gained notoriety primarily for reported incidents of sudden, unintended acceleration. CBS aired an infamous *60 Minutes* episode in November 1986, that delved into the topic. The program aired interviews with people who had sued the company as well as footage showing an Audi 5000 apparently accelerating sharply when the brake pedal was pushed. Soon after the show aired, however, an investigation revealed that *60 Minutes* had filmed the acceleration with the help of a consultant who had altered the transmission.[11]

Regardless of the television scandal, Dave believes that virtually all such problems are the result of human error, when someone accidentally steps on the wrong pedal. He thought that the Audi had gotten a bad rap. In fact, he felt so strongly that Audi was the victim of bad faith that he actually purchased an Audi 5000 for his personal use. The car was reliable and well behaved. After an investigation, the National Highway Traffic Safety Administration (NHTSA) declared the car safe. But it took fifteen years for Audi sales to recover.[12] One positive legacy of this sad episode is that Audi was the first car manufacturer to introduce a brake interlock mechanism—now a standard safety feature on all cars—in which drivers are required to depress the brake pedal before the car can be shifted out of park.

A Challenge with DeLorean

If Audi suffered from an image problem in the U.S. market, a unique sports car with gull-wing doors had a different problem. The DeLorean suffered from a star complex.

John Z. DeLorean (who died in 2005) was a flamboyant car industry figure with a fabled career in the industry and is best remember as the founder of the ill-fated DeLorean Motor Company. Before that, however, he was an automotive engineer whose star rose quickly through General Motors. He put a large stamp on Pontiac, which he is credited with transforming from a producer of cars for senior citizens to a manufacturer of powerful machines that appealed to young people looking for a fast, stylish car. DeLorean, trained as an automotive engineer, championed the introduction of the GTO (Gran Turismo Omologato), a hot rod that is remembered as the industry's first "muscle car."[13] It was released to great acclaim and sharp sales in 1964, and DeLorean, always a consummate self-promoter, rode its success. He took a lead role in marketing the car, pushing GTO's image as a youthful, hard-charging machine to the discomfort of Pontiac's stodgier executives. In 1965, DeLorean was promoted to lead Pontiac, becoming the youngest division head ever seen at GM.[14]

He did not, however, concentrate solely on Pontiac. He lived a high-profile lifestyle and traveled the world on promotional stints. He gained a reputation as a jet-setting playboy, appearing often in stylish clothes and with famous people. Within the staid confines of GM, he was seen as a rebellious maverick, but that didn't stop him from rising even further in the company. He was promoted again in 1969, this time to lead the Chevrolet division, which he did to much acclaim, achieving sales of three million vehicles for Chevrolet in 1972. That same year DeLorean was made vice president of GM's entire car and truck production, and he seemed on a fast track to the company's top leadership job. But in April of 1973, DeLorean abruptly resigned from GM. He was forty-eight years old, and he told the media that he wanted to break out of the constraints of Detroit's corporate culture.[15] Soon after, he gathered investors and started his own company, intent on building his dream sports car. Named simply the DMC-12 but known as "the DeLorean," the two-seater had gull-wing doors, a stainless steel exterior, and featured a V6 engine that was jointly developed by three European automakers: Renault, Peugeot, and Volvo.[16]

It was about this time that DeLorean asked for Dave's help. Dave's old friend from Mazda, Dick Brown, had signed on to work with DeLorean, and the company asked J.D. Power and Associates first to assist it in an effort to acquire the U.S. distribution rights to cars produced by Alfa Romeo. DeLorean invited Dave to go on a mission with some of his chief auto designers to visit the Alfa Romeo assembly plant near Milan. At the time, the militant Red Brigades were terrorizing Italy with violence and sabotage. During Dave's visit to the Alfa Romeo plant, the Red Brigades threatened an action and the DeLorean mission was hustled out the back door and evacuated in armored vehicles. The negotiations never got very far after that.

Along with the startling political situation, Dave recalls the Italy visit because he got a key glimpse into DeLorean's personality. Dave had known DeLorean's reputation as a mover and shaker. At a dinner in Milan, as the good wine and food flowed, DeLorean held court. It was clear he had a sharp mind, was eloquent, and was good at reading people to respond to them on their level. At the table, he was mannerly, but in charge. "He would issue very profound statements," Dave recalls. Dave recognized in DeLorean a personality type that "hungered to have impact and get the confidence of others."

DeLorean asked Dave to perform a product clinic for the car under conditions of strictest secrecy. J.D. Power and Associates received a prototype and went to Beverly Hills and other high-income areas of Los Angeles to conduct static focus groups on product styling and price points. Reaction by potential drivers to the car's design was very positive. To estimate what price buyers would be willing to pay for the car, J.D. Power contrasted the new DeLorean vehicle with the Corvette, the Porsche, and other sports cars of its class. Dave evaluated the surveys and suggested that the retail price be set at $12,000 (which provided the genesis of the name DMC-12). Dave also offered an analysis of initial sales volume, but the evaluations turned out to be moot.

Fraud by DeLorean was the culprit. The vehicle's production was to be done in Northern Ireland, and DeLorean both issued a prospectus to potential investors and sought funding from the British government. But DeLorean took the retail price suggested by the J.D. Power study and, unbeknownst to Dave, doubled it. While he was at it, DeLorean took the J.D. Power sales estimates and doubled those, too. "I didn't see it until after it was published," Dave says. When many months later he learned about the exaggerated numbers, he was very angry. It was clear to him that by distorting the facts, DeLorean was using the imprimatur of J.D. Power and Associates in its attempts to raise investment capital. At this point, Dave terminated his relationship with DeLorean. "John DeLorean betrayed us," he says. "He took our honest research numbers and twisted them to promote his increasingly desperate search for capital."

Dave was not surprised to hear of DeLorean's fall from grace. In 1982, DeLorean was arrested by the FBI for drug trafficking, and the DeLorean Motor Company collapsed in a swarm of lawsuits the same year. Brown, who had good relationships with the dealers, never got caught up in the lawsuits. In DeLorean's high-profile criminal trial, his defense claimed entrapment by federal agents, and he was acquitted of the drug trafficking charges by a jury, but he never again gained respectability. As for the DeLorean DMC-12 sports car, it achieved pop culture immortality when it was featured in the sci-fi *Back to the Future* movie series but otherwise was viewed as a failure. J.D. Power and Associates had a claim against the company when it went bankrupt, but the claim was never satisfied.

The Secret Lemon Problem

The success of J.D. Power and Associates' research presented another ethical dilemma for Dave and his clients. Both market researchers and manufacturers had to deal with the penchant by the media for bad news.

In 1999, Dave had to address what an article published in the *New York Times Sunday Magazine* called the "Secret Lemon Problem." At first Dave didn't want to release unfavorable IQS rankings to the public (though, of course, J.D. Power and Associates released the full details to corporate buyers of the syndicated surveys). "What we were finding was the press, especially the television news, would call up the day that we would announce a study, and they'd want to know the bottom-five makes," he told the *Times*. "Not surprisingly, this emphasis on the bad news upset manufacturers at the bottom of the list," wrote reporter Timothy Noah, "all potential J.D. Power customers. So, J.D. Power instituted a policy in which, with few exceptions, only above-average rankings in syndicated studies are made public, while companies that rank below average are listed alphabetically in press releases."[17]

Dave's goal in controlling the release of names was always to promote quality, not embarrass anyone. But this control had an unintended consequence. Even the hint of forbidden fruit inspired otherwise lazy reporters to become investigative news hounds and sniff out the forbidden information, which suddenly had the smell of real news. Once they did—and there were always those among the subscribers who were eager to embarrass the competition by leaking the results—the stories always revealed the bottom five. The media's focus on the lowest-scoring cars "was exactly the opposite of what I wanted to see," Dave says. "Everyone was upset with us." In 1989, *Automotive News* angered Dave by publishing a leaked copy of the complete IQS, including the lower-ranked models.

The leaks got so bad that on July 3, 1991, Dave wrote a candid letter to the presidents of a number of carmakers subscribing to the IQS. The letter crystallized Dave's philosophy about not generally releasing the names of car companies at the bottom of the rankings and requested that automakers honor their confidentiality agreements. Excerpts from the letter reveal his thinking:

> J.D. Power and Associates is proud of its contribution by providing reliable and useful measures to the industry, but we are greatly disturbed by the harm that is being done to the general industry image and especially to a few of the manufacturers that may end up near the bottom of our rankings on a particular survey when one or more of our subscribing clients have individuals on their staff release the reports to the press.
>
> At J.D. Power and Associates, we have always attempted to accentuate the positives to the press. We only show the top-ranking nameplates or, at most, those that are above industry average. This serves to stimulate us all to participate in the race to continue to improve quality and customer satisfaction. The press is always out to get the

"whole" story and some individuals in the client companies have taken it upon themselves to provide the entire management summary of our reports within minutes of receiving them. It appears as though the press gets the information before top management in their own company gets to read the report.

In the recently released initial quality survey (IQS), the top five or ten nameplates were released along with the bottom five. Within hours, this information was published in newspapers throughout Europe and Asia. This is unfortunate because the emphasis is often switched to the bottom five by the popular press and leads to misinterpretation of the findings. This type of "bootleg" release has the potential to harm even the manufacturer involved and has never contributed to clear understanding about the studies by consumers.

Information released "out-of-control" has tremendous potential for misinterpretation. . . . We are taking additional steps to stop the information leaks from whatever source, but we are asking our clients to help out in any manner you can to impress upon your employees the need to secure J.D. Power and Associates' written permission before the information is released. . . .

In the meantime, I am requesting that each of our clients help correct any possible violations of information control within their respective organizations. It is a serious matter, and *enough is enough*.[18]

When Dave could get them alone, the senior executives of the Big Three often confessed to him that they actually preferred to see all the rankings made public. This was a heresy they could not admit in public. "Most of the car company CEOs rose from finance and manufacturing, disciplines that favored data and analysis," Dave says. "The CEOs wanted to hear about real problems so they could correct them; they wanted to make decisions based on objective information and they were frequently frustrated in their ability to get that data from their own operations." Some of the CEOs privately complained to Dave that they often received unreliable research findings from marketing, engineering, parts and service, and other departments. The CEOs believed those findings to be biased to advance the narrow agendas of the departments sponsoring them. Dave recalls a CEO telling him that having independent market research studies available for scrutiny by everyone helped him make decisions.

When the media complained about this practice and virtually accused J.D. Power and Associates of keeping important information secret, Dave knew he needed to reconsider his policy. There were two threads to his response. First, public awareness was the very foundation of his conception of market research. Secrecy encouraged market researchers to emphasize the findings that suited them best and minimize or ignore the findings that were challenging. There was no integrity in that. "By putting our methods and findings in the public sphere for scrutiny by everyone, it kept everyone honest." By the turn of the millenium Dave had reversed his policy, and began releasing the entire list to the media.

The Power "Whatjamacallit"

The market research professionals at Ford were the most vocal critics of the statistical methodology underpinning the Customer Satisfaction Index (CSI). In 1985, one of the Ford statisticians actually produced an internal report attacking the CSI. J.A. Frechtling, Ford's manager of truck marketing research, in a report titled "The Power's Satisfaction 'Whatjamacallit,'" argued that the CSI not only didn't measure customer satisfaction, it wasn't even an index. In four pages of dense type, Frechtling criticized everything from the CSI's application of the Consumer Price Index to the relative weights the CSI assigned to specific measures. Many of the report's objections were trivial. For example, it criticized a standard ranking practice—not unique to J.D. Power—that skipped a ranking number when there was a tie. For example, if two vehicles were tied for, say, third place, the first four rankings would be listed as first, second, third, third. The next ranking would then jump to fifth and continue.

In response, Dave wrote an essay for his own monthly publication, the *Power Report*, titled "Customer Satisfaction Is Measured in the Eyes of the Beholder." Some excerpts from his essay illustrate both his steely determination (by defending the integrity of the CSI) and his humility (by extending an olive branch):

> Customer satisfaction is a top priority in the automobile industry today, but nobody can seem to agree on a definition of just what is customer satisfaction. . . .
>
> Our objective in developing CSI was to formulate a balanced, fair, consistent and objective measure. There were several assumptions we made before coming up with our definition of customer satisfaction and a technique to measure it.
>
> - In surveying car owners, we could only measure their perceptions and attitudes.
> - It is important for manufacturers to know what these perceived problems are.

- Car owners are, more often than not, unable to completely differentiate problems encountered because of the product design or quality and those problems caused by poor dealer service.
- Measuring absolute customer satisfaction is impossible—it has to be done on a relative basis because satisfaction is a dependent upon the level of expectation of each car owner, and these expectations are constantly changing.
- A full year of ownership with an average of 15,000 miles on the vehicle is an optimum point in time to survey the owners because the honeymoon period is over, as is the normal factory warranty. The owner also has had two or three servicing experiences. . . .

Using a detailed questionnaire and a complex formula to arrive at an index score takes much of the subjectivity out of our rankings. Our severest critics have access to the formula, as well as the database, and we welcome any constructive criticism to make the index system better reflect customer satisfaction as we define it.[19]

Frechtling's attacks on J.D. Power and Associates continued. At this point, it would have been understandable for Dave to dig in his heels and become defensive. Instead, he opted for transparency and used the momentum of the other side to his advantage. The more he could engage Ford in a dialogue about his methods the less J.D. Power could be ignored. Besides, Dave was humble enough to acknowledge that on occasion perhaps some of the criticism had actual merit. After all, there are many ways of measuring and analyzing market research information. He was prepared to accept the probability that the market research products

J.D. Power sold had room for improvement. He was eager for constructive feedback.

Dave found his opening in a November 1985 letter Frechtling sent to Linda Hirneise, J.D. Power's manager of client services. The blistering letter said:

> It is inconceivable to me how an organization purporting to include research professionals can call such balderdash an index . . . [an] index, your whajamacallit ain't!
>
> You will find it very easy to say that mine is just a very acute case of NIH (not invented here), but I am including another copy of my memo regarding your service "whatnot." Lord knows, you are located near many nests of competent statisticians. I would be very interested in seeing a critique of your data and my memo with it from a statistician competent in survey and index operations. To give you a start, I have enclosed two pages from the current (1985) ASA directory of members resident in California. If you spend a little time with the directory, you should be able to find someone fitting the bill. I'm looking forward to seeing some real progress made on substantive issues at Power. Of course, my subjective probabilities say [it's] a long shot.[20]

Although Frechtling's challenge to get an impartial statistician to pass judgment on the CSI and the "Whatjamacallit" was probably offered in sarcasm, Dave considered taking the challenge seriously. He wasn't afraid of letting a neutral statistician review his methodology if there was even a small chance doing so would neutralize some of Ford's objections. As he perused the directory of statisticians Frechtling had provided, Dave smiled. For on those very pages, he saw the name of one of his own associates. At that moment, Dave had the germ of an idea. He took a walk down the hall to visit Mark Rees, a statistician who had joined J.D. Power and Associates in 1982 and just so happened to be listed in that ASA directory.

Meanwhile, the Ford people behind the "Whatjamacallit" memo raised the stakes by hiring a professor of statistics from the University of Texas to review the J.D. Power methodology. Dave decided to cooperate with the professor and handed over the CSI algorithms, questionnaires, and data sets. The professor took six months to produce a report. In the end, the professor's report identified nine issues in the CSI that he felt were problematic from a statistical standpoint.

Ray Ablondi, the director of market research for Ford, requested an opportunity to present the report. Albondi proposed to deliver the report to Dave in person and, of course, Dave was agreeable. A breakfast meeting was set up in the boardroom of the Hyatt hotel in Westlake Village near the J.D. Power headquarters. Ablondi had requested that Dave come to the meeting alone, but on the day of the meeting, Dave brought along John Hammond, an expert in applied economics who had joined the company in 1987. A five-member Ford delegation flew out to California in a company jet. "Dave, we asked for this meeting because we wanted to share something we feel will help make the CSI more statistically reliable," said Joseph Kordick, who was acting as the "good cop" to Ablondi's "bad cop." Kordick, who retired in 1988 as vice president and general manager of Ford's Parts and Service Division, slid a one-inch binder across the polished surface of the boardroom table to where Dave sat. Tabbed in nine sections, the binder was filled with dense statistical arguments. "I appreciate the work you put into this," Dave said. "I'll have my statisticians get right on it and we'll get back to you."

The Ford delegates looked at each other. Dave sensed that they wanted to discuss the nine points immediately, but he was firm. "This will require considerable study. Maybe if I had my statistical team here we could get into it, but I'm simply not prepared to discuss the points raised by this report immediately. Let me get back to you." With that, before the breakfast Dave had ordered could even be served, the Ford delegation gathered their belongings and went back to the airport for their return flight to Detroit. The whole meeting took less than fifteen minutes. "I have no idea what they were expecting," Dave says. The bigger question was, what to do next? The argument would go back and forth forever unless Dave figured out a way to bring it to a close.

Two-Pronged Strategy

Dave and Mark Rees began a two-pronged strategy to engage the Ford critics in finding common ground on the intellectual underpinnings of the CSI and other J.D. Power studies. First, they would address the academic criticism of the methodology behind the CSI. Second, they would take on the popular attack of the CSI as inherently subjective.

In addressing Ford's engagement of the University of Texas statisticians, Dave decided not just to see Ford's bet but to also raise it. "Let's have some university statistics professors, or even the head of a statistics department, do some studies," he told Rees. "And while we're at it, let's add a respected academician from Ford's own backyard."

As a result, J.D. Power selected three highly regarded statistics professors, including one from the University of Michigan, and paid them each $5,000 to produce a statistical review of the methodology J.D. Power used for the CSI. The three academics were Dr. Edward Rothman, chairman in the department of statistics at the University of Michigan; Dr. Kenneth Koehler, professor in the department of statistics at Iowa State University; and Dr. Jagdish Sheth, professor of marketing and research at the University of Southern California. These three statisticians, working independently, were asked to examine the statistical foundations of the CSI with respect to the specific concerns raised by Ford, to perform such tests as they deemed appropriate, and to prepare a report assessing the accuracy of the J.D. Power methodology. "Basically, all we asked," Rees says, "was that the researchers examine our methodology and validate that it was a reasonable approach to generating an index."

If Ford researchers expected independent corroboration of their challenge that the J.D. Power and Associates methodology was statistically invalid, they were disappointed. All three scientists ran the raw data through their own statistical calculators and determined that the outcomes were basically identical to the results J.D. Power reported. "Qualitatively, our results are in substantial agreement with those obtained by J.D. Power," wrote Rothman. In response to a specific Ford objection that the CSI distorted outcomes by averaging customer experiences over the entire car line, Rothman wrote, "The overall results of the analysis on individual responses gives us basically the same results as the analysis on responses averaged over car line." All three agreed that J.D. Power used rigorous statistics in generating the CSI and that the CSI was scientifically valid and represented a reasonable way to generate an index measuring the experience of car owners.

Dave assembled the three reports in a three-inch binder and requested an opportunity to present the results to the Ford people in Detroit. Dave and Mark Rees presented the results to the senior managers at Ford. "None of the statisticians or consultants in the room could critique it," Rees says. "It ended the argument. What I learned is that listening to the customers and understanding their concerns is probably the best way to do business." The cost of hiring the three researchers was $15,000, but the value was priceless.

Customer Satisfaction Symposium

The second prong of Dave's response to criticism of the statistics underpinning the CSI and other J.D. Power studies took a page out of Michael Corleone's playbook: "Keep your friends close, but your enemies closer."[21] To that end, Dave convened a customer satisfaction symposium to discuss the statistical methodology used for J.D. Power studies and invited the market research professionals of all the car companies to participate.

The full-day symposium took place in 1986 at the North Ranch Country Club outside Los Angeles. All told, about forty people from GM corporate, the Buick and Chevrolet divisions, Ford, Honda, Toyota, BMW, and Mercedes, as well as potential subscribers, participated. All the attendees had a chance to share their views and vent a bit. Some vented more than others, and many of the comments were focused on the perceived subjectivity of the J.D. Power weightings.

A number of proposals and suggestions flowed from the symposium. "When we allowed everyone to present their own ideas on how the questions were to be weighted, it became evident that everyone had a different opinion," Dave says. "Some of the proposals were self-serving and taken under advisement, but some had merit and we were pleased to consider them." The agenda of the attendees was obvious: J.D. Power and Associates was a force to be reckoned with, it wasn't going away, and it was more in their interests to influence the methodology than to ignore it.

Rees was a witness to these proceedings. "The CSI, which the company had launched only a few years earlier, was often the focus of the most intense criticism," he says, explaining that the original CSI was really a summary metric of a series of cross-tabulated responses having to do with dealer service and the problems car owners experienced. The CSI sampled car owners by car model. The quality results of the individual models would then be weighted as a function of the sales volume of the particular model. "Based on these cross-tabulations," Rees says, "we assigned weights to each series of quality questions." For example, some areas were worth 30 percent; others were worth 40 percent. The weights were suggested by a data-driven framework, but the company could not escape the objection that the weightings were, in the end, subjective. The subjectivity, according to Rees, made it irresistible for critics of J.D. Power and Associates to attack the methodology. "When I gave presentations on the CSI, I found most of my time was spent arguing about the weights than the actual results." Rather than building confidence in the CSI, the subjective weighting became a distraction. "A lot of people challenged us on how we awarded those weights."

"We agreed to make some adjustments to our analytical process," Dave says. One recommendation was to apply the discipline of factor analysis to the problem. Rees believed factor analysis was the best tool to correlate the items on the CSI and to derive a meaningful expression of how car owners really experienced the quality of the car they had purchased twelve months earlier. Factor analysis is used as a means of data reduction through considering variables, both seen and unobserved. Through complicated mathematics, a large number of variables can be considered in one equation, sharpening the resulting analysis. The main question on the CSI—"How, overall, would you rate your satisfaction with your car?"—was used as the dependent variable. All the factors related to overall automobile satisfaction were then scored as independent variables. This analysis produced weightings that were not vulnerable to being criticized as "subjective."

That approach drew agreement from most of the participants. "Factor and regression analyses allowed us to have all the clients buy into our system," explains Rees. By doing so, the company could assign a weight to the effectiveness of each factor in determining the overall satisfaction rating. "None of the adjustments to the index changed the outcomes, but it gave the participants some ownership of the process and confidence that the weightings we used weren't arbitrary." At the end of the symposium, many attendees seemed more comfortable with the process. "I won't say all blessed the results, but many left feeling better about us."

In the following months, Dave Power and Mark Rees presented the changes made to the J.D. Power CSI to various audiences in Detroit and elsewhere. As a result, much of the previous criticism evaporated, and while the car companies from time to time continued to object to particular results reported by the CSI, IQS, and other studies, they rarely called into question the validity of the methodology itself. Dave's efforts paid off. J.D. Power and Associates could have taken a defensive stance in the face of relentless criticism, but instead, by choosing the path of transparency and engagement, it won over its critics and in a bold stroke cemented J.D. Power's legitimacy. "It was my privilege to have a ringside seat to see develop an independent, unbiased set of metrics that forced the auto industry to truly look at the quality of products and the levels of service that it delivered," Rees says. "Dave's work was the catalyst that changed the auto industry from competing on price and design to an industry that competed on quality and service."

But even as late as 1997, when Ford became a less-reluctant subscriber to J.D. Power and Associates studies, the grumbling didn't abate. Dave often received copies of internal Ford memos critical of his company from executives at various levels of the company who thought it would be helpful for Dave to see the unalloyed concerns. The following highlights, taken from one of these 1997 internal memos, underscore some of the reasons why Ford managers felt they should be suspicious of J.D. Power surveys:

- The Power Index calculations are formulated to magnify differences and deemphasize similarities among manufacturers, and data generally are presented without reference to their statistical significance.
- Ford has no control over the quality of research methods used by J.D. Power.
- Sample and composition is determined primarily by Power rather than customized to Ford needs and interests.
- Robustness of sample sizes is questionable compared with Ford's proprietary surveys.
- Timing of the Power surveys—the IQS in particular—is not well suited to Ford needs.
- Power surveys are syndicated among many manufacturers; one manufacturer cannot make changes without the knowledge and approval of all the manufacturers.
- Using Power data provides Ford with no better data than are available to any manufacturer.
- Unlike a typical market research company, J.D. Power also figures prominently as a source and publicist of awards to companies in the automotive and other industries. In addition to charging a price for survey data, J.D. Power also charges companies for the right to advertise awards created from the survey. We see an inherent conflict in the multiple roles of J.D. Power.[22]

Dave chalks up Ford's continuing reluctance to its struggles, even in 1997, to achieve competitive levels of product equality. "Ford staff members didn't understand that the customer—not the manufacturer—was now in charge," says Dave. "Today, top management has accepted this lack of control, and for Ford, quality has improved so that they now advertise their rankings when they deliver the quality their customers expect."

Gaming the System

As more studies were created and more customers began to rely on them, the influence of the J.D. Power ratings soared, and the stakes for carmakers and dealers rose along with it. By 1985, when the J.D. Power customer-satisfaction rankings were released, dealers saw increased traffic in the showrooms and rising sales of the top-ranked cars. In the late 1980s, one moribund car—the Buick LeSabre—saw an incredible increase in sales, nearly doubling the one-month sales over the same month the previous year,[23] after a high IQS ranking was advertised. Twenty years later, Buick tied with Jaguar at the top of the J.D. Power Vehicle Dependability Study in 2009, and in 2010 Buick announced sales growth of 61 percent, making it the fastest growing brand in the industry.[24]

The pervasive influence of the J.D. Power rankings created a troubling situation for Dave: some carmakers actually tied employees' individual compensation to their performance on the J.D. Power rankings. Generally, a high ranking on the CSI, for example, would result in a bonus, raise, or promotion. To Dave, this linkage was troubling even if it validated how his rankings were now the de facto standard for measuring something everyone agreed was important. "Tying monetary incentives to customer satisfaction scores is a double-edged sword," Jamey Power wrote in his book *Satisfaction*. "On one hand, any psychologist will tell you that the fastest way to get someone to conform to a desired behavior is to build a reward system around that behavior. While this may be fine for getting your child to eat broccoli, incentivizing customer-friendly behavior is more problematic. After all, what are you really paying them for? Are you paying your employees to treat customers better, or are you paying them for higher survey scores? Your goal is the former, but your employees may focus on the latter; and this is why we find so many resorting to begging customers to mark perfect scores on their surveys."[25] Paying employees for performance distracts them from focusing on satisfying the customers.

J.D. Power and Associates encouraged car dealers to focus on the customer's experience rather than a study score, but the message was often ignored by front-line managers and salespeople. "Instead of working to fix the problems, some dealerships took a short-cut by directly asking customers to give them a good rating when it came time to fill out their survey," says Jamey.

Eventually, significant sums of money came to be associated with the satisfaction rankings along with the prestige. Marketers had millions of dollars of income riding on the rankings. Dave knew that money always tempts some people to bend the rules, and it wasn't long before he saw evidence of people trying to game the system and undermine the integrity of the market research. It was a constant battle for J.D. Power and Associates to stay ahead of the cheaters.

J.D. Power had a number of advantages that inoculated it against such threats. The main bulwark was the company's total independence, which shielded its syndicated research from pressure from the automakers. The company went out of its way to provide not only the reality of objectivity, but also to promote it. For example, J.D. Power didn't directly select the car buyers who received its questionnaires. This critical task was delegated to R.L. Polk and Company, an independent third party, which performed the selection process.

Many of the attempts to game the process came at the response phase. Dave caught a handful of dealers bribing customers with offers of everything from a free tank of gas to free oil changes if the customer would just bring their blank survey to the dealership. Some parties duplicated and returned multiple J.D. Power questionnaires instead of just one. The goal was to fraudulently "stuff the ballot box" to manipulate the ratings. At one point, for example, Honda established an incentive program to reward dealers who scored above average on J.D. Power's rankings of dealers. Some dealers duplicated the questionnaires and submitted multiple entries, Dave recalls. What the miscreants did not know is that each questionnaire was individually tagged. The J.D. Power computers immediately flagged the attempts at duplication and the scheme was exposed.

One study called for J.D. Power to measure the experience of GM car dealers with General Motors Acceptance Corporation (GMAC), the lending arm of the company. Dave heard a rumor that some GMAC regional offices tried to influence dealer results by offering them consumer electronics. Dave made a few calls and put a stop to the practice, in the low-key, straightforward manner in which he handled all controversies. "My basic message was," he says, "that it was harmful for them as an organization to be indulging in such practices."

Other attempts to influence the rankings came at the carmaker level. A number of consulting firms offered services promising to improve a carmaker's results on the CSI and and IQS. "I am sure there were many well-meaning consultants that tried to help honestly but fell into the trap of believing that quality or satisfaction is something that you can spray on at the end," says Dave Sargent. "This is a seductive approach as it implies that there are low-effort ways to get high quality or satisfaction when there really aren't. I can't count the times that we were asked, 'We want to be number one next year, what do we do?' The answer invariably begins with 'Start ten years ago . . . '"

"What we found was that our most effective tool in improving quality was to do the work internally ourselves and use J.D. Power as a guide. GM actually had to do the hard work of listening to the customers and then acting on what it heard," says Roland Hill, who ended a thirty-two-year career at GM as director of quality before joining J.D. Power as a consultant in Detroit. "I believe that General Motors is better at providing high quality and customer satisfaction today because of Dave Power and J.D. Power and Associates."

CHAPTER NINE

CONTROLLED CONTROVERSY

Ever since his earliest days conducting research studies and providing insights to clients, Dave Power has had a knack for recognizing important facts that need consideration. Whether uncovering findings contrary to the company line or problems ignored by the people in charge, Dave has straightened his back and calmly said what needs to be said. Many have bristled at facing the unvarnished truth, but many others have recognized the value in Dave's ability and willingness to stir the pot, because they believed it was being done for the right reasons. Dave describes his role as simply laying out the facts respectfully and engaging with his auto industry colleagues in a measured exchange.

"If we're trying to change the thinking of the automobile industry, we have to be provocative," Dave explains. "We don't have an impact if no one gets excited about it one way or another. When you create controlled controversy, you don't go overboard. You might create a press release that has one or two items that get dealers or manufacturers a bit upset, but that's what gets people talking and thinking, and leads to change."

"You see this constant theme with Dave that he would be so far ahead in his thinking," says Chris Denove, who worked for J.D. Power heading up the company's auto retailing and Internet sales divisions. "It's like somebody playing chess: most people are looking one, maybe two moves ahead; Dave's looking five, six moves ahead. That was sometimes hard for clients to get their hands around."

Colleagues and clients have seen the value of Dave's accurate predictions. "It's a matter of how much confidence you have that what you're stating that may be controversial is true," says long-time J.D. Power and Associates executive Loretta Seymour. "This is where Dave based his opinions. The positive that happened with Dave is that his controversial positions came true."

"Dave is like sunlight," says Jac Nasser, former president and CEO of Ford Motor Company. "It's good when you have sunlight on what customers are thinking. Dave will be remembered for bringing a customer focus to how you measure quality and satisfaction."

While Dave has often taken on tough challenges to build his company's reputation and value, his underlying goal—recognized widely by clients, whether at the time they signed on for J.D. Power services or in hindsight—was always to help improve matters, from customer satisfaction to the client's bottom line. This was a position that motivated even his most controversial moves.

For instance, Dave's European clients, who had long been guided by engineers who seemed begrudging to the notion of serving customers, had to swallow hard when Dave pointed out their need to change. "Part of the threat that he represented to the interior organization was that, after listening to Dave's presentation, product planning understood that the J.D. Power organization knew more about Audi in the U.S. market than Audi's own product planning group," explains Gunnar Larsson, former vice president of product development at Saab and general manager of Volvo's Monitoring and Concept Center in California before serving in research and development and on the management board at Audi. "That caused an awkward feeling for the Audi planners.

They didn't like the idea that someone outside the company would know more about the cars than someone inside the company." But Dave proved his message with data, gaining the respect and understanding of technical people. "Even engineers started to understand that what they knew was not enough to please the customers," Larsson adds. "The way an engineer thinks is more about the production side, until the customer receives the product. . . . We were more focused on things gone wrong rather than things gone right." When Dave started measuring customer satisfaction, automakers' eyes were opened to a new way of gauging their success. For Dave, helping automakers become more successful gave him the greatest satisfaction.

Such an altruistic focus, even if it comes from an entrepreneurial angle of creating a unique, must-have service, won the respect—sometimes reluctant—of the vast majority of critics who encountered Dave and his work. Even those who did not agree with Dave on all his views appreciated Dave's willingness to engage on the issues.

"We used to have wonderful debates," recalls dealer John Bergstrom, chairman and CEO of Bergstrom Corporation in Neenah, Wisconsin. "Well, Dave is not argumentative, so they were really wonderful discussions. Dave is someone who cares about what people think of him when he's criticized, but he doesn't show it. He has his own set of values and doesn't change them."

Building Media Relations

Controversy is the coin of the realm in media empires, and early in his career Dave saw the value in making the most of research findings that surprised, alarmed, or engaged clients. In 1973, when the *Wall Street Journal* broke the news that Dave's research had uncovered Mazda's serious problems with the O-rings in its rotary engines, Dave quickly realized it would be beneficial to have other media in on the story, too, and he didn't waste a moment in capitalizing on the front-page splash. "The next day we sent it to the other journalists. We went to the major business publications, and the *New York Times*, the *L.A. Times*, the *Chicago Tribune*. We sent it to automotive journalists. I knew some of them, not all of them. We sent it to *Fortune* magazine, *Businessweek*, and I think *Automotive News,* too.

"It was a short article, but it had an impact that we couldn't have hoped for," Dave recalls. "Within forty-eight hours, it had gone all around the world. Europe covered it, Japan covered it—the two biggest auto manufacturing centers outside the United States."

"Media was an early supporter of Power," recalls one longtime Detroit auto journalist. "We in the media began to take those numbers and surveys and press releases a bit more seriously than the Detroit auto companies did." He recalls that by the early 1980s, "it began to sink in that this was important, groundbreaking stuff and that Power was way out in front of anyone else."

Along with solid data, it was Dave's personality and his approachability—paired with the attitude of a quiet maverick—that brought in media coverage of J.D. Power's work. "He's a pretty charismatic guy," the journalist adds. "He has always struck me, whether at a public event or a one-on-one on the phone, as being down-home and personal. He always stood his ground, would never waver. When he felt he was right, he had no problem telling the auto companies, 'Hey, this is what the data showed us.'"

Dave has always been genuine but purposeful in his friendliness toward the automotive media. "People loved to chat with him," recalls former director of publications John Rettie, himself an automotive journalist but one who directed the J.D. Power and Associates publications for a decade in the 1990s. "I think at times he would probably tell them things or talk with them perhaps more than he should have done, from a corporate research point of view, which is why automotive journalists loved chatting with him."

"In dealing with the media, he was always candid, never guarded at all. Always very up front," says the Detroit automotive journalist. "Obviously, that plays a role in building a relationship with the media, too."

Rettie identifies a key trait that Dave and reporters had in common: "Journalists have always liked controversy, and Dave likes controversy and likes stirring things up. I think that's part of his modus operandi right from word one. So there's always been a mutual respect for each other from that point of view. Which is why the more journalists stir things up and are more forthright with their questions, the more Dave seems to appreciate them."

Some of Dave's most engaging media professional exchanges were with Joseph B. White from the *Wall Street Journal*; Matt DeLorenzo, formerly of *Road and Track;* and Paul Ingrassia, who has written several popular books on the auto industry and is currently managing editor of Thomson Reuters. Ingrassia recalls meeting Dave at a National Automobile Dealers Association event in New Orleans and was struck by Dave's relaxed demeanor. "I thought he was a nice, regular guy. What I expected was something of a Dale Carnegie type," recalls Ingrassia. Instead, he "reminded me of Peter Sellers." Ingrassia watched Detroit's reaction to Dave with interest, seeing a "tipping point" for Dave's influence in 1986 to 1988. "A lot of things were dawning on the executives in Detroit. His was no longer just a voice in the wilderness, and he could be ignored only at a company's peril."

Publicizing the results of J.D. Power and Associates surveys had a salutary benefit for Dave's company as it bolstered the effects of the brand being mentioned in advertising. "J.D. Power and

Associates was arguably the first market research firm to make its findings public and, without question, the most sophisticated in its ability to work with the media to advance its strategic goals," says Bill Young, former president of Volkswagen North America who also worked for J.D. Power. By promoting the results to the media, Dave could not only reach those decision makers, but also extend the brand and bring transparency to the J.D. Power rankings. Young notes, "Dave was very clever in using the media to get his message directly to the top executives of the car companies, successfully bypassing the market research professionals who frequently represented barriers."

Bringing the results into the public—shining the sunlight on heretofore internal automotive workings—brought Dave much respect from industry journalists. "Dave basically invented customer satisfaction," says Csaba Csere, former editor of *Car and Driver* magazine. "He created an outside, independent organization that provided an accurate measure of quality. And because he did it well, his measures had a great deal of credibility. Before Dave Power came along, there was no independent measure of quality in the automobile industry."

By focusing on quality for the customer, Dave was seen by leading journalists not only as shining light on an insular industry, but also as a voice for change. "In my view, there were two analysts who changed the face of the car industry for the better," says Keith Crain, chairman of Crain Communications and the publisher of *Automotive News.* "One was Dr. Deming, who made a giant contribution to the Japanese car industry, and the other was Dave Power, who demonstrated that consumers could and should define quality. He's done a great service to American consumers by working to increase quality across the board. Everyone who owns or drives a car in America is in his debt."

Analysts Becoming Resources

Although Dave was the person journalists often aimed to speak with, over time it became more practical for the company analysts who headed up a study or closely followed a particular automaker to provide a quote to the media. This succeeded in making J.D. Power and Associates a go-to resource on all things automotive.

"I had a lot of friends [in the media], and some of them would call me up because they hated going through the PR lady, who was sort of a blockade for getting to Dave Power," recalls John Rettie wryly. "So I would sometimes send them to the right person without letting on that I was the conduit. Got my rear end chewed out a couple of times by the lady in charge of PR, but I also got praised by Dave Power a couple of times." Dave was, after all, a veteran of the end-around play.

The press calls came so fast and furiously, sometimes it fell to whoever was available to field the questions, whether or not that person was on top of the issue. "There might have been some instances where they said the wrong thing, or tried to say the right thing but it was printed the wrong way," Dave recalls. "We were still tight-knit and we talked to each other and knew what was going on. If somebody got a call, we'd discuss it and compare notes. It was generally a joint discussion with two or three staff members." That preparation and openness led the Power staff to gain respect from journalists, says Dave, but it was a two-way street. "We respected what they were doing for us," he says. "It was the press that delivered our message."

Dave was diligent in responding to reporters who desired information, but he was also diligent in responding when reporters wrote something he considered inaccurate or a misrepresentation of his company or its research results. On August 15, 1994, Jim Mateja, who covered the automobile industry for the *Chicago*

Tribune, wrote an article titled "J.D. Power Speaks: Chrysler Listens." It created the impression that the IQS included frivolous categories, the only purpose of which was to generate advertising claims. Although the response sent to Mateja in reaction to the article was signed by Patty Patano, J.D. Power's director of marketing and special projects, the hard-hitting sentiments were Dave's.

The note pointed out that Mateja had not contacted J.D. Power for comment, and "Chrysler's desire to 'cram for the J.D. Power and Associates exam,' so to speak, has certainly gained a great deal of attention." However, the note said, "We cannot support Chrysler's approach to achieving quality, i.e., determining quality according to a single survey."[1] Quality, as had been proven many times by other automakers' measured reactions to low IQS scoring, came over time by listening to the customer and then improving quality control processes.

But the letter also defended IQS categories and noted that the article had erroneously mentioned ergonomic issues that were not part of the study's eighty-nine problem categories:

> Contrary to what was reported, this study rates problems, not how consumers feel about the location of cupholders or ashtrays. This is a gross misrepresentation of this important study, and we regret that you did not contact us for clarification. The wide range of surveys that you indicate we do are each done for a specific reason and not to create advertising claims. Placement of knobs, switches, and cupholders are evaluated in another study but not in the Initial Quality Study.[2]

The letter concluded that a study such as the IQS, which reported ratings by a company's customers, would inevitably put a company at odds with the results, and J.D. Power's response did not result from a "popularity contest" but rather the desire to set the record straight.

It helped that the media, especially the business press covering the auto industry, quickly saw that J.D. Power was a source of independent data in a world where much of the data from the industry was seen as self-serving. "J.D. Power and Associates was an entirely new thing and he was treated as news by the media," said Ben Bidwell, former chairman of Chrysler Motors, in the media-industry magazine *Brill's Content* in 1999. "Stories began to appear, and over time there appeared to be some public acceptance that [Dave's] word was gospel."[3]

Making Readers CarSmart

While the media often reported their survey results, Dave and his staff sought many avenues to build overall awareness of J.D. Power and Associates' work among the general car-buying public. One major effort in the mid-1990s resulted in a new publication. Dave entered into an experiment with the Hearst Corporation, publisher of *Good Housekeeping, Popular Mechanics,* and dozens of other well-known titles, to produce a magazine featuring J.D. Power content. The magazine was called *CarSmart,* and its first issue also featured a long profile of Dave, titled "The Power of Power." "A J.D. Power ranking can make or break a car," the profile began, "which is why the car companies love-hate the man and his machine." The winter 1995 issue displayed the J.D. Power seal on the cover and also included such articles as "281 J.D. Power Car and Truck Rankings for Quality, Satisfaction, Dependability."

Three test issues of *CarSmart* were published before Dave terminated the experiment because he became uncomfortable with the blurring of the line between editorial content and advertising.

Many of the clients felt that Hearst sales people threatened bad J.D. Power rankings if they did not buy ad space. "*CarSmart* could have been very good for us," Dave says, "but in the end, Hearst couldn't guarantee the level of integrity we required."

Sharing a Provocative View with Industry Insiders

Years before his Hearst experiment, Dave was communicating directly to auto industry insiders through his subscription-based newsletter known widely as the *Power Report*.

In the May 1989 edition of the *Power Report*, Dave made waves when he detailed his growing concerns about automotive retailing by comparing selling cars to selling television sets.

> What manufacturer has the best quality television set today? What brands have the best quality in terms of reliability and trouble-free operation? Which brands have the poorest reputation for reliability? . . . Where are most of the television sets sold in the U.S. built today? Is there any significant difference in sets coming from Singapore, Hong Kong, Taiwan or South Korea and those that come from Japan? . . .
>
> When it comes time to buy a new television set today, just how much concern do consumers have about these factors? Indeed, they have become non-issues. Where do consumers go today to buy television sets? Certainly not to the factory-franchised Zenith or Magnavox dealer![4]

After setting up this scenario, Dave asked the reader to consider this question: "Can this happen to the automobile industry?" Is it really conceivable that car buyers in the near future will no longer visit traditional car dealers but find what they need in a wide variety of retail experiences? As the article continued, Dave answered his own question:

> Yes. In fact, it has already begun to happen. Like it or not, approve of it or disapprove of it, it is happening faster than many think. It is beyond the control of manufacturers, distributors, and dealers, individually or collectively.[5]

In the world of electronic retailing, Dave had seen how the market responds enthusiastically to consumer-driven forces, and the dramatic effect this has had on retailing. The world of automobile retailing, he suggested, can and will go the same route. He noticed early on that the automobile manufacturing costs were becoming a smaller and smaller percentage of the retail price of each vehicle, while the costs of distributing, marketing, and selling cars kept increasing. Some of this dynamic flowed out of the process improvements implemented by the car manufacturers. Some of it flowed from improved quality, improvements that were often a direct result of the CSI results released by J.D. Power and Associates. And some of it was due to the rising costs of advertising, marketing, inventory management, and the way new cars are distributed.

The consumer-driven retailing environment Dave envisioned was available for all to see on used car lots just by reviewing how dealers arranged the inventory on their lots. Do they put all the Toyotas in one aisle, Fords in the other, and Chryslers lined up on the other side of the lot? No, they put all the sedans together, the compacts together, and the pickup trucks together. Why? The used car dealer would say, "Because customers arrive at the car lot already knowing what category of car they want to buy and want to compare available models." The new car franchise system, however, still forces consumers to go from dealer to dealer to look at competitive cars. "Through the franchised dealer system," Dave wrote in 1989, "the effort has been to minimize competitive disadvantages rather than to rethink the utility of the system itself."

Falling on Deaf Ears

Even before his seminal editorial on franchising published in the May 1989 issue of the *Power Report*, Dave was highlighting what he believed was the instability of the franchise system in his speeches and writing. In 1968, Dave suggested that the way new cars were retailed in the U.S. was increasingly inefficient and contributed to the decline of the domestic automobile industry. To any audience that would listen, Dave argued that there were simply too many car dealerships and that the franchise system, while designed to protect the economic interests of car dealers, actually threatened the long-term profitability of their dealerships.

By 1980, it had become obvious to Dave that the automobile retailing-franchise system no longer served the goals for which it was designed. Both the economics that supported the franchise system and the customer behavior that was emerging made the status quo increasingly difficult to defend. The main issue, according to Dave, was that the car industry had dramatically improved the ability to build cars at a low cost. The industry had wrung most inefficiencies out of the process of manufacturing cars, increasing quality in the bargain. But the way new American cars were distributed and sold had barely changed in fifty years. That stagnation was affecting dealer profitability and innovation.

J.D. Power and Associates also had been among the first to point out the impact of dealer consolidation and the growing significance of megadealers. However, the megadealers themselves—and the new imports setting up their new franchise systems—generally stuck to the principle that what had worked in the past would work in the future. "The bet has been that the consumer would go along with it," Dave says. "That has become a bad bet."

But automobile quality, as tracked and spurred on by J.D. Power, was rising across all manufacturers, and Dave found even more urgency in his perception that retailing and franchising would have to change. The marketplace, as defined by the people he was surveying, was seeking better ways to buy cars, and the growing power of online technologies was providing new opportunities. Dave repeatedly wrote about dealer issues and sought every opportunity to engage J.D. Power more deeply in the auto dealer community. "Manufacturers wanted to keep the status quo, but the world has changed," Dave says. "Manufacturers will have to adjust. They cannot afford to buy out redundant dealers. There has to be some accommodation of the distribution process to make it economically feasible. There is pressure on the industry to change, but the pressure is not necessarily coming from within. The primary pressures are consumer behavior and economics as dealer profitability declines."

He continued to bring up the topic, and it was no secret that Dave felt a sea change was overdue. "When I'd speak, people would challenge me, but I felt I just had to keep hitting away at it."

Denove says Dave's role as a "revolutionary agent of change" often created a "love-hate" relationship with the dealers. At the same time, Denove believes Dave was always cognizant of the need to not just sound the alarm bell but also give clients the tools to succeed in changing times. Dave's message to dealers, Denove says, was, "Embrace change while the opportunities are there; don't just stick your head in the sand."

Next Exit, the Auto Megastore

It was in the spirit of helping the industry and its retail mechanism that, on October 28, 2003, Dave published an opinion piece titled "Next Exit, the Auto Megastore" in the *Wall Street Journal*. His goal was to give a wake-up call to everyone involved in automobile retailing. In that goal, he was successful. The auto industry woke up, all right. The commentary created more criticism than anything else Dave had ever written. He had clearly hit a nerve.

It is worthwhile to consider not only what the *Wall Street Journal* published, but also what it did not publish. The commentary Dave submitted was considerably more nuanced than the shortened version that was published. The entire text of the commentary as Dave submitted it is reprinted below. The underlined sections did not appear in the published version.

> When people ask me to predict the future of automotive retailing, I'm tempted to say, "Take a look at Allis-Chalmers." The fact is, you've probably never heard of Allis-Chalmers, a popular tractor manufacturer that helped mechanize America's small farms. Allis-Chalmers disappeared along with dozens of other farm equipment manufacturers in recession-driven consolidations of the mid-20th century.
>
> Or I might say, "Visit your friendly GE television dealer." You can't do that either. Franchised dealers and their repair operations went away after solid-state circuitry arrived and made TVs more or less reliable for life.
>
> I could be clever and say, "Let's ask the 50,000 or so U.S. automotive dealers." Only there aren't 50,000 new car dealers in this country anymore. There are less than half that.

Competitive and economic forces have squeezed that peak number down to less than 22,000 outlets owned by only 14,000 individuals.

By that measure, every day fewer people have a stake in how I answer the question. I do have an answer, and the short version is: "Wal-Mart." I'm not predicting that Wal-Mart is going to end the insular automotive retailing business, although if our current outdated state franchise laws were reformed, they could. I'm using Wal-Mart as a code word for how dynamic retailing can and should be. The Wal-Mart model foretells how much power the retailer and his customer can wield over what, when, where and how goods are purchased when the barriers of inefficient distribution are removed.

That same power has never been present in automotive retailing for several good reasons that have outlasted their merit. The franchise system was designed in part to preserve the manufacturer's control over vehicle distribution and pricing while entrusting sales and service to local entrepreneurs who would do it best. To counter-balance control by the manufacturers, dealers joined forces to enact protective state franchise laws. Today, there is a hefty price for those artificial and anachronistic controls, and they add about 30 percent to the base cost of a manufactured vehicle. That's right. Post-assembly marketing and distribution costs can represent nearly a third of the price of a new vehicle purchased today through a franchised automotive dealer. Over the last 30 years, manufacturers have become quite adept at excising the inefficiencies out of the manufacturing process. If distribution costs don't diminish, they will consume an even greater share of the consumer dollar. You might think that consumers wouldn't tolerate that. You'd be right. There is a battle brewing in automotive distribution. It is a struggle that will transform automotive *franchising* into automotive *retailing*. It is a change that will produce new outlets and give the retailer and his customer ultimate control over what, when, where and how vehicles are purchased. It is a very big battle and yet, the outcome is inevitable.

I, and others, have been saying as much for some time. I have many friends who are happy, successful auto dealers, and they don't begrudge my point of view. Many of them just think I'm wrong. They've heard this prediction so often that, to them, this is yesterday's war, falsely warned and never waged. It's true: old habits and old laws tend not to change very easily. The old order hasn't toppled with a single assault or an isolated event. It survived the nascent Auto Nation revolution. It outlasted the initial Internet uproar. Where is his long-awaited loud-trumpeted future?

It's right under your nose.

Recessions always hasten transformation, and the most recent one is no different. During market contractions, stronger players pull out all the stops to protect their market share at the expense of the weaker. Where is today's contraction, you might wonder, when vehicle sales are near all-time highs and dealers are coasting on solid profitability? Masked, perhaps, by the extraordinary new-car incentives still being offered to support sales. Manufacturers will not sustain these giveaways. Economic reality has a way of reappearing, and continued consolidation is inevitable. Just ask Allis-Chalmers.

<u>How far would you go to make a great deal of a new car? Now, how far would you go for an oil change? You probably answered these questions quite differently and illustrated my next point for yourself. The automotive industry has made dramatic improvements in product quality, reliability and technical performance. Vehicles need less service, less often, from factory-authorized technicians. The de-coupling of sales from service, a result of superior product quality, cuts to the very core of the franchise rationale.</u>

Franchise laws are overdue for overhaul, and increasing numbers of dealers would like to lead the change. These are the multi-franchise dealers, who suffer greatest from the inefficiencies of the current system. In the vernacular of the automotive industry, these owners operate more than one "store," none of them true stores where customers can comparison-shop across makes under one roof. When the European Union's antitrust commission repealed old rules preventing dealers from selling competing brands, Virgin Cars flew out of the gate with the world's first multi-brand auto department store, which opened just this May in Manchester, England.

The 30,000 square foot "Megastore" offers 25 automotive brands under one roof at very competitive prices in a friendly, relaxed atmosphere. Vehicles are not grouped by brand, but by themes such as "crowd pleasers," "thrills," "first class," and "adventure."

They sold 150 vehicles in their first six weeks. Not surprisingly, they predict a glorious future selling up to 60,000 cars a year through 12 stores within seven years. Imagine what American consumers would do if, heartened by product quality, assured of price discounts, completely informed and confident in their choices, they could shop for cars the way they've always wanted to. <u>Just ask your friendly GE television dealer.</u>

Dealership ranks are declining, and not just among the small and under-capitalized. To be sure, some dealers are simply cashing out of their high-value real estate. In any event, it is difficult for any enterprise to thrive when profit margins shrink and inventory costs rise. Our own studies show that more than one-fourth of the people who walked out of a new-vehicle dealership without buying said they did so mainly because they didn't like the way the salesperson handled their business. <u>I have to believe that satisfied salespeople produce satisfied customers; satisfaction is the product of satisfaction.</u> With its high cost and high pressures, the current system hardly serves or satisfies anyone.

Changes like these don't happen quickly, but it will seem like overnight to the inattentive or unprepared. In another 10–15 years, consumers will have many more choices of where they can shop for new vehicles. The dealers who prevail will be those among today's hearty crop who have the wisdom to understand and the initiative to adapt to these unstoppable forces. What happens when information and access are finally unleashed to empower the retailer and his customer to control what, when, where and how goods are purchased? Ask Wal-Mart.[6]

Dave received hundreds of letters, emails, faxes, and phone calls from car dealers, car company executives, and people associated with the automobile industry, including car buyers. Many of the letters excoriated Dave for biting the hand that fed him. A response from Ford executive Stephen G. Lyons, president of the Ford Division, was typical of the negative tone:

> Your letter in the *Wall Street Journal* has created quite a negative reaction from many Ford dealers. I have received numerous dealer e-mails concerned with both the tone and the direction of the article. The question of why or should we continue to do business with J.D. Power has been raised by many of the dealers.
>
> I have read your article and the implication is that the current dealer structure does not meet the needs of the consumer. We disagree with that assertion. Clearly, one of our competitive advantages is the strength of our dealers. Ford Division's 3,800 dealers and their 220,000 employees offer quality service, shopping convenience, and product selection. We both know that this is a unique and demanding business and the dealer has successfully stood the test of time.[7]

Other letters that Dave received were more supportive. A well-regarded consumer marketing consultant praised Dave's vision:

> Your "Manager's Journal" column in the October 28th issue of the *Wall Street Journal* was right on the mark. It's too bad that the U.S. automotive industry is unlikely to pay much attention to it. . . . The impression I've had is that this message has fallen on deaf ears. The sorry state of the U.S. automotive industry today largely reflects the inbred, short-sighted, "hero du jour" approach . . . which has characterized its management style. Congratulations on a well-reasoned and courageous column![8]

"When was the last time you heard about a customer being lied to by Wal-Mart?" an executive at a car leasing company in Maryland wanted to know. He sent Dave these words of encouragement:

> The "not all dealers are bad" defense simply doesn't work anymore. There are enough shenanigans going on at the dealerships to warrant low scores on any comfort meter. There is enough deception, misinformation, slanted truths and outright fraud occurring to generalize about the retail segment of the industry.
>
> In the vehicle leasing business it seems a day does not pass without hearing from prospects and customers about their dissatisfaction with the dealer experience. There are independent leasing companies that operate throughout the country that owe their very existence to the inefficient, incompetent and dishonest atmosphere created at dealerships. You and your company are taking heat for understating dealer weakness. Don't back down. No one else in the industry is willing to address the issue.

Response to Criticism

The passion his commentary aroused surprised not only him but also everyone at the company. "I heard Dave give that basic talk many times, and it never created controversy," says J Ferron, a former J.D. Power and Associates senior partner, "but seeing it in print on the *Wall Street Journal* opinion page made it appear that Dave was calling for a brand new distribution system that would leave existing car dealers in the lurch." The commentary became a lightning rod for all the fissures in the retailing end of the automobile industry. "It was like poking at a hornet's nest,"

Dave recalls. "What really made the dealer community furious is when I wrote 'If you don't believe me, talk to Wal-Mart.' They called me the Darth Vader of the auto industry."

Dave sees his commentary as an attempt to simply point out the shift he saw happening—as he always did by interpreting the results of his market research work—not to instigate a change. And his opinions came from more than forty years of observing the industry; in fact, he had seen signs of retailing problems even in his first job at Ford Tractor. "I saw the changes going on in agriculture that changed the tractor business," he recalls. "And I also remember the tug of war on the family farm, trying to compete with the mechanized farm. They just couldn't stop the tide that was changing. I think my understanding of that was very helpful in saying it's going to happen in the auto industry as well."

A week after his column appeared, Dave attempted to explain his remarks in a letter to the editor of the *Wall Street Journal*. The *Journal* declined to publish the letter, but *Automotive News* did publish Dave's follow up as part of a November 17, 2003, feature, "Letters on the Power Debate":

> I would like to clarify my Oct. 28 Manager's Journal column in the *Wall Street Journal*. There has been some confusion over my comments, and I welcome the opportunity to provide my perspective again.
>
> With the advent of real-time information and significant advances in technology, the world is changing on many fronts. Consumers are becoming more knowledgeable and more time-sensitive, and their expectations continue to rise. Many institutions are adapting to those new dynamics, and the automotive industry is not insulated from those forces.

In the 1980s, the automotive industry responded to the coming of the megastores and public ownership. In the early 1990s, consolidation in the retail ranks began and continues. Today, consumers are the catalysts for additional changes in automotive retailing.

Armed with real-time information, consumers are demanding the right product in the right place and at the right time. I believe inefficiencies in the manufacturer distribution system are an area that could be improved to address these consumer issues. The primary point of my column was to stimulate dialogue about those new forces.

I said in my submitted column to the *Wall Street Journal* that post-assembly marketing and distribution costs can represent nearly 30 percent of the price of a new vehicle purchased today through a franchised automotive dealer. Unfortunately, that statement was edited out of the column due to space restrictions and has created some misunderstanding of my point.

Some believed I was referring to dealer margin, but this is not the case. While the exact percentage is open to debate, when you add it all up, the sales, marketing and distribution system reflects a substantial indirect cost to new vehicles. Costs related to advertising and incentives, floor-plan assistance, and fleet and field support can be reduced significantly by leveraging timely consumer information.

That is not happening today, as dealers are burdened by excess production of less-desirable products. As we all know, the longer a product remains on a dealer's premises, the more likely it is to create increased warranty costs.

Some publications have also misrepresented my analogy of Wal-Mart. I used Wal-Mart an example of a highly efficient retail system that uses technology and real-time information to reduce costs and increase consumer value. It has the ability to control what products it receives and when it receives them—all directly tied to consumer demand.

Unfortunately, many readers misconstrued my mention of Wal-Mart as an attack on the current automotive franchise system. I did not nor do I advocate Wal-Mart selling new cars and trucks in towns across America. Wal-Mart was used simply as example of a retailer in control, dictating what, where and when product is needed.

I do believe that many consumers would prefer to comparison shop for new vehicles under one roof. The winds of change are blowing, perhaps with more intensity in the United Kingdom. I mentioned in my column an experiment in which Virgin Cars in Manchester, England, is selling 25 automotive brands under one roof.

That will be an interesting test of consumer acceptance of a new retailing concept in the United Kingdom. In fact, across the United States, that concept has been used for many years to organize and display used cars and trucks by vehicle type.

Retailing changes have been occurring slowly in the United States. In the 1980s, Martin Swig was a pioneer and a vanguard of a new trend in automotive retailing with his San Francisco Autocenter, which operated 17 franchises under one roof. I remember Paul Tamraz saying in the late 1980s when he built his multimake Motor Werks facility in Barrington, Illinois, that "many makes at one location is the only way to go." Just last year, Roger Penske with his new North Scottsdale, Arizona, facility took that concept to the next level.

During the next 10 to 15 years, there will be changes in the manufacturer distribution system and other restrictive controls because consumers will drive the change. Dealers who are listening to those consumers will endorse and respond to the change to their benefit.

I know many dealers who are good friends and excellent retailers. They are adapting to those changing forces, taking great care of their customers and making outstanding contributions to their communities.

If manufacturers and dealers are to prosper in the future, they must be ever sensitive to the changing attitudes of the consumer. That was the premise of my column in the *Journal*. I look forward to continuing the dialogue as the automotive industry adapts and prospers in the years ahead. It is our goal to help the industry thrive and survive in an era of change.[9]

On November 24, 2003, the late Tom Nemet, owner of Nemet Auto Group, a large dealership in New York City, wrote a letter to *Automotive News* in defense of Dave's commentary:

. . . For those of my fellow dealers clamoring for Power's head, I urge you to first ask yourselves a few simple questions before marching toward the guillotine, basket in hand: Do you sell and service today a significantly better quality product within your franchise? Do you see a correlation between the improvements in the quality of the product you sell and independent consumer feedback generated over the past few decades? And, looking to the future, do you believe manufacturers will pay more attention to your lone voice or to the collective views of the thousands of customers surveyed annually by J.D. Power?

The David Power I know has done more for our business over the past 30 years than probably any other person in our industry. I don't agree with his ideas about changing our franchise laws, but I do believe he is being attacked unfairly simply for expressing his views. This brilliant and decent human being has provided an invaluable service that directly improved our bottom lines. He developed a mechanism by which important information—consumer feedback—reached manufacturers, information that they could accept or ignore. The availability of unbiased consumer data has enabled manufacturers to act on consumer desires and thus to provide us with the best-selling, most reliable products in the world. And in the process he has helped our industry prosper and created hundreds of thousands of jobs for Americans. Instead of asking for his head, we ought to be grateful.[10]

A few weeks before he passed away on July 4, 2010, Nemet reflected on his long relationship with Dave. "The Big Three should have listened to Dave a lot earlier," he said. "Had they done so, they would have built smaller cars, safer cars, more fuel-efficient cars to compete with the Japanese. The entire course of the auto industry may have been different."

Bay Area retailer Martin Swig, who Dave had mentioned in his follow-up, also submitted a letter that ran in *Automotive News*, on December 1, 2003:

I am shocked by the venomous reaction to J.D. Power III's recent remarks about the cost of marketing and distributing automobiles and his suggestion that we all could learn from Wal-Mart.

Are they shooting the messenger?

Twenty years ago, I opened the San Francisco Autocenter, a Wal-Mart-style multifranchise auto mall. It featured American, Asian and European makes, plus all the normal used-car, parts and service functions.

The *New York Times* and *Time* magazine hailed it as the dealership of the future. Customers loved it. Other dealers loved it. Manufacturers tolerated it because San Francisco is such a tough place to do business.

It was exactly what Dave Power is proposing now. In 1983, no one screamed that it was unfair.

We are in a changing world. . . . Power saw the magnitude of coming changes clearer than anyone else. He helped the industry change and adapt. I think he deserves a respectful hearing. . . .[11]

Wisconsin dealer John Bergstrom says he is relieved that Dave's image of the big-box model of selling cars like home electronics has not yet come to pass. "I'm very happy that he wasn't right. The big-box model wouldn't work because of the constant service demand," he says. "We agreed on almost everything except for the vision that a person could sell all of those products out of one store."

In the twenty-five years since his first published views on the franchise system in the *Power Report* in 1989, Dave hasn't really changed his views. Certainly the time frame of his prediction can be amended—"I'd stretch it out from 2015 to 2025," he says today—but the signs of trouble are even more evident. "The franchise system got a big blow when General Motors and Chrysler filed for bankruptcy [in 2009]," he says. "It allowed them to give up on the contracts they had, and the franchise system is a contract, so they got rid of some of the dealers and kept others. The ones that lost their franchise didn't get anything for it."

The situation caused a rift in the dealer community. The dealers' industry group saw a few hundred of its members taken out, but a number of other members benefitted by the reduction in competition. Some who were stripped of their dealerships fought the system and got their franchises back. "To me, that's a sign that the franchise system needs to adapt," Dave observes, "and the consumer will be in control from now on. The manufacturers and dealers have to understand that and adapt to it."

In the last few years, the margin has been squeezed even further, and the only way dealers have been able to gain profits is through finance and insurance—the "F&I" department—which sells consumers all the extras: accessories, options, extended warranties, undercoatings, safety glass, mechanical insurance, and more. "They've really marked those things up," Dave notes, "but that aggravated the consumer."

It's like the seemingly endless process of buying a home, Dave says. There is the mortgage broker, the real estate broker, the title insurance, the mortgage insurance. "All those things really run the cost up."

Considering what's next has also been an evolving task, due to the ubiquity of the Internet. Dave no longer believes that the big-box retailer with all the brands under one roof is the ultimate new model. "That will be an interim solution," he says, "and we're not there yet. Ultimately, it will be online shopping." Even today, many people pre-shop for their cars before setting foot on a car lot. "Anyone who's fluent with a home computer can look at all the models of different makes and run their own judgment on them and decide they want the Camry, but they also want to look at the

Accord and the Impala." Then a person can shop prices at two or three dealers before choosing one to go to for a test-drive.

Dave believes the F&I department is also going to move online. "You'll get the best price ever, because it's costing less to do it. That's streamlining all the costs involved in buying a car."

He points out that retailing has always been very dynamic, and you can see this type of change happening with other products, such as home electronics. "We went from Sears to Best Buy to Amazon and the Apple store today."

As these changes happen, entrepreneurs will continue to try out new approaches, and there will be winners or losers. But it will be the efficiency of the Internet that will drive that evolution, and some day a buyer may not even step into a dealership. "Eventually," he says, "they could deliver it to the home."

A Network to Give Dealers the Power of Information

Dave was always determined to position J.D. Power and Associates as part of the solution, rather than to simply air the automobile industry's problems. But he understood their issues, and saw that one of the biggest hurdles facing auto dealers and manufacturers was a lack of up-to-the-minute transactional information. To the extent such information was available, mistrust prevented it from being shared. In the early 1990s, Dave began to conceptualize a strategic product that would eventually be known as the Power Information Network (PIN), a system of data collection, reporting, and analytical tools for the auto industry based on point-of-sale data. The network arose out of Dave's observation that dealers were lacking current information, but it was one of his earliest business memories that reminded him what needed to be done.

"In 1946, I worked in one of the first supermarkets, when I first got my social security card," Dave recalls. "I saw for the first time a checkout counter at the supermarket and watched the change that took place due to information. Later, as I continued to watch the supermarket industry, I saw that they were collecting the information off the cash register and the scanning process. Having information like that could create a process, and understanding that process would make it more efficient. When you make it more efficient, it lowers prices. The ones who get most efficient get the profits as well."

Some forty-five years later, Dave recalled those lessons and thought this system should be used in the auto industry. He wanted more information than what was on the customer satisfaction survey or the dealer survey. He wanted on-the-spot details on retail sales, "instead of the archaic program where they sent in the warranty cards." With that, manufacturers and dealers could put the appropriate product on the lot, "instead of shipping the cars out and finding they have excess inventory and have to run incentive programs to move the product."

In creating PIN, Dave wanted to gather as much information as possible—selling price, vehicle details, cost—and report it back to the manufacturer, so the factories could adjust production to what was selling. Two elements came together to make PIN a reality. First, from one of Dave's early clients, MSI Data Systems, he got the idea that a data-driven approach could transform an industry; MSI Data Systems marketed a store ordering system for supermarkets, the forerunner of what would turn into the barcode-enabled inventory system that revolutionized the packaged goods industry. Second, Dave realized that auto dealers were capturing enormous amounts of quality financial data every time they sold a car. One application was obvious. Everyone had the utmost interest in knowing the average prices of new and used vehicles by model, sales year, and condition, but the existing resources for such information—NADA, Kelley Blue Book, etc.—were little more than semi-scientific estimates. Dave knew there would be a market for definitive pricing information based on real-time sales.

Dave started working on PIN in 1990, billing it as a "value-added information resource that collects, interprets, and enhances" automotive point-of-sale transaction data for the benefit of retailers, manufacturers, and other interested parties. Here's how it works: PIN gathers daily point-of-sale transaction data for both new and used cars directly from the dealers. It also gathers more than two hundred and fifty key observations for each vehicle transaction, such as cost, profit, finance, lease, and trade-in statistics. Dave's vision was to aggregate all these data points into a supercharged database to give dealers up-to-the-minute pricing information, and to help them understand sales patterns and market conditions. With such information, for the first time, dealers would be able to take real-time data and benchmark their performance against competitors to improve the overall efficiency of their operations.

Dave studied how such transactional data gathering was conducted in the grocery industry and saw ways to improve the business model. The companies that worked with the grocery industry actually paid the businesses for their data. Dave didn't want to follow that model. "We wanted to trade data for context: we would repay the dealers who allowed us to use their data by giving them actionable knowledge." Why would any car dealer go for that deal? One sales pitch went like this: if you have a lot of loose lumber in the backyard, give us that lumber and we will use some of it to build you a nice shed where you can keep your tools. In other words, J.D. Power would take the loose information lying around and put it together in terms of broad market information and industry velocities.

The benefits would be immediate across every dealer function, such as inventory, for example. Unlike most mom-and-pop retail stores, even large dealers still have no reliable way to judge how many cars of what model and color to order. "Many dealers still place orders using sales from the previous year," Dave explains. "If a dealer sells one hundred white cars one year, it simply orders one hundred more of the same color the next. This primitive system leads to both overstocking and missed sales." There's no way for the dealership to know whether there will be a demand for one hundred white cars this year. Conversely, those one hundred white cars might take the place of cars that the dealer might sell at a higher margin. Cars that languish on the lot quickly lose value, a condition known as "lot rot."

PIN represented an ambitious leap for J.D. Power and Associates. Working with data information provider Reynolds and Reynolds, a company well known to car dealers, Dave proposed to give dealers unprecedented access to industry information. Even so, he realized that PIN would be a tough sell. Automobile dealers are notoriously wary of sharing information (a legacy of their adversarial relationship with car manufacturers) and resistant to technological changes. "Many dealers were worried that a tracking system might reveal flaws in the individual dealerships," says Jamey Power. A third concern was revealing information to competitors. "The larger dealers," recalls Dave, "felt their data was ten times or one hundred times more valuable than their competitors in the local market."

When Dave began PIN, it was the era of the dot-com boom, when technology investment was yielding incredible results, and start-up companies were exploding overnight to become giants with massive initial public offerings on Wall Street. Dave saw that trend and badly wanted to ride it. But he was ahead of the thinking within his own company, and the program also met with resistance within J.D. Power and Associates. Some objected to the sharp turn away from the company's main business, which was booming, and to the massive funds needed for staff and development projects that diverted resources from the firm.

"A lot of people internally thought he was crazy," notes Loretta Seymour, because the program was drawing so much investment money from company coffers.

"That's why he started it in a separate office, ten miles or so away from the main office," explains John Rettie, who was editorial director when Dave began working on PIN. "It was very controversial . . . but he persevered and said it had a future." It did not take off as envisioned; it did not become a darling of the Internet IPO set. Still, Dave's passion remained with PIN, and he spent much of his time working with its staff, even as the company's research services continued catapulting J.D. Power and Associates into a powerhouse consulting firm on a robust growth curve.

Dave's enthusiasm and frustration over PIN was reflected in a January 1997 memo to Steve Goodall. In the memo, Dave reinforced his vision for PIN, advocated for more progress, and personally committed himself to the effort:

> PIN has been a long-term investment opportunity . . . over the past six years. Most of the industry observers and client companies' management, as well as leading car dealers themselves, view PIN as a noble but futile experiment. It is my belief that this investment will have a much greater impact on the overall growth and profitability of J.D. Power and Associates than our CSI and IQS surveys. It is encouraging that five or six of the leading car manufacturers are now interested in participating with our pilot California

program. In 1997, we have the potential to show the industry how valuable this information will be to everyone, including the consumers. While many hurdles lie ahead, this is the year to tell our California story before venturing to other states and regions.

As in some of our other practice areas, PIN is making some progress, but results are not fast enough. The sign-up and turn-on of the additional dealers went well in the middle of 1996, but fell way short of 200 additional franchises, our goal in the fourth quarter of 1996. To date, this year we have not done any better, even though we have added staff. The key target was to have 1,200 of the 3,200 franchises in California reporting before we aggressively pushed out to other states. . . .

In the weeks and months ahead, I personally will become more active with the PIN project, because it needs to be shifted into high gear.[12]

Dave realized that rolling out on a national basis was too great a challenge. The resource need was prohibitive and the resistance from manufacturers, large dealers, and the data companies was daunting. "I said let's pull back to California and get the state of California up and running," Dave recalls. It worked, and they expanded the model to twenty-eight of the top metropolitan areas across the country. Finally, the wheels started to turn and propel the PIN team on their uphill course.

PIN took far longer to gain traction than Dave had anticipated, but by the company's fortieth anniversary, it was profitable and providing valuable information to more than 7,500 franchise dealerships in the thirty-five biggest markets in the U.S., representing about 75 percent of national sales volume. Business reporters relied on the data from PIN, marketed by J.D. Power and Associates as "the industry's premier source for real-time automotive monthly retail sales data."

One observer who immediately understood Dave's vision was Graham Phillips, a former Ogilvy & Mather advertising executive who relied on Dave as a guide to the automobile industry. "I saw PIN as an enormously powerful system to aggregate real-time information on which vehicle production and retail sales could be based," he says. Had things worked out a little bit differently, PIN could have become as big and important to the auto retail market as Nielsen is to media, according to Phillips. "I could see that Dave was frustrated at how difficult it was to make PIN as pervasive as he knew it could be."

While Dave might have been exasperated at the way PIN was struggling and the time it took for acceptance of the service to take hold, slowly the data began to accumulate and earn the interest of potential customers.

"In recent years, the Power Information Network really shook up the retail establishment," recalls a Detroit auto journalist, "because it was a direct pipeline to the dealers on actual transaction prices, which most of the time have nothing to do with MSRP [manufacturer's suggested retail price]. For the first time ever, there was a way to find out what your competitors were charging and getting, what dealers across the country were charging and getting." But, the journalist says, it was difficult for the industry to swallow yet another "fundamental change" concept from Dave Power. "There's a widespread sense in the industry that this was a revolutionary thing."

"Dave was willing to stand up to his peers at the company because his vision was strong," recalls Herb Williams-Dalgart, a senior director at J.D. Power and Associates, "and all of us still with the company are very glad he did, because it remains a powerful asset of the company. To this day, we are generating new products from that model. It just took a long time to build it."

As the Power Information Network matured and began to fulfill Dave's vision, it also became attractive to potential investors who had long been asking Dave for the keys to J.D. Power and Associates. By the mid-2000s, Dave was eyeing retirement, and J.D. Power's primary suitor, the McGraw-Hill Companies, was taking an in-depth look at every aspect of the company—that included PIN. "I think McGraw-Hill had the most interest in that part of the company," says Loretta Seymour. "Financially it was a strong contributor with very few competitors."

Fielding Suitors

Dave had seen the potential for PIN and had seen how much capital investment was required to effectively add a new service to this large but still family-run and privately funded business. As J.D. Power and Associates bootstrapped its growth and diversified, it began to take seriously the solicitations for partnership or purchase of the firm.

The board had been steadily bringing more structure and discipline to the organization—while fending off purchase solicitations—but in 2004 they began to discuss in earnest the idea of selling the firm. Coming off a torrent of growth and an increased complexity of the firm that taxed the energies of leadership, the family faced an intricate set of choices about its future. Jamey recalls that finding a large, well-capitalized suitor who could take the company to the next level seemed like the best approach, to both meet the interests of the family and ensure the ongoing success of the business. "We wanted to find a good way to recapitalize the company so that it could continue on its growth trajectory."

On March 7, 2005, nearly forty years after the company had begun around a kitchen table, J.D. Power and Associates announced its sale to the McGraw-Hill Companies. Making the announcement at an event at J.D. Power's headquarters in Westlake Village, California, Dave described the search for a partner who "could allow us to continue with our vision" of independence, impact, and integrity. He then sat down with Terry McGraw, great-grandson of that company's founder, and a signing ceremony took place that was simulcast to all J.D. Power offices across the globe. "Dave Power is a founder," McGraw said respectfully. "He defied odds. He did things. He worked long hours. He would not be denied." McGraw noted a parallel path with his firm, formerly run by his forebears but now a publicly traded company. Throughout its history, he said, integrity had been a guiding principle. Jamey reminded the assemblage of the company's incredible reach. "We've transformed mighty industries," he said, "and transformed how customers are served."[13]

Fifty Years of Independence, Impact, and Integrity

Dave Power's life has spanned the evolution of the automotive industry from the postwar might of gleaming, chrome-fendered behemoths to the influx of imports and the gas-crisis-fueled compact cars to the near dismantling and ongoing reinvention of Detroit. It's an evolution that would have occurred without Dave, but the auto industry would not have had the benefit of understanding the voice of the customer and reacting to it. Jeremy Main, author of *Quality Wars*, wrote, "David Power is a transformative figure in the U.S. auto industry. He set the standard for judging the quality of automobiles. Power made it perfectly clear to the manufacturers how their efforts to improve quality were rated by their customers and how well or poorly each manufacturer's efforts stacked up against the competition." Dick Colliver, former senior marketing executive for both Mazda and Honda, has called Dave "an icon" for his contribution to the industry building a higher quality, safer product. "The manufacturers that listened to him first benefitted most," says Colliver. "He had a major impact."

The greatest impact, however, surely must be that the overall baseline of car quality would not be where it is—around the globe—had Dave and his team of associates not systematically documented the grievances of drivers, then thoughtfully analyzed and presented the data in a way that empowered automakers to act. "His whole focus on things gone right and things gone wrong has permeated the industry," comments Gary Cowger, former president of General Motors. "In GM's case, it had a profound effect on how we looked at the car from an engineering and manufacturing perspective." Bob Reilly, former COO of American Isuzu Motors Inc., notes, "The automobile industry would grant that Dave is primarily responsible for the primacy and development of customer satisfaction."

Executives, insiders, and experts across the automobile industry—and indeed other industries that J.D. Power and Associates has helped burnish to higher levels of customer satisfaction—are quick to offer accolades to Dave and his vision. However, despite logging a half-century in the automotive industry and amassing a collection of crystal balls that symbolize his visionary abilities, the person who spontaneously came up with the mantra for his firm—"independence, impact, and integrity"—is not ready to repose in the reflective glow of legacy quite yet. "In fifty years, we've gone from the manufacturing era to the information-driven economy," Dave says. "The shift has been dramatic and difficult for the automobile industry, and there is still a long road ahead." It's clear through his ongoing involvement that he hopes his outspoken views and vision for the industry's future will still be heeded. It's also clear those views will continue to come from an autonomous thinker, a sort of benevolent, influential gadfly, a person who, with veracity and sincerity, has always stepped back to let the data speak for itself.

AFTERWORD

After more than fifty years working with the automobile industry, and many other industries in both the very early and later parts of my career, I would not trade my experiences for anything in the world. It is interesting to me now to look back across those years, to all the people with whom I've worked and all the engagements that had a formative effect on my thinking, and then to look forward, because the future holds more fascinating, challenging changes.

I am sure many people would credit their early career experiences as forming the track of their work, and I can point to many, varied experiences that helped me build my company and become an effective contributor to the industry served by it. I don't feel I have any special wisdom that allowed me to do what I did, but these experiences gave me the big picture; plus, I was fortunate to be exposed to the auto industry at a time of great change, before many people in the industry realized what they were going through.

First, I feel fortunate to have begun my career at the Ford Tractor Division, which many might find surprising, because it was a niche far removed from the main automobile company. But it was precisely that situation that made it so valuable. I began in the business after a recession, at a time when the agricultural world was experiencing vast change. Ford's agriculture machinery business would need to change with it, but it was stuck in an existing model. Ford had a small tractor that had been a best seller after World War II, and its success led it into a period of complacency. Ford Tractor did not have any product development arm to look at what was happening to the state of agriculture. In the 1950s, agriculture shifted from a nation of small family farms to industrial farming, and Ford Tractor didn't see it happening or imagine what was ahead. Working in their finance department, I was tasked with pricing the tractors and implements and trying to forecast volume estimates. I handled dealership audits and saw dealers struggling with the shrinking demand for their product. I analyzed the company's two-step distribution system and found it unsustainable. These projects gave me insight into the tractor market—I could see the future consolidation that eventually resulted in one major farm equipment brand—but the experience also gave me my first understanding of the automobile industry. I recognized that the same two-step distribution system was also destined to fail the automakers. I saw the need to anticipate consumer demands and respond to consumer desires. It was a tremendous overview of what was happening in the industry, and I was able to comprehend it before many of the executives did.

Other influences came together in the early years of my career. My Coast Guard experience greatly prepared me for running my own business, and for recognizing my own strengths. I began to fully understand the role and responsibility of leadership, and the value of teamwork. I read the works of leading thinkers and business writers, for instance discovering how important it was to look to the future and analyze trends, as my friend Alvin Toffler did so well. How the forces of change would influence business people and their organizations was an incredibly valuable lesson I gained from Peter Drucker's writing. And my early exposure to one of the automobile industry's largest marketing firms, McCann-Erickson's Marplan, showed me that the existing model of market research and consumer surveying needed to change with the times.

In my fifty-year career, I have seen the American economy move from a manufacturing era to an information-driven one. The shift has been dramatic, and it has been difficult for the automobile industry to adjust. In the 1940s and 1950s, management executives controlled their future. Today, that is no longer the case. I believe J.D. Power and Associates played a significant part in showing the industry how the world was changing around them and in helping them adapt.

We began with the premise that the manufacturer should listen to the voice of the customer. What manufacturers heard resulted in improvement of car quality and overall ownership experience across the industry. At the same time, the technology tools of the information age helped us broadly distribute information on quality to consumers, further empowering them. As everyone gets more information—both manufacturers and consumers—they make better decisions.

Communication has gone global and information is instantaneous. This provides new challenges for people in the auto industry—but it also provides tremendous opportunities for understanding the customer. Recently, we saw the value of information sharing and widespread analysis. J.D. Power studies revealed a slump in auto quality between 2010 and 2011. At that point, the automakers turned to dealers to help them analyze and correct the trend. It also affirmed to me that our consumer surveys and data are as important as ever, if not more so.

Today, the auto industry overall is doing pretty well, and I believe that's due largely to increases in quality, and the quality advances are due in turn to the fact that the automakers ultimately learned how to listen to their customers. Currently, Ford is on an impressive run of success, and Honda continues on its reliable path of producing a quality product. Hyundai certainly found its way but must understand that expectations for them to maintain a position at this level are high. Nissan is somewhat quietly finding its own path. Toyota and Volkswagen—who have both had their troubles in the recent past—are doing better. Chrysler also seems to be on an upswing. General Motors is still struggling to emerge from their problems that culminated in bankruptcy, but signs are very positive for that company as well.

It is fascinating to study trends from the point of view of a long career. Early on, I learned that proprietary market research could never help a company appreciate broad trends across an entire industry; only a global view could accomplish that. Now that information is flowing so much more freely, forward thinkers must envision what effect that will have on the future of their industries.

A few thoughts about the future I envision: Overall, I believe that dealerships will continue to adapt to industry changes and remain viable, especially if they are savvy and embrace emerging trends, as so many of my friends in retail do. They will be operating in an era of customers empowered by the Internet and even more freely available data. This is an especially important issue in metropolitan markets, where there might be multiple dealers of each brand within shopping range. The reliability of a car will continue to increase to the point that the warranty will no longer be as vital to the equation. Used cars will remain important. Also, industry people should never underestimate the power of the consumer to seek out and grab a good deal. Customers are already willing to drive many miles to buy a car if it's the one they want and the best deal they can find, and this trend will only expand.

Today, most people still want to touch the car before they make such a large purchase. However, with the quality levels of most brands so much higher than they were—and relatively equal across many competing models—this will become less of an issue to the consumer. I can see the day when new cars are primarily ordered and purchased sight unseen and delivered directly to the customer's door. This dynamic evolution will have ripple effects through every facet of the industry, from manufacturing and assembly to marketing and finance.

I believe that, in the future, organizations will be less worried about proprietary information, because of the advantages they will receive from freely flowing information providing a broader understanding to industry trends. Approval for buyer financing is now happening electronically and instantaneously, and this technology-enabled change has reinvigorated that segment of the industry. I sit on the board of directors of Dealertrack Technologies, the foremost company in providing computerization and digitization of financing data. Eventually, the entire process will be digitized and available immediately, completing a trend toward open, industry-wide sharing of financing information. I am more bullish on the pace of this change than many of my fellow board members, but when it happens, the free flow of information will allow everyone to do a much better job.

When you make projections, timing is always key. Perhaps at times I have overestimated the rate of change, but I continue to believe that anticipating change rather than responding to it is the path to continued—even expanding—success. The great danger for any industry, I feel, is that it is easy to see a change happening after the fact but difficult—if not impossible—to effectively adjust to it at that point. A lot of people and organizations are blindsided by change and go out of business. When you run into a recession, like the deep one we are going through now, it is often too late to adjust. If there is any lesson from my career that can help a business survive and thrive in today's environment, it is to keep adapting and adjusting as fast as possible, because change is coming more rapidly than ever.

It is my hope that the work I produced during my career—and that is being carried on today at J.D. Power and Associates—will continue to help the individuals who design, engineer, produce, sell, and service vehicles succeed through understanding, responding to, and even anticipating the voice of the customer.

J.D. Power III
March 2013

NOTES

Chapter One

1. "Autos: Gamble on the Rambler," *Time*, December 19, 1955. http://www.time. com/time/magazine/article/0,9171,861782,00.html.
2. McMahon, Fr. Michael. "The Jesuit Model of Education," Edocere, retrieved December 17, 2012. http://www.edocere.org/articles/jesuit_model_ education.htm.
3. Levitt, Theodore. "Marketing Myopia," *Harvard Business Review*, July–August 1960, 50.
4. Johnston, Russ. *Marion Harper: An Unauthorized Biography* (Chicago: Crain Books, 1982), 8.
5. Lockley, Lawrence C. "Notes on the History of Marketing Research," *The Journal of Marketing*, 14, no. 5, April 1950, 733.
6. Svetich, Kim. "More Power to You," *California Business,* September 1991, 49.
7. Camp, Charles B. "Wankel Engine's Durability is Challenged by Research Firm; Mazda Attacks Data," *Wall Street Journal*, May 7, 1973.

Chapter Two

1. Dolan, Matthew. "To Outfox the Chicken Tax, Ford Strips Its Own Vans," *Wall Street Journal*, September 23, 2009. http://online.wsj.com/article/ SB125357990638429655.html.
2. Taylor, Alex. *Sixty to Zero: An Inside Look at the Collapse of General Motors—and the Detroit Auto Industry* (New Haven: Yale University Press, 2010), 15–16.
3. Bryne, John A. "The Man Who Invented Management," *Businessweek*, November 27, 2005. http://www.businessweek.com/stories/2005-11-27/ the-man-who-invented-management.
4. Holusha, John. "W. Edwards Deming, Expert on Business Management, Dies at 93," *New York Times*, December 21, 1993. http://www.nytimes.

com/1993/12/21/obituaries/w-edwards-deming-expert-on-business-management-dies-at-93.html?pagewanted=all&src=pm.

5. Aguayo, Rafeal. *Dr. Deming: The American Who Taught the Japanese About Quality* (New York: Simon & Schuster, 1990), 253.

6. "Biography: W. Edwards Deming," The W. Edwards Deming Institute, retrieved January 13, 2013. http://deming.org/index.cfm?content=61.

7. Holusha, "W. Edwards Deming."

8. "Opinion: The Disease of the Future," *Time,* 96, no. 5, August 3, 1970. http://www.time.com/time/subscriber/article/0,33009,876677,00.html.

9. "Alvin Toffler: Still Shocking After All These Years," *New Scientist,* March 19, 1994, 22–25.

10. Ibid.

11. Martin, Douglas. "Walter B. Wriston, Banking Innovator as Chairman of Citicorp, Dies at 85," *New York Times,* January 21, 2005. http://www.nytimes.com/2005/01/21/obituaries/21wriston.html?_r=0

12. "Walter Wriston Biography," *The Walter B. Wriston Archives,* retrieved April 9, 2013. http://dca.lib.tufts.edu/features/wriston/about/bio.html.

13. September 17, 1991, memo to Dave Power from Gun Dukes.

14. April 28, 1988, letter to Lloyd Reuss from Dave Power.

15. April 9, 1991, letter to James Fitzpatrick from Dave Power.

16. February 14, 1989, letter to stockholders from Roger B. Smith.

17. Meiners, Jens. "Dr. Piëch's Legacy: Hits and Misses from a Distinguished Career," *Car and Driver,* February 2011. http://www.caranddriver.com/features/ferdinand-piechs-career-with-volkswagen-group-feature.

18. Andrews, Edmund L. "Chief of BMW Leaving Post in a Shake-Up," *New York Times*, February 6, 1999. http://www.nytimes.com/1999/02/06/business/international-business-chief-of-bmw-leaving-post-in-a-shake-up.html

19. Ibid.

20. Ibid.

21. Landler, Mark. "Volkswagen Ousts a Chief Who Had Seemed a Survivor," *New York Times,* November 8, 2006. http://query.nytimes.com/gst/fullpage.html?res=9D07E1DF1E3FF93BA35752C1A9609C8B63.

Chapter Three

1. LaReau, Jamie. "The Death of Oldsmobile," *Automotive News* 81, September 25, 2006, 62.

2. Bunkley, Nick. "Pontiac, 84, Dies of Indifference," *New York Times,* October 30, 2010. http://www.nytimes.com/2010/10/30/business/30pontiac.html?pagewanted=all&_r=0.

3. Wojdyla, Ben. "The Top Automotive Engineering Failures: Oldsmobile

Diesels," *Popular Mechanics*, April 5, 2011. http://www.popularmechanics. com/cars/news/vintage-speed/top-automotive-engineering-failures- oldsmobile-diesels.

4. Taylor. *Sixty to Zero*, 155.

5. Moore, Thomas. "'The GM System Is Like a Blanket of Fog,'" *Fortune,* February 15, 1988. http://money.cnn.com/magazines/fortune/ fortune_archive/1988/02/15/70199/.

6. Zesiger, Sue. "GM's Big Decision: Status Quo," *Fortune,* February 21, 2000. http://money.cnn.com/magazines/fortune/fortune_ archive/2000/02/21/273868/index.htm.

7. Sonnenfeld, Jeffrey A. "How Rick Wagoner Lost GM," *Businessweek,* June 1, 2009. http://www.businessweek.com/managing/content/jun2009/ ca2009061_966638.htm.

8. "The Driving Force Behind Ford's Success Profile: Under Donald E. Petersen, Design, Direction and Timing Have Merged to Make the Firm the Most Profitable Auto Company in History," *Los Angeles Times,* October 31, 1989. http://articles.latimes.com/1989-10-31/business/fi-246_1_ford-design.

9. "CEO of the Year 1989," *Chief Executive*, July 1, 1989. http://chiefexecutive. net/ceo-of-the-year-1989.

10. February 15, 1988, letter to Dave Power from D.E. Petersen.

11. "Topics of the Times; the Legacy of Henry II," *New York Times,* September 30, 1987. http://www.nytimes.com/1987/09/30/opinion/topics-of-the-times- the-legacy-of-henry-ii.html.

12. "Henry Ford 2d Is Dead at 70; Led Auto Maker's Recovery," *New York Times,* September 30, 1987. http://www.nytimes.com/1987/09/30/obituaries/henry- ford-2d-is-dead-at-70-led-auto-maker-s-recovery.html?pagewanted=all&src=pm.

13. Iacocca, Lee A. *Iacocca: An Autobiography* (New York: Bantam Books, 1986), 134.

14. "Art Collector, Benefactor Walter Chrysler Jr. Dies," *Washington Post (Pre-1997 Fulltext),* September 19, 1988. http://pqasb.pqarchiver.com/ washingtonpost/access/73632812.html?FMT=ABS&FMTS=ABS:FT&date= Sep+19%2C+1988&author=&desc=Art+Collector%2C+Benefactor+Walter+C hrysler+Jr.+Dies.

15. Schlesinger, Jacob M. and Amal Kumar Naj. "Chrysler to Buy Renault's Stake in AMC; Seeks Rest of Company—Purchase of All of Car Maker Would Have a Value of Up to $1.11 Billion," *Wall Street Journal,* March 10, 1987.

16. Welch, David. "Bob Lutz Retires from GM. Long Live His Influence," *Businessweek,* March 2, 2010. http://www.businessweek.com/ stories/2010-03-02/bob-lutz-retires-from-gm-dot-long-live-his-influence.

17. Cseser, Csaba. "Bob Lutz Takes His Flashy Act to GM," *Car and Driver,* November 2001. http://www.caranddriver.com/columns/csaba-csere-bob- lutz-takes-his-flashy-act-to-gm-column.

18. "Chrysler Vice Chairman to Retire July 1," *New York Times,* May 22, 1998. http://www.nytimes.com/1998/05/22/business/chrysler-vice-chairman-to-retire-july-1.html.

19. Sass, Rob. "In Monterey, Classics Turn Bankable," *New York Times,* August 19, 2010. http://www.nytimes.com/2010/08/22/automobiles/collectibles/22PEBBLE.html

20. Iacocca, *Iacocca,* 285.

21. June 8, 1987, letter to Dave Power from Bennett E. Bidwell.

22. Krebs, Michelle. "Market-share Scramble," *Automotive News,* June 8, 1987, E30.

23. May 23, 1989, letter to Dave Power from Bennett E. Bidwell.

24. John, Pearley Huffman. "Translating 'Top Gear' into American, Again," *New York Times,* November 21, 2010. http://www.nytimes.com/2010/11/21/automobiles/21TOPGEAR.html?pagewanted=all.

25. "New Look for Top Gear Magazine as TV Show Returns," BBC Worldwide Press Releases, October 21, 2002. http://www.bbc.co.uk/pressoffice/bbcworldwide/worldwidestories/pressreleases/2002/10_october/top_gear_newlook.shtml.

26. Elder, Scott. "Last Stand at Edo Bay," *National Geographic,* retrieved April 9, 2013. http://ngm.nationalgeographic.com/ngm/0210/feature2/online_extra.html.

Chapter Four

1. Adelson, Andrea. "People Buy the Cars He Says They Like," *New York Times,* October 16, 1997. http://www.nytimes.com/1997/10/16/automobiles/people-buy-the-cars-he-says-they-like.html.

2. Taylor, Alex. "More Power to J.D. Power," *Fortune,* May 18, 1992. http://money.cnn.com/magazines/fortune/fortune_archive/1992/05/18/76421/index.htm.

3. October 17, 1990, notes for presentation to Mazda dealerships representatives in Tokyo, Japan.

4. Denove, Chris, and James D. Power IV. *Satisfaction: How Every Great Company Listens to the Voice of the Customer* (New York: Portfolio, 2006).

5. "Honda Plans Auto Plant in Marysville," *The Blade,* January 11, 1980, 1. http://news.google.com/newspapers?nid=1350&dat=19800110&id=ED1PAAAAIBAJ&sjid=jQIEAAAAIBAJ&pg=4089,5492580.

6. Hartford, Bill. "Driving the New Volvo 760 GLE," *Popular Mechanics,* 158, no. 2, August 1982, 112.

7. Translation of *Kvalitet Fakta* provided in September 17, 1991, memo to Dave Power from Gun Dukes.

8. September 17, 1991, letter to Lennart Jeansson from Dave Power.

9. *Kvalitet Fakta:* Quality Information System. 1998, no. 3, May 13, 1996, 12.

10. Lippert, John, Alan Ohnsman and Rose Kim. "Billionaire Chung Proving Hyundai No Joke Aiming for BMW," *Bloomberg Markets Magazine,* March 1, 2012. http://www.bloomberg.com/news/2012-03-01/billionaire-chung-proving-hyundai-luxury-no-joke-in-drive-to-top-bmw-cars.html.

11. Gock, William. "10 Cars That Deserved to Fail," *Popular Mechanics,* retrieved July 18, 2012. http://www.popularmechanics.com/cars/news/pictures/10-cars-that-deserved-to-fail#slide-8.

12. Mateja, Jim. "Full-speed (and All-wheel-drive) Ahead for Audi," *Chicago Tribune,* February 11, 1996. http://articles.chicagotribune.com/1996-02-11/travel/9602110200_1_audi-a4-quattro-snow.

13. Denove and Power, *Satisfaction,* 248.

14. Chang, Peter. "How Hyundai Made the Grade," *Automotive News* 78, no. 6105, August 2, 2004, 30H.

15. Carroll, John. "U-Turn," *American Way,* December 1, 2005. Reprint Management Services #1-13912511.

16. Denove and Power, *Satisfaction,* 249–250.

17. "Japan's Top Three Automakers Set Global Output Records in 2012," *Japan Times,* January 29, 2013. http://www.japantimes.co.jp/news/2013/01/29/business/japans-top-three-automakers-set-global-output-records-in-2012/#.UXA42oJ1FhA.

18. James, Wanda. *Driving from Japan: Japanese Cars in America.* (Jefferson, North Carolina: McFarland & Company, Inc.), 222.

19. "Mitsubishi Reveals More Defect Coverups," *Automotive News,* June 2, 2004. http://www.autonews.com/apps/pbcs.dll/article?AID=/20040602/REG/406020707&template=printart

20. Kanner, Bernice. "Jaguar Revs Up," *New York* 20, no. 34, August 31, 1987, 23.

21. Dale, Michael H. "How We Rebuilt Jaguar in the U.S.," *Fortune,* April 28, 1986. http://money.cnn.com/magazines/fortune/fortune_archive/1986/04/28/67474/index.htm.

22. Ibid.

23. Davidson, Andrew. "UK: The Davidson Interview—Nick Scheele," *Management Today,* February 1, 1999. http://www.managementtoday.co.uk/news/412259/UK-Davidson-Interview---Nick-Scheele/?DCMP=ILC-SEARCH.

24. Priddle, Alisa. "Tata Buys Jaguar and Land Rover from Ford," *Car and Driver,* March 2008. http://www.caranddriver.com/news/tata-buys-jaguar-and-land-rover-from-ford-car-news.

25. "Mercedes-Benz M-Class—1998 Motor Trend Truck of the Year," *Motor Trend,* retrieved January 30, 2013. http://www.motortrend.com/oftheyear/truck/112_9712_mercedes_benz_m_class_truck_of_the_year/viewall.html.

26. Kurylko, Diana T. "Hubbert's Last Hurrah: M-B Quality," *Automotive News* 78, no. 6105, August 2, 2004, 3.

Chapter Five

1. Allen, Leslie J. "The First Dealers: From Humiliation to Retail Success," *Automotive News* 81, supplement, September 25, 2006, 6.
2. Stoffer, Harry. "Government Tips Scales for Dealers, Automakers," *Automotive News* 81, supplement, September 25, 2006, 26.
3. Ambrose, Kevin. "Washington D.C.'s Top 5 Surprise Snowstorms," *Washington Post,* January 19, 2012. http://www.washingtonpost.com/blogs/capital-weather-gang/post/washington-dcs-top-5-surprise-snowstorms/2012/01/16/gIQAPwOoAQ_blog.html.
4. Sorge, Marjorie. "Big Three Find Common Bond: QS-9000 Marries Automaker Quality Standards," *WardsAuto,* March 1, 1995. http://wardsauto.com/news-amp-analysis/big-three-find-common-bond-qs-9000-marries-automaker-quality-standards.
5. Horovitz, Bruce. "Riney Grasps for Ring, but Saturn May Bring Him Down to Earth," *Los Angeles Times*, March 17, 1990. http://articles.latimes.com/1990-03-17/business/fi-294_1_hal-riney.
6. "At Saturn, What Workers Want Is . . . Fewer Defects," *Businessweek,* December 1, 1991. http://www.businessweek.com/stories/1991-12-01/at-saturn-what-workers-want-is-dot-dot-dot-fewer-defects.
7. "Suddenly, Saturn's Orbit Is Getting Wobbly," *Businessweek,* February 27, 1994. http://www.businessweek.com/stories/1994-02-27/suddenly-saturns-orbit-is-getting-wobbly.
8. Chappell, Lindsay. "GM's Fling with Saturn Rankled Many at Chevrolet," *Automotive News: Chevrolet 100,* October 31, 2011, 184. http://lb2.ec2.nxtbook.com/nxtbooks/crain/an_20111031_chevy100/index.php?startid=184#/186.
9. Ibid.

Chapter Six

1. Osborne, D.M. "Deconstructing Power," *Brill's Content,* June 1999.
2. "G.M. Sells Suzuki Stake in Its Effort to Raise Cash," *New York Times* (November 17, 2008). http://www.nytimes.com/2008/11/18/business/18suzuki.html?_r=0.
3. Ibid.
4. January 6, 1986, acceptance letter to Dave Power from Syd Havely.
5. Ingrassia, Paul. *Crash Course: The American Automobile Industry's Road to Bankruptcy and Bailout—and Beyond* (New York: Random House, 2010), 65.

6. Italia, Robert. *Great Auto Makers and Their Cars* (Minneapolis: The Oliver Press, 1993), 131–141.

7. Ingrassia, *Crash Course*, 66.

8. Italia, *Great Auto Makers*.

9. Ibid.

10. Ingrassia, *Crash Course*, 72.

11. Johnson, Greg. "Agency Followed 'Simple' Equation for Honda Success," *Los Angeles Times*, July 29, 1999. http://articles.latimes.com/1999/jul/29/business/fi-60563.

12. "Mazda Announces Luxury Sales Channel: Amati," press release from Maureen Nelson, August 20, 1991.

13. Ibid.

14. Lamm, Michael. "Firsthand Report: Driving the Isuzu I-Mark and P'up," *Popular Mechanics* 156, no. 1, July 1981, 73.

15. Gunn, Richard. *Trucks & Off-Road Vehicles* (St. Paul, Minnesota: Motorbooks International, 2004), 113.

16. Taylor, Richard. "Blind Taste Test," *Popular Mechanics* 167, no. 11, November 1990, 44.

17. Shwiff, Kathy. "Isuzu to End Car Sales in North America in 2009," *Wall Street Journal*, January 30, 2008. http://online.wsj.com/article/SB120172584463929557.html.

18. Kiley, David. *Getting the Bugs Out* (New York: Wiley & Sons, 2002), 122.

19. Kiley, *Getting the Bugs Out*, 116.

20. July 29, 1985, memo to all Saab-Scania of America Employees from Robert J. Sinclair.

21. January 27, 1989, letter to Robert J. Sinclair from Dave Power.

22. "Spyker Sues GM for $3B Over Saab Bankruptcy," *Chicago Tribune*, August 6, 2012. http://articles.chicagotribune.com/2012-08-06/business/sns-rt-us-spyker-generalmotors-saabbre8750js-20120806_1_zhejiang-youngman-lotus-automobile-saab-automobile-saab-bankruptcy.

23. Magnusson, Niklas. "Saab Hometown Prays for Revival with China Electric Push," *Bloomberg*, January 25, 2013. http://www.bloomberg.com/news/2013-01-24/saab-hometown-prays-for-revival-with-china-electric-push.html.

24. "The 50 Worst Cars of All Time: 1985 Yugo GV," *Time*, September 7, 2007. http://www.time.com/time/specials/2007/article/0,28804,1658545_1658533_1658529,00.html.

25. Miller, Edward. "Would You Go for a Yugo Costing $3,990?" Associated Press, February 15, 1985. http://www.apnewsarchive.com/1985/Would-You-Go-For-A-Yugo-Costing-$3-990-/id-c358d27ea03d06112017240c00792969.

26. Ibid.

27. Pace, Eric. "Armand Hammer Dies at 92; Industrialist and Philanthropist Forged Soviet Links," *New York Times,* December 12, 1990. http://www. nytimes.com/1990/12/12/obituaries/armand-hammer-dies-at-92-industrialist-and-philanthropist-forged-soviet-links.html?pagewanted=all&src=pm.

28. Dean, Paul. "A Year-End Review: Tying Up Some of the Loose Ends from '84: A Wild and Crazy Car," *Los Angeles Times,* January 1, 1985. http://articles. latimes.com/1985-01-01/news/vw-10382_1_malcolm-bricklin.

29. "Yugo Importer Bricklin Files for Bankruptcy Liquidation," Associated Press, August 22, 1991. http://www.apnewsarchive.com/1991/Yugo-Importer-Bricklin-Files-for-Bankruptcy-Liquidation/id-a607ed10b9f23258 53e2b09ceabc9ef8.

30. Ibid.

31. Levin, Doron P. "Importer of Yugo Seeks Protection," *New York Times,* January 31, 1989. http://www.nytimes.com/1989/01/31/business/importer-of-yugo-seeks-protection.html.

32. "South Korea Dumps the Past, at Last," *Economist,* November 9, 2000. http:// www.economist.com/node/420816?zid=293&ah=e50f636873b42369614615 ba3c16df4a.

33. Ravenhill, John. "From National Champions to Global Partners: Crisis, Globalization, and the Korean Auto Industry," *Crisis and Innovation in Asian Technology* (Cambridge, United Kingdom: Cambridge University Press, 2003), 128.

34. June 26, 1996, letter to C.S. Lee from Dave Power.

35. O'Dell, John. "Huntington Dealership in Daewoo's U.S. Debut," *Los Angeles Times*, September 29, 1998. http://articles.latimes.com/1998/sep/29/business/ fi-27413.

36. Lim, Bomi. "S. Korea Pardons Daewoo Group Founder Kim Woo Choong," *Bloomberg,* December 30, 2007. http://www.bloomberg.com/apps/news?pid= newsarchive&sid=aNn72K19F3x8.

37. Mateja, Jim. "Peugeot's U.S. Exit May Be Omen for Other Small Importers," *Chicago Tribune,* August 7, 1991. http://articles.chicagotribune. com/1991-08-07/business/9103260509_1_peugeot-motors-kim-derderian-high-mileage.

38. Ibid.

Chapter Seven

1. Fisher, Lawrence M. "Gartner to Acquire Dataquest in $80 Million Bid to Expand," *New York Times*, November 29, 1995. http://www.nytimes. com/1995/11/29/business/gartner-to-acquire-dataquest-in-80-million-bid-to-expand.html.

2. January 2, 1997, memo to Steve Goodall from Dave Power.

3. Ibid.

Chapter Eight

1. Levin, Doron P. "Honda's Ugly Little Secret," *New York Times,* May 2, 1993. http://www.nytimes.com/1993/05/02/business/honda-s-ugly-little-secret. html?n=Top%2fReference%2fTimes%20Topics%2fSubjects%2fA%2fAutom obiles&gwh=E4463EC1D7CD01F6C4EE14D5DB9C1954.

2. Lynch, Steve. *Arrogance and Accords: The Inside Story of the Honda Scandal* (Irving, Texas: Pecos Press, 1997), 62.

3. March 14, 1983, letter to Y. Munekuni from Dave Power.

4. Lynch, *Arrogance and Accords,* 72.

5. Lynch, *Arrogance and Accords,* 148.

6. Lynch, *Arrogance and Accords,* 280.

7. November 11, 1998, letter to Dave Power from Jim Cardiges.

8. *Car: The Definitive Visual History of the Automobile* (London: Dorling Kindersley, 2011), 250.

9. Wimmer, Engelbert. *Motoring the Future: VW and Toyota Vying for Pole Position* (Houdmills, Besngstoke, Hampshire, U.K.: Palgrave Macmillan 2011), 40.

10. Lazarus, George. "Audi May Steer to New Ad Agency," *Chicago Tribune,* March 24, 1993. http://articles.chicagotribune.com/1993-03-24/ business/9303240237_1_audi-new-agency-ddb-needham-chicago.

11. White, Joseph B. and Dionne Searcey. "Audi Case Set Template for Toyota's Troubles," *Wall Street Journal,* March 12, 2010. http://online.wsj.com/article/ SB10001424052748704349304575115952186305536.html.

12. Ibid.

13. Bunkley, "Pontiac, 84, Dies of Indifference."

14. Ingrassia, Paul. *Engines of Change: A History of the American Dream in Fifteen Cars* (New York: Simon & Schuster, 2012), 167–189.

15. Ibid.

16. Lamm, John. *365 Sports Cars You Must Drive* (Minneapolis: Motorbooks, 2011), 101.

17. Noah, Timothy. "People's Choice Awards," *New York Times,* August 8, 1999. http://www.nytimes.com/1999/08/08/magazine/ people-s-choice-awards.html?n=Top%2fReference%2fTimes%20 Topics%2fSubjects%2fR%2fRatings%20and%20Rating%20Systems&gwh= 67A85837FE1406D98CA7B3C7268DB229.

18. July 3, 1991, letter prepared for data merge from Dave Power.

19. Undated J.D. Power and Associates presentation "Customer Satisfaction Is Measured in the Eyes of the Beholder."

20. November 5, 1985, memo to Linda Hirneise from J.A. Frechtling.
21. Doyle, Charles C., Wolfgang Mieder, and Fred Shapiro. *The Dictionary of Modern Proverbs* (New Haven: Yale University, 2012), 87.
22. January 30, 1997, memo to Steve Goodall, Chance Parker, and Dave Power from Bill Davis.
23. Taylor, "More Power to J.D. Power."
24. September 1, 2010, news release "Chevrolet, Buick, GMC and Cadillac Sales Decline 11 Percent from 2009 Cash-for-Clunkers Level." http://www.sec.gov/Archives/edgar/data/1467858/000119312510203702/dex991.htm.
25. Denove and Power, *Satisfaction*, 226.

Chapter Nine

1. August 19, 1994, letter to Jim Mateja from Patricia A. Patano.
2. Ibid.
3. Osborne, "Deconstructing Power."
4. "The Automobile Market in Transition—Are You Ready?" *The Power Report on Automotive Marketing* 11, no. 5, May 1989.
5. Ibid.
6. October 3, 2003, J.D. Power III, "*Wall Street Journal* Submission."
7. November 3, 2003, letter to Dave Power from Stephen G. Lyons.
8. October 29, 2003, letter to Dave Power from John H. Bissell.
9. November 17, 2003, letter to the editor of *Automotive News* from Dave Power. http://www.autonews.com/article/20031117/SUB/311170734#axzz2Qss9E2zQ.
10. November 24, 2003, letter to the editor of *Automotive News* from Thomas Nemet.
11. December 1, 2003, letter to the editor of *Automotive News* from Martin L. Swig.
12. January 2, 1997, memo to Steve Goodall from Dave Power.
13. March 7, 2005, video, "The McGraw-Hill Companies Announcement Ceremony."

INDEX

ABOUT THE AUTHORS

Sarah Morgans has spent more than a decade documenting the history and culture of some of the country's most storied corporations, organizations, and individuals. She served as the editor of more than a dozen authorized histories, including those of Ford Motor Company, NASCAR, the Kentucky Derby, the New York Giants, Humana, Dover Corporation, and CBRE, as well as entrepreneurs Wayne Huizenga, Gerald Hines, and Gary Milgard.

Bill Thorness is a Seattle-based writer and editor who has authored three books, contributed to many others, and writes regularly for the media. He reported for more than a decade in the business press before becoming a freelance writer. As an editor, he has worked with authors ranging from psychologists to teenagers to historians. Although he's more likely to commute by bicycle today, he can still tell you the engine displacement and stock modifications of his first car, a 1969 Grand Prix, which literally got him through high school.